# Good Words Fast

## The unique thesaurus for business writers, journalists, copywriters and more

**Oliver Dirs**

LIDBROOK
PRESS

*Good Words Fast* is also available as an e-book for computer, tablet and phone.

Good Words Fast:
The Unique Thesaurus for Business Writers, Journalists, Copywriters and More



Published by Hilltop Language Ltd
under the Lidbrook Press imprint



ISBN: 978-1-5272-6289-8

Editor: Louise Dirs

Cover design by G. M. Fernández

LIDBROOK PRESS

## Preface: A different kind of thesaurus

The English language has so many handy turns of phrase, yet as writers we often struggle to put them to good use when rushing to meet a deadline. It can be hard to switch from 'work' to 'creative' mode to make our copy stand out. Unfortunately, regular thesauri frequently fail to provide the inspiration we seek.

*Good Words Fast* addresses this problem in two unique ways. First, it complements a conventional thesaurus by focusing on the most common terms that writers need alternatives for, such as 'improve', 'deteriorate', 'impressive', 'significant' and 'problem', as well as business-specific terms like 'profit' and 'sustainable'. Under 1,100 such entries, *Good Words Fast* provides a huge depth and range of genuinely useful words and phrases, suitable for everything from detailed analyses to frothy features. Second, much of this book's content has been collected from a vast array of media, including print journalism, business publications, news broadcasting, financial reports and advertising, as well as everyday speech.

So in addition to standard synonyms, you'll find distinctive content to give your work sparkle and precision. Adjectives such as 'game-changing' and 'ahead of its time', nouns like 'learning curve' and 'watershed moment' and verbs such as 'make inroads' and 'take a hit'. In all there are more than 39,000 options.

While the focus is on a commercial context, all sorts of writers will benefit from this book. Business writers will appreciate entries such as *Investment, Unprofitable* and *Mitigate.* Journalists will gain from headings like *Criticism, Unexpected* and *Reconsider.* And copywriters will welcome entries such as *Advantage, Stylish* and *Feature.* Meanwhile, subeditors, copyeditors and translators into English will be spoilt for choice.

Entries are intentionally broad to provide the maximum assistance for writers in a hurry, with both related useful expressions and more direct synonyms. For instance, under *Disappointing* you'll find everything from 'damp squib' to 'devastating', while *Succeed* ranges from 'do well' to 'go down a storm' (see 'Using this book' overleaf).

I hope you find *Good Words Fast* a source of inspiration when chasing deadlines and a reminder that even the most mundane of texts can benefit from thoughtful use of language and a little flair.

Oliver Dirs

## Acknowledgements

I'd like to thank my wife Louise for her contribution to, advice on and patience with this book, which grew from a small project to help us with our translation and copyediting assignments into a reference work of more than 240 pages. Thanks also to Anna and Emily at Lidbrook Press for their help in getting this book over the line.

## Using this book

**Familiarise yourself with the content**

Flick through the book and get an idea of the kind of entries it lists (and doesn't list). This will allow you to make the most efficient use of the book, particularly when you're in a hurry. Each entry carries a 'see also' reference to key synonyms and related words to spark further ideas.

**Know how to use the words you find**

A sure way to lose credibility with your readership (or your copyeditor if you're lucky enough to have one) is to use fancy terms incorrectly or in the wrong context. Unlike a traditional thesaurus, entries in this book are intentionally broad in order to provide maximum inspiration and save time, and include related expressions as well as more direct synonyms. Moreover, many of the synonyms provided can't simply substitute the entry word. Indeed, rarely are any two words entirely interchangeable. If you're unsure exactly how to use a particular word or phrase, refer to a dictionary or see how it's used by reliable native English language sources such as authoritative news providers.

Note that transitive (takes an object) and intransitive (doesn't take an object) verbs are listed together in this book; for example, under *Increase* you'll find both transitive verbs such as 'raise' and intransitive verbs like 'rise'. So check if you're uncertain. In addition, some entries contain related words that can be used from a different perspective; for instance, *Recall* includes 'awaken' and 'ring a bell'.

### Can't find what you're looking for?

If you can't find the entry you're looking for, search for a more general term. For instance, if you can't find a main entry for 'government', look under 'authority' or 'leadership' instead. In the digital version you can, of course, simply use your reader's search function more broadly.

### Avoid inelegant variation

Inelegant variation (or 'elegant variation' as originally, ironically, termed) means sounding like you've swallowed a dictionary. Good writing is all about using the right words at the right time. Use 'good words' judiciously and they'll have greater impact.

### Definitions

Unlike a conventional thesaurus, entries in *Good Words Fast* are very broad to provide maximum inspiration. In most of this book's entries, where there is an overlap between definitions of a word, no differentiation is made between definitions. In some cases, however, where a word has a number of very different meanings, it is divided into two or more definitions. For example, *Ability* is not divided into separate definitions as its main meanings of 'skill', 'opportunity' and 'possibility' overlap. However, *Decline* is separated into two definitions as it carries the very different main meanings of 'decrease/deteriorate' and 'reject'. The focus is on the most commonly used definitions, particularly in a commercial context, with more obscure meanings omitted.

### UK vs US English

This book uses UK spelling (e.g. 'favourable', 'centre', 'organise' and 'fulfil'), while the style of the words and phrases generally aims to be 'international English' (neither strongly UK nor strongly US).

### Initial definite and indefinite articles

Synonyms are listed without initial definite and indefinite articles to make it easier to search alphabetically. So, for example, under the entry for *Insignificant* you'll find 'drop in the ocean' ('*a* drop in the ocean' is, of course, the correct expression) and under *All* you'll find 'works' ('*the* works' is correct). Once again, check if you're unsure about usage.

### Prefixes and suffixes

Prefixes and suffixes that can be added to in order to create other words are shown with asterisks. For instance, under *Automated* you'll find 'self-*****' (as in 'self-driving car', with a hyphen), while the entry for *Like* lists '*****esque' (as in 'a Picassoesque style of painting', without a hyphen).

### Compound words and hyphenation

#### *Nouns and verbs*

This book follows generally accepted style for compound nouns and verbs. Words like 'by-product', 'after-effect' and 'fine-tune' are usually hyphenated, while others such as 'mindset' are commonly written as one word.

#### *Adjectives*

Most of the compound adjectives listed in this book follow generally accepted hyphenation to join parts of speech. For example, 'tailor-made' combines a noun, 'tailor', and an adjective, 'made'. However, hyphenation only applies if the adjective is used before a noun. Where a compound adjective is likely to only be used after a noun, such as 'spot on', it is not hyphenated. Some compound adjectives, such as 'breathtaking', are listed unhyphenated, as is common.

### Parts of speech

Entry headwords are marked as nouns (n.), adjectives (adj.), verbs (v.), adverbs (adv.), determiners (det.), conjunctions (conj.), phrases (phr.), prepositions (prep.) and pronouns (pron.). In order to offer the greatest choice of terms, some entries for adjectives also include nouns, some noun entries contain verbal phrases, and so on.

---

# A

**Ability** n., see also Possibility, Skill
acumen, adeptness, aptitude, brilliance, calibre, capabilities/capability, capacity, chance, command, competence, credentials, dab hand, effectiveness, expertise, facility, flair, forte, genius, gift, ingenuity, innate ability, intelligence, knack, know-how, knowledge, mastery, means, natural ability, nous, opportunity, potential, power, proficiency, promise, prowess, resourcefulness, resources, scope, skillset, speciality, strength, strong point, strong suit, talent, what it takes, wherewithal

**Able (Be Able)** v., see also Capable
be allowed, be authorised, be capable, be effective, be ideally placed, be permitted, be possible, be possibly, be prepared, be up to, be well positioned, can, cope, could, have the ability, have the authority, have the opportunity, have the possibility, have the resources, manage, may, might

**Absence** n., see also Few, Insufficient
almost no, bereft, conspicuous absence, dearth, deficiency, devoid of, distinct lack, few and far between, gone, inadequacy, in short supply, lack, need, next to nothing, no, no real, no sign of, none, nonexistence, omission, paucity, scarcity, short of/on, short supply, shortage, shortfall, sparsity, thin on the ground, unavailability, vacuum, virtually no, want, zero

**Accept** v., see also Agree, Allow
abide by, acknowledge, admit, adopt, approve, be reconciled to, be resigned to, bear, believe, bow to (*e.g. pressure*), bury the hatchet, buy, come to terms with, concede, concur with, consent to, embrace, endorse, endure, face facts, face up to (reality), get, go along with, give the nod, grant, grin and bear it, heed, hear, let, live with, permit, put up with, receive, recognise, respect, roll with, rubber-stamp, shoulder, stand (for), stomach, swallow, take, take it as read, take it on the chin, take on board, take receipt, tolerate, trust, undertake, understand, welcome

**Accurate** adj., see also Correct, Specific
bang on, certain, definite, detailed, exact, factual, fair, faithful, faultless, indisputable, irrefutable, meticulous, on the button, on the money, perfect,

precise, precision, reliable, right, rigorous, sound, spot on, strict, true, true and fair, trustworthy, truthful, unerring, unquestionable, with pinpoint accuracy, without error

**Achieve** v., see also Do, Succeed

accomplish, achieve a goal, acquire, attain, bear fruit, bring about, bring off, bring to a conclusion, bring to fruition, carry off, carry out, carry through, complete, conclude, conquer, create, deliver (the goods), do successfully, earn, effect, engineer, establish, execute, finish, fulfil, gain, garner, get done (and dusted), get over the line, hit (the mark/target), implement, land, live up to, manage, mastermind, meet, not disappoint, obtain, orchestrate, perform, post, prevail, produce, pull off, put in place, rack up, reach, reach a landmark, reach a milestone, realise, record, see through, strike, triumph, win

**Achievement** n., see also Performance, Success

accomplishment, attainment, award, badge of honour, completion, conquest, coup, creation, crowning achievement, crowning glory, culmination, execution, exploit, feat, feather in one's cap, finest hour, fruition, fruits of labour, fulfilment, gain, (new) heights, implementation, kudos, landmark achievement, legacy, lifetime achievement, magnum opus, masterpiece, milestone, mission accomplished, no mean feat, prowess, quite an achievement, realisation, result, successful completion, triumph, turnaround, victory, win

**Acquire** v., see also Buy, Invest

achieve, acquire a stake, amass, assume, attain, bag, become the owner of, bring in, buy into, buy out, buy up, claim, earn, gain, get, get one's hands on, grab, make a purchase, make an acquisition, obtain, pick up, procure, purchase, receive, secure, seize, snag, snap up, source, take a stake in, take on, take over, take possession of, win

**Acquisition** n., see also Investment, Transaction

addition, asset, attainment, bolt-on acquisition, buy-out, buy-up, corporate acquisition, deal, move, ownership, possession, prize, procurement, purchase, strategic acquisition, takeover

**Act** v., see also Do, Implement

1. achieve, apply, carry out, deliver, effect, enforce, execute, get involved, get to grips with, go about, have an effect, impact, intervene, make progress, move, operate, perform, put in place, put into effect, react, respond, roll out, step in, strike, take action, take effect, take measures, take on, take steps, take the initiative, take the lead, take the plunge, undertake

2. adopt a role, appear, behave, conduct oneself, cut a [adjective] figure, fulfil a role, function, have a role, operate, play a part, seem, serve, take on

**Action** n., see also Activity, Implementation
achievement, business, course of action, dealings, development, drama, dynamism, efforts, endeavours, energy, engagement, enterprise, event, execution, gambit, incident, initiative, intervention, measure, move, movement, operation, performance, power play, procedure, proceedings, process, reaction, response, step, undertaking, work

**Active** adj., see also Busy, Enthusiastic
alert, at work, bustling, committed, current, dedicated, determined, driven, dynamic, eager, employed, endeavouring, energetic, engaged, enterprising, functioning, hard at work, hard-working, in action, in process, industrious, interested, involved, lively, occupied, ongoing, operating, passionate, preoccupied, proactive, purposeful, taking action, tireless, underway, working

**Activity** n., see also Industry, Work
action, area of business, area of expertise, assignment, business, business activity, business area, bustle, deployment, duties, efforts, endeavour, energy, enterprise, exercise, field of interest, function, hive of activity, interest, job, life, line of business, market, measure, movement, occupation, operation(s), project, pursuit, scene, scheme, sector, task, undertaking, venture

**Adapt** v., see also Adjust, Change
acclimatise, accommodate, alter, amend, be flexible, become accustomed to, calibrate, change/move with the times, comply, configure, conform, convert, customise, develop, evolve, find one's feet, fine-tune, fit (in/with), get used to, harmonise, modify, orientate, overhaul, rearrange, recalibrate, reconfigure, reform, remodel, reorganise, reshape, respond, rethink, revamp, review, revise, roll with, shape, show flexibility, suit, tailor, tinker, transform, transition, tune, tweak, update, upgrade

**Add** v., see also Boost, Contribute
add a dash of, adjoin, advance, amplify, append, attach, augment, beef up, bolt on, bring, bring to the party/table, bump up, complement, continue, enhance, enlarge, expand, extend, heighten, include, increase, infuse with, inject, intensify, introduce, magnify, make an addition, pepper, raise, slap on, spread, step up, strengthen, supplement, tack on, throw in

**Address** v., see also Manage, Resolve
approach, attend to, broach, clear up, concentrate on, confront, counter, deal with, engage with, fix, focus on, get on top of, get to grips with, grapple with, handle, iron out, look at, meet, meet head on, meet the challenge, navigate, nip in the bud, oversee, put right, rectify, regulate, remedy, repair, respond to, rise to the challenge, see to, settle, solve, sort (out), stop the rot, supervise, tackle, take care of, take the bull by the horns, treat, undertake, withstand

**Adequate** adj., see also Enough, Satisfactory
acceptable, all right, ample, appropriate, average, capable, competent, cutting it, decent, does the job, fair, fine, fit for purpose, good enough, it will do, mediocre, okay, ordinary, passable, presentable, reasonable, regular, requisite, respectable, so-so, standard, sufficient, suitable, tolerable, unexceptional, up to scratch

**Adjust** v., see also Adapt, Change
acclimatise, accommodate, alter, amend, balance, become accustomed, calibrate, change tack, configure, conform, correct, customise, enhance, evolve, fine-tune, fix, get used to, harmonise, hone, improve, modernise, optimise, overhaul, perfect, polish, readjust, recalibrate, reconfigure, rectify, refashion, refine, reform, regulate, rejig, rethink, revamp, review, revise, revisit, sharpen, tailor, tighten, tinker with, tune, tweak, update, upgrade

**Adjustment** n., see also Amendment, Change
adaptation, addition, alteration, conversion, customisation, development, enhancement, evolution, fine-tuning, improvement, innovation, makeover, modification, optimisation, orientation, overhaul, readjustment, recalibration, reconfiguration, rectification, refinement, regulation, rethink, review, revision, shift, tinkering, tweak, update, upgrade

**Administration** n., see also Authority, Management
1. care, charge, command, control, decision-making, direction, enforcement, guidance, governance, government, handling, jurisdiction, leadership, operation, orchestration, organisation, overseeing, oversight, power, regime, regulation, reign, rule, running, tenure, stewardship, supervision
2. agency, authorities, bureaucracy, committee, corridors of power, department, decision-makers, executive(s), government, leadership, ministry, officialdom, officials, powers that be, regime, those in charge/power, top brass

**Admire** v., see also Appreciate, Like
acclaim, adore, applaud, approve, be a fan of, be blown away by, be filled with admiration for, be impressed by, be in awe of, be mad about, be wild about, cannot speak highly enough of, celebrate, commend, credit, doff one's cap to, give credit to, glorify, hail, hand it to, have a good/high opinion of, have great admiration for, hold in high esteem, hold in high regard, idolise, laud, look up to, marvel at, pay homage to, pay tribute to, praise, prize, rate, respect, revere, think a lot of, think highly of, tip one's hat to, value, worship

**Advanced** adj., see also Complex, High-tech
ahead of its time, ahead of the curve, all-singing all-dancing, automated, bells-and-whistles, bang up to date, breakthrough, cutting-edge, digital, fancy, forward-thinking, future-proof, future-ready, futuristic, game-changing, groundbreaking, innovative, inventive, latest, leading, leading-edge, light years ahead, modern, new, new-look, next-generation, novel, pioneering, progressive, radical, revolutionary, sophisticated, state-of-the-art, technically advanced, technological, trailblazing, ultra-modern, updated, up-to-date, upgraded, very latest

**Advantage** n., see also Benefit, Strength
ace up one's sleeve, added advantage, aid, asset, assistance, beauty, big plus, blessing, boon, bonus, boost, competitive advantage/edge, convenience, dominance, edge, fillip, foothold, forte, head start, help, in the driving seat, joy, lead, leg-up, leverage, merit, party piece, perk, plus, plus point, power, resource, secret weapon, selling point, strong point, strong suit, superiority, supremacy, tailwind, trump card, upper hand, upside, usefulness, USP, utility, value, virtue, weapon

**Advertise** v., see also Announce, Promote
bang the drum, big up, champion, communicate, create a buzz, declare, disclose, display, emblazon, endorse, feature, flaunt, give the hard sell, herald, highlight, hype, inform, make known, market, notify, pitch, plug, present, proclaim, publicise, publish, push, reveal, sell, shout about, showcase, sponsor, spread the word, tout, trail, trumpet, vaunt

**Advertising** n., see also Communication, Marketing
ad, advert, advertisement, announcement, blurb, claim, commercial, declaration, endorsement, glitz, hard sell, hype, infomercial, pitch, plug, PR, presentation, proclamation, promotion, propaganda, public relations, publicity, razzamatazz, showcase, splash, sponsorship

**Advice** n., see also Help, Warning
advisory service, aid, assessment, assistance, caution, consultation, consulting, counsel, encouragement, forewarning, guidance, hack, idea, input, instructions, judgement, opinion, perspective, piece of advice, point of view, pointer, proposal, proposition, recommendation, sound advice, suggestion, support, take, tip, tip-off, tips and tricks, view, wisdom, word, word(s) of wisdom

**Advise** v., see also Help, Recommend
advocate, appeal to, caution, communicate, counsel, dissuade, encourage, exhort, forewarn, give advice, give input, guide, have the ear of someone, inform, inspire, instruct, keep posted, level with, notify, offer advice, offer an opinion, persuade, point out, preach, prepare, provide advice, provide information, prompt, steer, strongly advise, suggest, support, take the view, tell, urge, warn, weigh in on

**Affect** v., see also Affect Negatively, Cause
act on, affect deeply, alter, be at play/work, bear upon, bite, change, concern, drive, fuel, gain traction, have a bearing on, have an effect on, have an impact on, have an influence on, have implications for, impact, impinge on, influence, involve, kick in, leave one's mark, make a change, make a difference, make an impact, make waves, modify, move the needle, permeate, prompt, provoke, regard, relate to, shape, spark, spur, stimulate, take effect, touch, transform, trigger

**Affect Negatively** v., see also Damage, Hinder
adversely affect, afflict, assail, be costly for, blight, blindside, bring to one's knees, bruise, buffet, cripple, deal a (body/hammer) blow, dent, derail, detract from, devastate, diminish, disrupt, disturb, dog, doom, embroil, engulf, hammer, hamper, have a negative effect/impact/influence on, have on the ropes, hit, hit hard, hobble, hound, hurt, impact negatively, impair, imperil, impoverish, incapacitate, inflict damage, inhibit, knock, knock for six, leave in tatters, mar, overwhelm, plague, poleaxe, put on the back foot, put under pressure, rock, rock to one's core, scupper, send into meltdown, send reeling, set back, shackle, shake, spell trouble for, strain, strike, take a toll on, throw a spanner in the works, trouble, undermine, upset, weaken, weigh on, wound, wreck

**After** adv./conj./prep., see also Consequently, Result In
after-effect, afterwards, at a later date, at the end of, beyond, ensuing, following, following on from, hot on the heels of, in hindsight, in the aftermath

of, in the wake of, later, later on, looking back, next, on the back of, post-*****, subsequent to, subsequently, thereafter, upshot, when the dust settles

**Agile** adj., see also Efficient, Quick
active, adaptable, adept, adroit, alert, bright, brisk, bustling, deft, dynamic, energetic, fast, fast-moving, fast-paced, flexible, instant, just-in-time, lively, nimble, prompt, quick-witted, rapid, rapid-response, responsive, sharp, speedy, spirited, sprightly, swift, with agility

**Agree** v., see also Approve, Match
1. abide by, accede, accept, accord with, acknowledge, adopt, agree terms, assent, be aligned with, be in agreement, be amenable to, be in harmony, be in line with, be of the same opinion, be on board with, be on the same page, be pro something, be unanimous, be united, be willing, bow to, bury the hatchet, buy into, clinch a deal, coincide, come on board, come to an agreement, come to terms, comply, compromise, concede, conclude an agreement, concur, conform, consent, cut a deal, echo, enter into an agreement, fall into line, get on board with, give one's blessing, give the go-ahead, give the green light, go along with, grant, hammer out, harmonise, join forces, kiss and make up, land a deal, make a deal, make peace, okay, pander to, pencil in, permit, put aside one's differences, put pen to paper, reach a consensus, reach agreement, recognise, reserve, resolve one's differences, seal the deal, second, see eye to eye, settle, settle differences, shake on, side with, sign (an agreement), sign off on, sign up to, strike a deal, sympathise, undertake, unite around
2. align with, be consistent, be in line with, be similar, be the same, chime, coincide, comply, concur, conform, correlate, correspond, echo, harmonise, resonate with, tally

**Agreement** n., see also Approval, Contract
1. acceptance, accommodation, accord, accordance, acknowledgement, alliance, arrangement, assent, authorisation, backing, buy-in, compatibility, compliance, compromise, concession, consensus, consent, deal, endorsement, go-ahead, harmony, mutual understanding, negotiation, nod, okay, olive branch, pact, protocol, ratification, recognition, reconciliation, settlement, sign-off, transaction, treaty, truce, understanding, unison, unity
2. accordance, affinity, compatibility, compliance, concurrence, consistency, correlation, correspondence, match, similarity

**Aim** n., see also Ambition, Goal
aspiration, desire, destination, determination, dream, end, end goal, endeavour, expectation, focus, forecast, hope, horizons, idea, intent, intention, mission,

object, objective, plan, point, purpose, sights, stated aim, target, ultimate objective, vision, wish

**Aim** v., see also Focus, Intend
aspire, attempt, be determined, be keen, be resolved, bid, concentrate on, count on, design, endeavour, envisage, expect, eye, forecast, foresee, go after, go for, go for broke, have a crack at, have a stab at, have as a goal, have designs on, have in one's sights, have the intention, hope, look, look ahead to, look forward to, look to, make a bid, mean, plan, propose, pursue, push, seek, set one's sights on, shoot for, strive, take aim, target, try, undertake, venture, want, wish, work towards, zero in on

**All** adv./det., see also Complete, Entire
across the board, all and sundry, all bar none, all-encompassing, altogether, any, completely, comprehensive, each, each and every, entire amount, entirely, entirety, every, every last/single, everyone, everything, full, full complement, full works, fully, lock stock and barrel, total, totality, totally, utterly, whole, whole caboodle, whole hog, whole shebang, wholly, without exception, works

**Allow** v., see also Enable, Support
accept, acknowledge, admit, agree, approve, assent to, authorise, concede, condone, consent to, empower, endorse, give one's blessing, give permission, give the go-ahead, give the green light, give the nod, give the OK, give the thumbs up, go along with, grant, grant permission, green-light, help, indulge, let, license, live with, make possible, okay, open the door to, permit, provide the opportunity, provide the scope, put up with, recognise, relent, rubber-stamp, sanction, stand by, say yes, sign off on, take no action against, tolerate, turn a blind eye to, unlock, wave through

**Almost** adv., see also Approximate, Undecided
about, about to, all but, approaching, approximately, around, as good as, basically, bordering on, borderline, close, close but no cigar, de facto, essentially, hair's breadth, in effect, in the vicinity of, just about, just shy of, near-*****, nearly, nigh on, not far from/off, not quite, on the brink of, on the cusp of, on the point of, on the verge of, practically, relatively, roughly, substantially, to all intents and purposes, very nearly, virtually, well-nigh, within grasp, within reach, within sight, within touching distance

**Alternative** adj./n., see also Choice, Different
another, as opposed, assortment, backup, contingency, contrasting, equivalent, fallback, flip side, instead, left-field, on the other hand, opposite, option,

optional, other, other options, plan B, possible, potential, preference, refreshing, replacement, reserve, second, second choice, selection, substitute

**Always** adv., see also Continual, Permanent
24/7, all the time, as ever, come rain or shine, concertedly, consistently, constantly, continually, day in day out, doggedly, endlessly, eternally, ever, ever-present, every time, forever, for good, habitually, incessantly, invariably, perennially, perpetually, persistently, pervasive, regularly, relentlessly, repeatedly, resolutely, since time immemorial, steadfastly, stubbornly, through thick and thin, unfailingly, without exception, without fail

**Ambition** n., see also Aim, Objective
appetite, aspiration, big ambitions, big picture, big plans, commitment, delusions of grandeur, desire, determination, dream, drive, eagerness, energy, enterprise, enthusiasm, fire in one's belly, get-up-and-go, goal, high hopes, hope(s), horizons, hunger, initiative, intention, intent, keenness, lofty ambitions, longing, mission, mojo, motivation, optimism, passion, plan, pretensions, resolve, target, ultimate objective, vision, wish, yearning, zeal

**Amend** v., see also Adjust, Improve
adapt, alter, calibrate, change, convert, correct, customise, develop, edit, enhance, fine-tune, fix, hone, make a change, make a modification, make an amendment, modify, optimise, overhaul, put right, recalibrate, reconfigure, rectify, redesign, refine, reform, rejig, remedy, remodel, reorganise, repair, reshape, rethink, revise, revisit, rework, ring the changes, shake up, switch up, transform, tweak, update, upgrade

**Amendment** n., see also Adjustment, Change
adaptation, addition, alteration, clarification, correction, development, edit, enhancement, fix, improvement, makeover, modification, optimisation, rectification, redesign, reform, remedy, repair, rethink, review, revision, reworking, shake-up, tweak, update, upgrade

**Amount** n., see also Level
abundance, bulk, capacity, chunk, cost, dose, entirety, expense, extent, helping, load, magnitude, mass, measure, no less than, number, percentage, portion, price, proportion, quantity, quota, ratio, result, scale, scope, score, size, slice, some (*e.g. some £1 million*), sum, tally, tidy sum, toll, to the tune of, total, value, volume, weight, whole

**Analyse** v., see also Assess, Understand
appraise, break down, calculate, catalogue, check out, conduct an analysis, consider, crunch the numbers, decipher, delve into, determine, dig deeper, dissect, do one's homework, drill down into, estimate, evaluate, examine, explore, figure out, gauge, get to the bottom of, get to the heart of, inspect, interpret, investigate, judge, lift the lid, look into, make of, monitor, pick over, ponder, pore over, probe, put under the microscope, reflect on, review, scour, screen, scrutinise, shed light on, shine a light on, subject to analysis, study, think through, unpack, unpick, verify, weigh (up)

**Analysis** n., see also Assessment, Evaluation
breakdown, calculation, conclusion, consideration, deep dive, detective work, due diligence, enquiry, examination, exploration, findings, hindsight, insight, inspection, interpretation, investigation, judgement, number crunching, opinion, picture, report, review, screening, scrutiny, search, soul-searching, study, test, understanding, verification, view

**And** conj., see also However
additionally, alike, along with, alongside, also, as is, as well, as well as, at the same time, besides, both, by the same token, combined with, coupled with, equally, furthermore, in addition, in combination with, in conjunction with, in equal measure, including, it should be added that, likewise, meanwhile, more than that, moreover, not only...but also..., not forgetting, not to mention, on top of that, one might add that, parallel to, plus, secondly, similarly, to boot, together with, too, what is more, while

**Anger** n., see also Disappointment, Unhappiness
acrimony, animosity, annoyance, bitterness, discontent, displeasure, disapproval, dissatisfaction, enmity, exasperation, frustration, furore, fury, hostility, huff, ill temper, indignation, infuriation, ire, irritability, irritation, outcry, outrage, rage, rancour, resentment, storm, umbrage, uproar, upset, vexation, vitriol, wrath

**Anger** v., see also Upset, Worry
affront, aggravate, annoy, antagonise, bait, be a red rag to a bull, cause outrage, displease, enrage, exasperate, excite, fan the flames, gall, get someone's back up, goad, hit a nerve, incense, incite, incur someone's wrath, inflame, infuriate, irritate, leave aghast, make someone angry/mad, make someone's blood boil, needle, offend, outrage, pique, provoke anger/fury, rankle, rile, rub up the wrong way, ruffle feathers, stir up, touch a nerve, vex, wind up

**Angry** adj., see also Disappointed, Unhappy
affronted, aggrieved, annoyed, apoplectic, bad-tempered, bitter, bristling, cross, disgruntled, displeased, enraged, exasperated, fed up, frustrated, fuming, furious, heated, hostile, hot under the collar, impassioned, incensed, indignant, infuriated, irate, irritated, livid, mad, miffed, offended, on the warpath, outraged, raging, resentful, riled, seething, ticked off, up in arms, upset

**Announce** v., see also Advertise, Say
affirm, articulate, assert, call, claim, communicate, declare, disclose, disseminate, divulge, explain, express, give notice, herald, issue, make an announcement, make known, make public, nail one's colours to the mast, notify, outline, present, proclaim, publicise, publish, put forth, reiterate, release, remark, report, reveal, set out, shout about, shout from the rooftops, signal, spread the word, state, stress, tell, trail, trumpet

**Annoying** adj., see also Disappointing, Worrying
aggravating, annoyance, disruptive, disturbing, exasperating, frustrating, galling, getting on one's nerves, grating, inconvenient, infuriating, irksome, irritating, jarring, maddening, nagging, niggling, nuisance, pain, pesky, source of frustration, troublesome, trying, upsetting, wind-up

**Anticipate** v., see also Estimate, Forecast
aim, assume, await, await eagerly, bank on, bargain for, be a step ahead, be braced for, be confident, be dying to, be excited, be hopeful, be prepared for, believe, bet, brace for, calculate, call for, can't wait for, come as no surprise, conjecture, count on, envisage, expect, fear, foresee, guess, have a feeling, have a hunch, have faith in, head off, hope, hotly anticipate, imagine, look ahead, look for, look forward, prepare for, plan for, predict, pre-empt, presume, price in, put money on, reckon, rely upon, second-guess, see, see coming, suppose, surmise, suspect, target, think, think likely, trust

**Apologise** v., see also Regret
admit error, apologise unreservedly, ask forgiveness, ask someone's pardon, atone, be apologetic, be contrite, be sorry, concede, confess, excuse oneself, express regret/remorse, hold one's hands up, issue a mea culpa, make amends, make up for, offer excuses, recant, repent, retract, rue, say sorry

**Appeal** n., see also Excitement, Interest
1. affinity, allure, attraction, attractiveness, beauty, captivation, certain something, charisma, charm, draw, fascination, glamour, glitz, je ne sais quoi,

likeability, magnetism, pull, seduction, seductiveness, selling point, sparkle, temptation, USP, X factor
2. bid, call, claim, clamour, demand, entreaty, overture, plea, proposal, request

**Appear** v., see also Emerge, Start
1. allude to, augur, be apparently, be on the face of it, be ostensibly, be seemingly, be set to, be suggestive of, bode, come across as, create the impression, evoke, give/create the impression, have the air, have the appearance, hint, imply, insinuate, intimate, look as though, look like, make for, promise, reflect, resemble, seem, set to be, shape up, show every sign of, smack of, sound, strike one as, suggest
2. arise, arrive, arrive on the scene, be released, be revealed, become known, blow up, break (through), burst onto the scene, come to light, crop up, develop, drop, erupt, gain attention, land, loom, materialise, occur, originate, rear its head, spring up, surface, turn up

**Appearance** n., see also Impression, Start
1. aesthetic, air, aspect, aura, demeanour, facade, first impression, front, illusion, image, look(s), look and feel, manner, optics, outward appearance, presentation, semblance, veneer
2. advent, arrival, breakthrough, debut, emergence, introduction, manifestation, onset, presence, presentation, rise, unveiling

**Apply** v., see also Use
1. administer, affect, be applicable, be appropriate, be relevant, bring to bear, carry out, concern, deploy, employ, enact, exercise, exploit, have a bearing, impact, implement, impose, involve, make use of, pertain, practise, put into practice, put to use, refer, regard, relate, utilise, wield
2. appeal, ask, claim, demand, enquire/inquire, make a claim, make an application, request, seek, solicit, submit an application/a request

**Appoint** v., see also Assign, Employ
allot, arrange, assign responsibility, authorise, charge with, choose, commission, delegate, designate, elect, engage, entrust, establish, give responsibility, give the nod, hire, install, name, nominate, parachute in, promote, put in charge, put in place, recruit, select, settle on, take on, task with

**Appreciate** v., see also Increase, Like
1. acknowledge, admire, applaud, approve of, be alive to, be appreciative, be aware, be conscious, be grateful, be indebted, be obliged, be sensitive to, celebrate, cherish, commend, comprehend, consider important, count one's

blessings, endorse, enjoy, favour, hail, have admiration for, hold in high esteem, know, put things in/into perspective, praise, prize, rate highly, recognise, regard highly, relish, respect, sympathise with, take account of, take one's hat off to, thank, treasure, understand, value (highly), welcome
2. climb, gain, go up in value, grow, improve, increase in value, rise

**Approach** n., see also Attitude, Method
action, avenue, concept, course, course of action, culture, ethos, framework, game plan, manner, means, mindset, modus operandi, organisational culture, outlook, path, pathway, perspective, plan, playbook, point of view, procedure, process, road map, route, school of thought, set of values, solution, stance, standpoint, strategy, style, tack, tactic, take, technique, thinking, tone, value set, values, viewpoint, vision, way

**Approach** v., see also Address, Manage
1. accommodate, adopt an approach, adopt an attitude, attend to, come at, deal with, embark on, ensure, focus on, get to grips with, grapple with, handle, look at, navigate, proceed, resolve, respond to, rise to the challenge, see to, set about, tackle, take steps, think about, treat, undertake, work on
2. advance, be almost here, be on the horizon, beckon, close in on, draw near, get closer, inch closer, loom, near, soon be here, threaten
3. consult, contact, make an approach, make overtures, request, sound out, suggest, talk to

**Appropriate** adj., see also Correct, Right
acceptable, applicable, apt, at home, befitting, compatible, conducive, consistent, convenient, corresponding, deserved, done thing, fit for purpose, fitting, geared towards, good, good fit, go-to, horses for courses, ideal, in keeping, in one's comfort zone, just right, just the thing/ticket, legitimate, made for, meeting with approval, one's cup of tea, only right, opportune, optimal, optimum, perfect, pertinent, proper, purpose-built/designed/made, quite right, relevant, right and proper, satisfactory, spot on, stacks up, successful, suitable, suited, suit down to the ground, tailored, tailor-made, ticking all the boxes, to taste, true, up one's street, useful, well-judged, well-suited

**Approval** n., see also Agreement, Decision
admiration, acceptance, appreciation, authorisation, backing, blessing, confirmation, consent, endorsement, go-ahead, green light, licence, liking, mandate, nod, okay, permission, praise, ratification, sanction, scope, stamp of approval, support, thumbs up, validation

**Approve** v., see also Agree, Like
accept, action, advocate, allow, applaud, approve of, authorise, back, buy into, commend, confirm, consent to, enable, encourage, endorse, favour, get behind, give approval, give one's blessing, give permission, give one's seal/stamp of approval, give the go-ahead/nod, give the thumbs up, go along with, grant, green-light, license, okay, pass, permit, praise, ratify, recommend, rubber-stamp, sanction, say yes, sign off on, subscribe to, support, validate, welcome

**Approximate/Approximately** adj./adv., see also Almost, General(ly)
approaching, around, at a guess, ballpark figure, bordering on, close to, crude, estimated, general, generally, imprecise, in the ballpark of, in the region of, in the vicinity of, just over/under, more than, more or less, near, nearly, nigh on, not far off, odd, or so, relatively, rough, roughly, roughly speaking, some (*e.g. some £1 million*), somewhere around, (there or) thereabouts, verging on

**Area** n., see also Division, Sector
1. activity, arena, aspect, bracket, breadth, business, domain, environment, expanse, extent, field, footprint, forum, front, industry, landscape, line, market, niche, part, place, pocket, portion, radius, range, realm, scene, scope, section, setting, site, space, sphere, stage, subject, territory, trade, world, zone
2. city, district, environment, landscape, locality, location, neck of the woods, neighbourhood, part, pocket, quarters, region, section, setting, site, surrounding area, surroundings, territory, town, vicinity, zone

**Argument** n., see also Conflict, Opinion
1. altercation, animosity, battle, battleground, beef, bickering, bone of contention, case, clash, controversy, deadlock, debate, defence, deliberation, difference of opinion, disagreement, disapproval, discontent, discussion, dispute, divide, exchange, face-off, falling-out, feud, gripe, hostility, impasse, misunderstanding, quarrel, row, run-in, spat, squabble, stand-off, tiff, wrangle
2. case, claim, contention, grounds, hypothesis, idea, justification, logic, rationale, reason, reasoning, theme, theory, thesis, view

**Aspect** n., see also Factor, Feature
angle, attribute, bit, building block, characteristic, circumstance, component, detail, element, facet, front, ingredient, measure, nature, parameter, part, phase, perspective, portion, position, property, quality, respect, section, sector, segment, share, side, situation, strand, tranche

**Assess** v., see also Analyse, Consider
appraise, calculate, check, check out, conduct an assessment/evaluation, deduce, determine, estimate, evaluate, examine, explore, explore options, figure out, forecast, gauge, grade, inspect, investigate, judge, look into, look over, make of, measure, monitor, pore over, probe, rank, rate, regard, review, screen, scrutinise, shine a light on, size up, study, survey, take account of, take into consideration, test, understand, value, verify, view, weigh (up)

**Assessment** n., see also Analysis, Forecast
appraisal, barometer, calculation, check, consideration, deduction, determination, discretion, due diligence, estimate, estimation, evaluation, exploration, gauge, grading, insight, inspection, investigation, judgement, measurement, opinion, outlook, ranking, rating, reckoning, review, screening, scrutiny, valuation, view, weighing-up

**Asset** n., see also Advantage, Wealth
1. ace, ace up one's sleeve, attribute, benefit, blessing, boon, fillip, forte, godsend, good point, help, importance, plus, resource, secret weapon, skill, strength, strong point, support, utility, value, virtue, weapon
2. belongings, capital, equity, estate, funds, goods, holdings, means, money, possessions, property, resource, valuables, value, worth

**Assign** v., see also Appoint, Employ
allocate, allot, allow, ascribe, attribute, authorise, charge, choose, commission, delegate, designate, earmark, elect, empower, entrust, give, give responsibility, hire, name, nominate, place, post, put in charge, put in place, recruit, select, set aside, specify, task with

**Assignment** n., see also Project, Work
allocation, appointment, authorisation, brief, commission, deployment, designation, distribution, duty, job, mission, nomination, obligation, office, position, post, recruitment, remit, request, responsibility, selection, task, undertaking

**Assortment** n., see also Range, Variety
all kinds/manner of, armoury, array, arsenal, batch, breadth, broad spectrum, choice, cohort, collection, combination, cornucopia, crop, cross section, diversity, everything from…to…, gamut, group, heady mix, kaleidoscope, line-up, medley, menu, mixture, offering, package, portfolio, product range, raft, repertoire, roster, scope, selection, spectrum, stable, suite, team, …to name but a few, wide range

**Assume** v., see also Consider, Forecast
1. anticipate, be a given, believe, conclude, estimate, expect, guess, have a hunch, have a suspicion, have an inkling, imagine, infer, make an assumption, postulate, presume, presuppose, speculate, suspect, suppose, surmise, take for granted, take it, think
2. accept, adopt, embrace, shoulder, take on, take over, take responsibility for, undertake

**Assumption** n., see also Basis, Expectation
acceptance, anticipation, argument, belief, bias, conclusion, confidence, conjecture, conviction, estimate, guess, hunch, hypothesis, inference, opinion, preconception, prejudice, premise, presumption, speculation, supposition, suspicion, theory, thought, understanding

**Attempt** n., see also Aim, Test
best efforts, best endeavours, best shot, bid, crack, effort(s), endeavour(s), enterprise, exertion, experiment, foray, go, Herculean effort, level best, nice try, one's all, one's best, project, pursuit, push, shot, stab, struggle, tilt, try, undertaking, valiant effort, venture

**Attempt** v., see also Aim, Endeavour
aspire, bid, buckle down, chip away at, dig deep, do one's best, do one's damnedest, exert oneself, experiment, get stuck in, give it a go, give it one's all, give it one's best shot, go after, go for, go for broke, have a crack, have a go, have a shot, have a stab, have a try, hope, leave no stone unturned, make a bid, make a fist of, make an effort, make a foray into, move heaven and earth, plan, pull out all the stops, pursue, push for, put one's best foot forward, put one's heart (and soul) into, put one's mind to, roll up one's sleeves, seek, set one's sights on, shoot for, step up (to the mark/plate), strive, struggle, target, try, undertake, venture

**Attitude** n., see also Approach, Opinion
angle, appearance, belief, character, core values, corporate culture, culture, demeanour, disposition, DNA, ethos, inclination, manner, mantra, maxim, mentality, mindset, mood, organisational culture, outlook, perspective, philosophy, point of view, position, stance, standpoint, strategy, take, temperament, tendency, thinking, thought process, tone, values, view, viewpoint, vision, way

**Attract** v., see also Admire, Like
appeal to, be a hit with, be a magnet for, beguile, bewitch, bring, bring in, captivate, capture the imagination, catch the eye, charm, coax, court, draw, draw attention, draw in, enchant, endear, engage, enthral, entice, fascinate, get attention, grab, gravitate towards, hook, interest, intrigue, invite, lure, pique the interest of, play well with, pull, seduce, spellbind, suck in, tempt, turn heads, win over, woo, wow

**Attraction** n., see also Excitement, Interest
affinity, allure, appeal, attractiveness, beauty, captivation, certain something, charisma, chemistry, charm, desirability, draw, enticement, fascination, glamour, glitz, je ne sais quoi, likeability, lure, magnet, magnetism, pull, seduction, seductiveness, sparkle, temptation, USP, X factor

**Attractive** adj., see also Entertaining, Good
adorable, alluring, appealing, attention-grabbing, beautiful, beguiling, blissful, breathtaking, captivating, charismatic, charming, dapper, dazzling, debonair, delectable, delightful, desirable, divine, drop-dead gorgeous, easy on the eye, enchanting, endearing, enthralling, enticing, entrancing, enviable, exciting, exquisite, eye-catching, fascinating, fetching, fine, flamboyant, flawless, glamourous, glitzy, glossy, good-looking, gorgeous, handsome, head-turning, high-end, iconic, impressive, interesting, inviting, irresistible, jaw-dropping, joy to behold, likeable, looker, lovely, magnificent, mouthwatering, must-have, must-see, pleasant, pleasing, pretty, pristine, seductive, sexy, sleek, sought-after, stunning, striking, stylish, suave, sublime, sumptuous, tantalising, tasteful, tempting, thing of beauty, to die for, trendy, unmissable, upmarket, vibrant, winning, wonderful, wow factor

**Authentic** adj., see also Real
accurate, actual, attested, authoritative, bona fide, candid, certain, confirmed, convincing, certified, credible, earnest, faithful, frank, genuine, heartfelt, honest, honest-to-goodness, kosher, legitimate, natural, official, original, proper, pure, real deal, real McCoy, real thing, real-life, reliable, signed-up, sincere, true, true colours, true-to-life, trusted, trustworthy, truthful, undisputed, unmistakeable, unquestionable, valid, verified, veritable

**Authorisation** n., see also Approval, Confirmation
accreditation, authority, backing, consent, credentials, empowerment, endorsement, entitlement, freedom, go-ahead, green light, leave, licence, mandate, nod, okay, permission, permit, power, right, sanction, say-so, scope, stamp of approval, support, thumbs up, validation

**Authorise** v., see also Approve, Certify
agree to, allow, commission, confirm, consent to, empower, enable, endorse, entitle, give authority, give the go-ahead, give the green light, give the nod, give the thumbs up, give permission, grant power, grant the right, green-light, legalise, let, license, mandate, okay, pass, permit, ratify, rubber-stamp, sanction, sign off on, support, validate

**Authority** n., see also Leadership, Power
1. authorisation, clout, command, consent, control, dispensation, domination, dominion, force, gravitas, grip, guidance, influence, jurisdiction, management, mandate, mastery, might, muscle, permission, predominance, prerogative, reign, responsibility, right(s), rule, say, scope, seniority, stature, strength, supremacy, sway, weight
2. administration, aficionado, agency, connoisseur, corridors of power, council, establishment, executive (authority), expert, government agency, local authority/government, municipality, officialdom, officials, powers that be, professional, regulator, regulatory authority, specialist, top brass, watchdog

**Automated** adj., see also Advanced, High-tech
AI, app-based, artificial intelligence, automatic, autonomous, computer-based/controlled, computerised, computer-operated, connected, digital, driverless, electronic, intelligent, mechanical, networked, online, pre-programmed, programmable, programmed, remote, remote-controlled, robotic, self-***** (*e.g. self-driving*), smart, unmanned, web-based

**Average** adj., see also Normal, Typical
bog-standard, bread-and-butter, common, common-or-garden, commonplace, decidedly average, everyday, humdrum, in-between, indifferent, intermediate, mainstream, mean, mediocre, medium, middle-of-the-road, middling, midway, moderate, not bad, nothing special, ordinary, pedestrian, rank-and-file, regular, run-of-the-mill, so-so, standard, standardised, standard-issue, uneventful, unexceptional, usual

**Avoid** v., see also Prevent, Stop
abstain from, avert, avoid like the plague, bypass, circumvent, deflect, defend against, distance oneself from, divert, dodge, dodge a bullet, duck, elude, escape, eschew, evade, fend off, get round, give a wide berth to, give something a miss, guard against, head off, ignore, keep away from, manage to avoid, refrain from, run a mile from, shake, shake off, shun, shy away, sidestep, skip, stave off, stay away, steer clear of, swerve, ward off, withdraw from

**Award** n., see also Achievement, Success
accolade, best, citation, decision, distinction, feather in the cap, first place, first prize, gong, honour, judges' decision, medal, nomination, number one, praise, presentation, prize, ranking, recognition, result, reward, silverware, title, top prize, top ranking, top spot, triumph, trophy, verdict, victory, win

# B

**Bad** adj., see also Negative, Weak
abysmal, adverse, amiss, appalling, atrocious, awful, bad news, below par, costly, counterproductive, damaging, dangerous, defective, deficient, detrimental, diabolical, dire, disappointing, disastrous, dismal, dodgy, dreadful, excruciating, feeble, flawed, found wanting, hapless, half-hearted, harmful, horrendous, horrific, ill-judged, imperfect, immoral, in a bad place, inadequate, ineffective, inept, inferior, insufficient, lacking, lacklustre, lousy, low-quality, malign, miserable, not a good look, not fit for purpose, not good, not up to scratch, not working, pathetic, poor, poor-quality, ropey, rough, sad, second-class, second-rate, shabby, shambolic, shoddy, sorry, subpar, substandard, suspect, terrible, toxic, unacceptable, unfit, unfortunate, unimpressive, unpalatable, unsatisfactory, wanting, woeful, wrong

**Balance** v., see also Lessen, Offset
adjust, balance out, bring equilibrium, cancel out, compensate for, counteract, counterbalance, equalise, even out, even up, harmonise, level out, level up, make up for, mitigate, moderate, more than make up for, neutralise, nullify, outweigh, readjust, rebalance, redress, square, stabilise, steady, strike a balance, temper

**Bankruptcy** n., see also Decline, Failure
administration, collapse, crash, default, demise, destitution, filing for bankruptcy, financial collapse, financial failure, financial ruin, going bust, going to the wall, going under, inability to pay, insolvency, liquidation, meltdown, non-payment, receivership, ruin

**Based** adj., see also Basis, Depend
arising from, born of, built, centred, constructed, derived, established, focused, founded, located, oriented, placed, positioned, predicated, premised, related, rooted, secured, situated, stemming from, supported, underpinned

**Basic** adj., see also Easy, Simple
back-to-basics, bare-bones, beginner's, bog-standard, cardinal, central, chief, classic, core, crucial, crude, default, down-to-earth, elementary, entry-level, essential, fundamental, grass-roots, indispensable, inherent, innate, intrinsic,

introductory, key, main, necessary, no-frills, no-nonsense, pared-back, primary, primitive, principal, quick-and-dirty, requisite, rough-and-ready, rudimentary, self-explanatory, simplistic, spartan, standard, straightforward, uncomplicated, underlying, unfussy, unsophisticated, vital

**Basis** n., see also Approach, System
agreement, arrangement, assumption, authority, backbone, base, bedrock, centre, centrepiece, core, core element, cornerstone, crux, essence, foothold, footing, foundation(s), framework, ground(s), groundwork, heart, infrastructure, justification, key, keystone, lifeblood, mainstay, method, nucleus, origin, parameters, pillar, platform, premise, presumption, principle, root, starting point, structure, support, theory, underpinning, way

**Be** v., see also Happen, Represent
account for, amount to, appear, be alive, be in place, be located, be present, become, boast, comprise, constitute, denote, do, embody, emerge, endure, epitomise, exist, feature, find oneself, give the impression, go on, last, live, look as though, look like, make for, occur, persist, personify, prevail, promise to be, prove (to be), reflect, remain, see happen, seem, serve as, set to be, shape up to be, stand for, stay, survive, transpire, turn out

**Because Of** phr., see also Therefore
as, as a result of, attributable to, by dint of, by reason of, by virtue of, caused by, courtesy of, driven by, due to, for that reason, fuelled by, given, in light of, in view of, now that, on account of, on the back of, on the grounds that, owing to, resulting from, since, thanks to, through

**Before** adv./conj./prep., see also Past, Previous
ahead of, ahead of time, at one time, beforehand, earlier, earlier on, ex-*****, forerunner, foretaste, former, formerly, historically, hitherto, in advance of, in anticipation, in the build-up/lead-up/run-up to, in the past, on the eve of, pre-*****, predating, previously, prior, sooner, until/up to now

**Begin** v., see also Innovate, Launch
activate, appear, arise, be a catalyst for, be born, be first, be in its infancy, blaze a trail, blow up, break new ground, bring about, broach, cause, come into existence, commence, conceive, creep in, cut one's teeth, dawn, debut, embark on, emerge, enter upon, erupt, establish, fire the starting gun, fire up, found, get cracking, get going, get the ball rolling, get the show on the road, get underway, give birth to, give rise to, herald, hit the ground running, inaugurate, induce, initiate, inspire, instigate, institute, introduce, jump-start, kick in, kick

off, kick-start, kindle, lay the foundations, lay the groundwork, light the fuse, make a start, mount, open, originate, pioneer, precipitate, premier, proceed, provoke, rear its head, scratch the surface, set about, set in, set in motion, set to, sow the seed(s), spark, spawn, start, start from scratch, start life, start off, start out, start up, stem from, stimulate, take off, take root, take the initiative, trigger, undertake, unleash, unveil, usher in

**Beginning** n., see also Innovation, Introduction
advent, baptism (of fire), birth, breakthrough, catalyst, commencement, creation, curtain-raiser, dawn, dawning, day one, debut, early days, embryonic, emergence, establishment, first steps, flying start, foothold, foundation(s), genesis, germ (of an idea), get-go, green shoots, groundwork, inauguration, inception, infancy, initiation, inroads, inspiration, just the beginning/start, kick-off, launch, launch pad, nascent, off, onset, opening, origin, outset, preface, prelude, premiere, rise, root(s), source, springboard, square one, start, start of something (big/great), starting point, start-up, tip of the iceberg, top, unveiling

**Belief** n., see also Approach, Confidence
acceptance, assumption, attitude, concept, conclusion, consensus, conviction, core values, corporate culture, creed, determination, doctrine, ethos, expectation, faith, feeling, fundamental belief, guess, hope, hypothesis, idea, ideology, impression, inkling, judgement, knowledge, mantra, maxim, mentality, mindset, notion, opinion, organisational culture, outlook, perspective, philosophy, point of view, position, principles, resoluteness, school of thought, self-belief, stance, suspicion, tenacity, tenet, theory, thinking, trust, understanding, values, view, viewpoint, vision, way of thinking

**Believe** v., see also Think, Trust
accept, be a (firm) believer, be certain of, be confident, be convinced of, be minded to, be of the opinion, be of the view, buy, conclude, consider, deem, espouse, expect, feel, have belief, have confidence, have faith, have no doubt, hold, judge, maintain, postulate, presume, reckon, regard, remain confident, sense, speculate, strongly believe, suppose, suspect, swear, take the view, understand

**Beneficial** adj., see also Effective, Good
advantageous, appropriate, benign, boon, constructive, convenient, encouraging, favourable, fortunate, *****-friendly (*e.g. family-friendly*), fruitful, helpful, ideal, invaluable, lucky, manna from heaven, of benefit/help/service, opportune, positive, productive, profitable, promising, reassuring, rewarding, suitable, supportive, timely, useful, valuable, welcome

**Benefit** n., see also Advantage, Help
added benefit, aid, asset, assistance, beauty, beneficial effect, blessing, bonus, boon, boost, contribution, convenience, dividends, favour, fillip, gain, godsend, good, interest, joy, merit, pay-off, perk, plus, profit, selling point, service, shot in the arm, silver lining, strength, support, tonic, upside, use, usefulness, utility, value, virtue, welcome addition, win, win-win, worth

**Benefit** v., see also Help, Support
advance, aid, assist, be an advantage, be good for, bolster, boost, capitalise, complement, contribute to, do a favour, do good, do the world of good, do wonders for, empower, enable, enhance, enrich, facilitate, favour, further, gain, gain an advantage/benefit, improve, make possible, make the most of, pay (off), pay dividends, profit, promote, prosper, provide/receive a benefit, provide/receive a shot in the arm, provide the means, reap benefits/dividends/rewards, reinforce, serve, strengthen, take advantage, thrive, turn to one's advantage, use, utilise, welcome

**Best** adj., see also Good, Successful
ace, beacon of, benchmark, best ever, best of both worlds, best-selling, best yet, beyond compare, blue-chip, champion, choice, class-leading, cream, cream of the crop, crème de la crème, elite, excellent, exemplary, favourite, finest, first, first-class, first-rate, flagship, foremost, frontrunner, go-to, gold standard, greatest, greatest of all time, high-performance, high-performing, incomparable, inimitable, invincible, jewel in the crown, leading, legendary, matchless, most suitable, number one, of choice, optimum, out of sight, outstanding, paragon, peerless, perfect, pick, pick of the bunch, pinnacle, pre-eminent, preferred, premium, prime, range-topping, record, record-holding, second to none, setting the standard, simply the best, standout, strongest, superior, superlative, supreme, terrific, top, top spot, top-flight, top-of-the-range, top-quality, ultimate, unbeatable, unbettered, unequalled, unmatched, unparalleled, unrivalled, unsurpassed, utmost, very best, world-beating

**Better** adj., see also Good, Improvement
above and beyond, ahead of, better than ever, cut above (the rest), enhanced, far better, going from strength to strength, have the edge, head and shoulders above, higher, higher-quality, improved, improving, light years ahead, miles ahead, miles better, more effective, more fitting, more suitable, more valuable, much-improved, new and improved, onwards and upwards, optimised, perfected, preferable, preferred, recovered, refined, revamped, sharper, streets ahead, stronger, superior, tweaked, updated, upgraded

**Big** adj., see also Extensive, Many
abundant, almighty, ample, aplenty, astronomical, awesome, behemoth, blockbuster, boundless, bountiful, broad, bulky, bumper, capacious, colossal, colossus, comprehensive, considerable, copious, dominating, enormous, epic, expansive, exponential, eye-watering, formidable, gargantuan, generous, giant, gigantic, ginormous, goliath, grand, great, heavy, hefty, Herculean, huge, humungous, immeasurable, immense, imposing, impressive, in force, innumerable, jumbo, king-size, large, large-scale, largish, legion, leviathan, limitless, major, mammoth, massive, mighty, monster, monstrous, monumental, mountain, of epic proportions, of huge proportions, omnipresent, outsize(d), oversize(d), overwhelming, plentiful, prodigious, roomy, seismic, significant, sizeable, spacious, staggering, strong, substantial, supersize(d), sweeping, swingeing, thumping, titanic, towering, tremendous, vast, voluminous, whacking (great), whopping, wide, wide-ranging, widespread

**Blame** v., see also Complain, Criticise
accuse, admonish, attack, attribute blame, blast, blow the whistle on, brand, call out, censure, chastise, chide, condemn, demonise, denounce, express disapproval of, find fault with, hold responsible, hold to account, impute, incriminate, lambaste, lay at someone's door, lay the blame, pass the buck, pin the blame on, point the finger, rebuke, reprimand, reproach, round on, scapegoat, take aim at, take issue with, take to task, throw under the bus, turn on, upbraid, vilify, villainise

**Bold** adj., see also Brave, Strong
adventurous, audacious, bold as brass, bold move, bold statement, bravado, brazen, buccaneering, cheeky, chutzpah, confident, cool, courageous, daring, dauntless, defiant, do-or-die, emboldened, enterprising, eye-catching, fearless, feisty, gung-ho, gutsy, heroic, in-your-face, intrepid, irrepressible, irreverent, not shy, ostentatious, overt, plucky, punchy, resolute, self-confident, spirited, sticking one's neck out, swashbuckling, throwing caution to the wind, tough, unafraid, unabashed, unashamed, undaunted, unflinching, valiant

**Boom** n., see also Growth, Upturn
advance, blossoming, boom in business, boom period, bonanza, boost, bounce, bubble, burgeoning, development, economic boom, expansion, explosion, flourishing, gold rush, golden age, golden era, good days, good times, heyday, high economic activity, improvement, increase, momentum, pickup, proliferation, prosperity, purple patch, rally, rapid/strong growth, renaissance,

resurgence, rise, spike, strengthening, success, surge, swell, turnaround, upsurge, upswing, upward trend

**Boost** n., see also Benefit, Increase
acceleration, addition, advance, aid, assistance, bolstering, bounce, catalyst, complement, encouragement, enhancement, escalation, expansion, explosion, fillip, growth, help, impetus, improvement, intensification, jump, leap, lift, momentum, mushrooming, pick-up, rally, ramp-up, rebound, resurgence, rise, shot in the arm, spike, springboard, spurt, step-up, stimulus, strengthening, support, surge, swell, thrust, tonic, turbocharging, upping, upgrade, upturn

**Boost** v., see also Increase, Strengthen
accelerate, add to, advance, aid, amplify, assist, augment, beef up, bolster, broaden, build up, bump up, buoy, complement, crank up, deepen, develop, dial up, drive (up), elevate, enhance, enlarge, enrich, escalate, expand, extend, facilitate, fortify, foster, fuel, further, galvanise, heighten, hike, improve, inflate, inspire, intensify, lift, magnify, make bigger, make more, power, promote, provide a boost, provide a shot in the arm, raise, ramp up, ratchet up, reinforce, scale up, send through the roof, spur, step up, stoke, supercharge, supersize, support, sustain, take to the next level, turbocharge, up, upgrade

**Boring** adj., see also Average, Weak
anodyne, banal, bland, drab, dreary, dry, dull, dull as ditchwater, insipid, humdrum, lacklustre, like watching grass grow, like watching paint dry, long-winded, mind-numbing, monotonous, mundane, not exactly setting pulses racing, pedestrian, prosaic, repetitive, run-of-the-mill, same old, staid, stale, sterile, strait-laced, stuffy, tame, tedious, tiresome, trite, uneventful, unexciting, unimaginative, uninspiring, uninteresting, well-worn, yawnsome

**Brand** n., see also Company, Reputation
badge, brand message, brand name, brand platform, business, company, designer, emblem, fashion house, hallmark, kind, label, line, logo, make, maker, marque, moniker, name, quality, sort, stamp, tag, trademark, type, variety

**Brave** adj., see also Bold, Tough
adventurous, audacious, confident, cool, courageous, daring, dauntless, defiant, determined, doughty, enterprising, fearless, feisty, fortitude, gritty, gutsy, heroic, indomitable, intrepid, irrepressible, laying one's neck on the line, lionhearted, never-say-die, plucky, resolute, spirited, unafraid, undaunted, unflinching, valiant

**Brief** adj., see also Small
abrupt, all of a sudden, at a glance, before you know it, blunt, concise, condensed, cursory, curt, ephemeral, fleeting, hasty, in a flash, in a nutshell, in conclusion, in summary, momentary, over in a flash, quick, short, short and sweet, short-term, short-lived, snappy, succinct, summarised, summary, swift, temporary, terse, to the point, whistle-stop

**Broad** adj., see also Large, Varied
all-embracing, all-encompassing, all-purpose, all-round, ample, blanket, broad-based, broad-brush, broad church, catch-all, comprehensive, covering all bases, disparate, diverse, eclectic, exhaustive, expansive, extended, extensive, far-reaching, general, generous, great, immense, inclusive, multifaceted, non-specific, open-minded, overarching, sweeping, umbrella, universal, unspecific, vast, versatile, voluminous, wide, wide-ranging, widespread

**Business** n., see also Activity, Work
1. business concern, business empire, chain, company, concern, conglomerate, corporation, employer, enterprise, entity, entrepreneur, establishment, firm, group, institution, legal entity, manufacturer, multinational, operation(s), operator, organisation, outfit, partnership, player, practice, private enterprise, producer, provider, setup, small business, SME, subsidiary, team, trader, unit, venture
2. big business, business activity, business area, business model, business sector, commerce, craft, dealings, economic activity, enterprise, field, game, industry, line of business, line of work, livelihood, market, occupation, operations, profession, sales, sector, trade, trading

**Businessperson** n., see also Business, Investor
baron, business figure, business leader, businessman, businesswoman, CEO, chief executive, dealmaker, dealer, director, employer, entrepreneur, executive, financier, founder, industrialist, magnate, manager, merchant, operator, owner, player, professional, serial entrepreneur, shareholder, sole trader, trader, tycoon, wheeler-dealer

**Busy** adj., see also Active, Enthusiastic
a lot on one's plate, abuzz, at work, beavering away, besieged, bustling, buzzing, chock-a-block, chocka, crowded, employed, energetic, engaged, engrossed, enterprising, flurry of activity, frantic, frenetic, frenzy of activity, hard at it, hard at work, hard-working, hectic, hive of activity, inundated, industrious, involved, juggling tasks, maelstrom of activity, manic, multitasking, nonstop, occupied, on the go, otherwise occupied, overloaded,

overwhelmed, packed, preoccupied, run/rushed off one's feet, snowed under, swamped, tied up, thriving, unavailable, underway, up to one's ears, whirlwind of activity, working

**Buy** v., see also Acquire, Pay

amass, bag, become the owner of, buy into, buy out, buy up, come by, fork out for, gain, get, get one's hands on, go on a spending spree, go shopping for, grab a bargain, hoover up, invest in, look for, make a purchase, make an acquisition, make an investment, obtain, open one's chequebook, open one's wallet, order, pick up (a bargain), plough money into, procure, purchase, put money into, secure, shop (for), sign on the dotted line, snag, snap up, source, take on, treat oneself to

# C

**Calculate** v., see also Assess, Measure
according to one's calculations, add up, anticipate, appraise, assume, bank on, compute, consider, count, crunch the numbers, determine, do the maths, do the sums, estimate, evaluate, extrapolate, figure (out), forecast, gauge, guess, intend, judge, quantify, reckon, rely on, run the numbers, suppose, tally, tot up, total, work out

**Calm** v., see also Lessen, Reduce
abate, allay, alleviate, appease, assuage, balance, calm fears, compose, cool, dampen, de-escalate, dial down, diffuse, dilute, ease, ease concerns, lighten, lull, minimise, mitigate, moderate, mollify, offset, pacify, placate, quell, quiet, quieten, reassure, rein in, relax, relieve, settle (down), simmer down, smooth, soften, soothe, stabilise, steady, steady nerves, stem, subdue, take the edge off, take the heat out of, take the sting out of, temper, tone down

**Can (Be Able)** v., see also Capable
be able, be allowed, be authorised, be capable, be effective, be ideally placed, be permitted, be possible, be prepared, be up to, be well positioned, cope, could, have the ability, have the authority, have the opportunity, have the possibility, have the resources, manage, may, might

**Cancel** v., see also Close, Stop
abandon, abolish, abort, annul, axe, bin, block, break off, call it a day, call off, call time on, can, cut, cut short, delete, discontinue, ditch, do away with, drop, eliminate, end, eradicate, freeze, halt, hold fire, kick into the long grass, kill off, knock on the head, negate, neutralise, nullify, override, postpone, pull, pull the plug on, put an end to, put on hold, put on ice, quash, remove, render invalid, render null and void, repeal, rescind, reverse, revoke, rule out, scrap, shelve, shut down, snuff out, stand down, strike out, suppress, suspend, terminate, torpedo, veto, void, wipe slate clean, withdraw, write off

**Capable** adj., see also Possible, Skilled
able, accomplished, adept, bright, competent, consummate professional, distinguished, effective, efficient, exceptional, experienced, expert, gifted,

good, having the ability, having the know-how, having what it takes, highly capable, ideally placed, impressive, intelligent, knowledgeable, masterful, masterly, more than a match, more than capable, multitalented, practised, professional, proficient, qualified, respected, seasoned, skilful, smart, talented, trained, up to (the job), versatile, veteran, well positioned, well versed

**Capacity** n., see also Ability, Extent

1. acumen, aptitude, bent, calibre, capability, competence, competency, effectiveness, efficiency, facility, genius, gift, intelligence, knack, potential, power, readiness, resources, skill, skillset, strength, talent, wherewithal
2. content, dimensions, magnitude, proportions, quantity, range, room, scale, scope, size, space, volume
3. duty, function, job, occupation, office, position, post, responsibility, role

**Capital** n., see also Investment, Money

assets, bank balance, big bucks, budget, capital injection, cash, coffers, equity, finances, financial clout, financial muscle, financial resources, funds, means, readies, resources, riches, wealth, wherewithal

**Careful** adj., see also Precise, Serious

alert, apprehensive, assiduous, attentive, belt-and-braces, cagey, calculating, cautious, choosy, circumspect, conscientious, conservative, considered, correct, deliberate, diligent, discerning, erring on the side of caution, exacting, fastidious, gingerly, guarded, hedging one's bets, heedful, hesitant, judicious, meticulous, mindful, non-committal, on one's toes, painstaking, particular, playing it safe, precautionary, prudent, reluctant, rigorous, safe, scrupulous, shrewd, strict, taking care, tentative, thinking twice, thorough, treading carefully, twitchy, vigilant, wary, watchful, with kid gloves

**Categorise** v., see also Describe, Distinguish

allocate, allot, alphabetise, arrange, bracket, brand, call, catalogue, class, classify, dub, file, grade, group together, have down as, index, label, lump together, name, number, organise, pigeonhole, put down as, put into groups, rank, sort, stereotype, systematise, tag, tar with the same brush, typecast

**Category** n., see also Group, Type

band, bracket, class, classification, demographic, denomination, department, designation, division, family, genre, grade, grouping, kind, label, league, level, pigeonhole, rank, section, same boat, sector, segment, series, set, sort, status, tier, variety

**Cause** n., see also Reason, Start

1. basis, catalyst, culprit, driver, driving force, explanation, foundation, genesis, grounds, impetus, incentive, inspiration, justification, key driver, mainspring, motivation, motive, origin, originator, precursor, rationale, root, root cause, source, spark, springboard, stimulation, stimulus, trigger, underlying cause
2. aim, belief, concern, conviction, goal, ideal, ideology, intent, mission, objective, principal, purpose

**Cause** v., see also Provoke, Start

activate, arouse, be a catalyst, begin, bring about, catapult, compel, create, drive, effect, elicit, energise, engender, evoke, fan, fire up, fuel, generate, give rise to, herald, ignite, incite, induce, inflict, influence, inspire, instigate, kick off, kick-start, kindle, launch, lay the foundations for, lead to, make for, mobilise, motivate, move, occasion, pave the way for, precipitate, produce, prompt, result in, rouse, set off, sow the seeds, spark, spawn, spur, stimulate, stir up, stoke, trigger, unleash, usher in

**Cautious** adj., see also Precise, Serious

alert, apprehensive, assiduous, attentive, belt-and-braces, cagey, calculating, careful, choosy, circumspect, conscientious, conservative, considered, correct, deliberate, discreet, erring on the side of caution, exacting, fastidious, gingerly, guarded, hedging one's bets, heedful, hesitant, judicious, keeping one's powder dry, meticulous, mindful, non-committal, on one's toes, on the lookout, painstaking, particular, playing it safe, precautionary, prudent, reluctant, rigorous, safe, scrupulous, shrewd, strict, taking care, tentative, thinking twice, thorough, treading carefully, twitchy, vigilant, wary, watchful, with kid gloves

**Celebrate** v., see also Praise, Remember

come together, commemorate, commend, dedicate, drink to, fete, gather, hail, have a celebration, have a get-together, have a party, hold a ceremony, hold celebrations/commemorations, honour, keep, look back on, mark, observe, party, recall, recognise, recollect, rejoice, revel, revere, toast, value

**Central** adj., see also Important, Main

at the heart of, at the crux of, basic, bedrock, central plank, centrally located, centre, centre stage, centremost, *****-centric, chief, core, cornerstone, defining, dominant, essential, focal, foremost, front and centre, front-line, fundamental, going to the heart of, heart of the matter, inner, innermost, instrumental, internal, key, key tenet, linchpin, mainstay, middle, midway, overriding, paramount, pertinent, pivotal, predominant, primary, prime, principal, salient, significant, vital

**Centre** n., see also Basis, Focus
axis, beating heart, bedrock, bullseye, capital, central plank, central point, centre of attention, centre stage, centrepiece, core, crux, epicentre, essence, eye of the storm, focal point, foundation, front and centre, front line, fulcrum, haven, heart, highlight, home, hot spot, hub, inside, interior, kernel, key element, key tenet, keystone, mainstay, mecca, meeting point, middle, midpoint, nerve centre, nexus, nub, nucleus, one-stop shop, root, soul, source, stronghold, thrust, very heart

**Certain** adj., see also Confident, Likely
absolute, adamant, assured, banking on, beyond a shadow of (a) doubt, black and white, bound to, cast-iron, categorical, certified, clear, clear-cut, conclusive, convinced, counting on, cut and dried, dead cert, decisive, definite, dependable, determined, emphatic, established, fail-safe, fait accompli, firm, foolproof, foregone conclusion, genuine, gimme, given, guaranteed, hard-and-fast, incontrovertible, inevitable, ironclad, irrefutable, nailed-on, never/not in doubt, positive, predictable, resolved, rock-solid, safe in the knowledge, satisfied, secure, settled, shoo-in, solid, sure, sure thing, sure-fire, tried-and-tested, true, trusty, unambiguous, unavoidable, undeniable, undisputed, undoubted, unmistakable, unquestionable, unshakable, untroubled, unwavering, watertight, with certainty, without a shadow of a doubt, without doubt

**Certainty** n., see also Reliability, Strength
assurance, belief, certitude, clarity, confidence, conviction, dependability, faith, firm foundations, forgone conclusion, gimme, inevitability, knowledge, necessity, no doubt, open and shut case, peace of mind, proof, reassurance, security, shoo-in, solidity, solidness, sound basis, soundness, stability, steadfastness, steadiness, strong foundations, support, sure thing, trust

**Certify** v., see also Authorise, Guarantee
accredit, affirm, approve, assert, assure, attest, authenticate, bear witness, confirm, corroborate, declare, document, endorse, license, okay, pledge, promise, ratify, reassure, reinforce, rubber-stamp, sanction, substantiate, support, swear, testify, underline, validate, verify, vouch

**Challenge** n., see also Competition, Difficulty
1. acid test, adversity, battle, big ask, bind, bumpy road, challenging situation, challenging times, complication, concern, conundrum, dilemma, glitch, hassle, headache, headwind, hitch, hurdle, issue, moment of truth, mountain to climb, obstacle, plight, potential banana skin, predicament, question mark, quandary, reality check, scourge, setback, situation, struggle, tall order, teething

problems, test, testing times, threat, trial(s), tribulation, trouble, uphill battle/task
2. argument, attack, confrontation, defiance, dispute, dissent, objection, opposition, protest, provocation, query, question (mark), squaring up, threat, throwing down the gauntlet, ultimatum

**Challenging** adj., see also Complex, Difficult
ambitious, arduous, asking a lot, beset by problems, big ask, bold, bruising, brutal, challenging times, daunting, demanding, exacting, formidable, fraught with difficulty, gruelling, hard, have one's work cut out, imposing, labour-intensive, moment of truth, mountain to climb, onerous, not easy, not straightforward, out of one's comfort zone, posing a test, presenting a challenge, problematic, stimulating, strenuous, tall order, taxing, testing, thought-provoking, time-consuming, tough, tough-going, tricky, trying, uncomfortable, unenviable, up against it, uphill (battle/task)

**Change** n., see also Adjustment, Variation
about-face, adaptation, addition, advance, alteration, amendment, break, changing of the guard, contrast, conversion, correction, customisation, departure, development, difference, evolution, flip-flop, flux, improvement, innovation, makeover, modernisation, modification, move, new era, new look, overhaul, pivot, realignment, rearrangement, reboot, recalibration, reconfiguration, reform, replacement, rethink, revamp, reversal, revision, revolution, sea change, seismic shift, shake-up, shift, step change, substitution, swap, switch, tipping point, transformation, transition, turnaround, turning point, tweak, update, upgrade, U-turn, volte-face, watershed moment, whole new ball game

**Change** v., see also Adjust, Amend
acclimatise, accommodate, adapt, alter, calibrate, change tack, chop and change, comply, configure, convert, customise, develop, diverge, diversify, effect change, evolve, exchange, flip, fluctuate, habituate, harmonise, improve, introduce, make a change, make over, mark a turning point, modernise, morph, move on, move with the times, mutate, overhaul, overturn, pivot, reach tipping point, readjust, reboot, recalibrate, reconfigure, redo, refine, reform, regenerate, reinvent, rejig, reimagine, remodel, renew, reorganise, replace, reshape, reshuffle, restructure, restyle, rethink, revamp, reverse, review, revise, revisit, revolutionise, ring the changes, rip up, shake up, shape, shift, shuffle, skew, swap (out), switch, switch up, tinker with, tip the balance, trade, trade in, transform, transition, turn around, tweak, twist, update, upend, upgrade, vary

**Change One's Mind** v., see also Change
back down, back-pedal, backtrack, climb down, come around, flip-flop, go back on, have a change of heart, have a rethink, have second thoughts, make a U-turn, overturn, reappraise, reassess, reconsider, re-evaluate, re-examine, rehash, relent, renege, rethink, retract, review, review one's position, revise, revisit, rework, row back on, see in a new light, sleep on, take a step back, take another look at, take back, think again, think better of, think over, think twice

**Chaos** n., see also Crisis, Instability
anarchy, bedlam, circus, clamour, commotion, confusion, debacle, devastation, disarray, disaster, discord, disorder, disorganisation, disquiet, disruption, fallout, farce, farrago, fiasco, hysteria, lawlessness, madness, maelstrom, mayhem, meltdown, mess, misrule, muddle, pandemonium, perfect storm, shambles, throes, tumult, turmoil, unrest, unruliness, upheaval, uproar

**Characteristic** n., see also Aspect, Feature
attribute, calling card, component, distinction, distinguishing feature, DNA, element, essence, facet, factor, flavour, foible, hallmark, individuality, ingredient, je ne sais quoi, mark, nature, party piece, peculiarity, personality, point, property, quality, quirk, selling point, signature, speciality, stamp, strength, strong point, trademark, trait, uniqueness, USP, virtue

**Cheap** adj., see Deficient, Small
1. affordable, attractively priced, bargain, bargain-basement, budget, cheap as chips, competitive, competitively priced, cost-effective, cut-price, cut-rate, dime a dozen, dirt-cheap, discounted, economical, economy, fair, good value, going for a song, inexpensive, keenly priced, knock-down, low-cost, low-priced, marked down, moderate, moderately priced, next to nothing, on sale, peanuts, pittance, reasonable, reduced, rock-bottom, shoestring, slashed, snip, song, steal, thrifty, value (for money), won't break the bank
2. cheap and nasty, inferior, low-quality, poor, poorly made, poor-quality, second-rate, shoddy

**Check** v., see also Monitor, Stop
1. analyse, ascertain, audit, certify, check out, conduct checks, confirm, double-check, ensure, examine, eyeball, inquire into, inspect, investigate, look at, look into, look over, make sure, note, perform checks, probe, research, review, screen, scrutinise, study, test, validate, verify, vet
2. arrest, block, combat, counteract, curb, foil, frustrate, halt, hinder, hold back, impede, inhibit, limit, obstruct, prevent, reduce, restrain, stymie, suppress, thwart

**Choice** n., see also Assortment, Decision
1. alternative, call, crossroads, cup of tea, determination, election, evaluation, judgement, nomination, option, outcome, pick, preference, prerogative, selection, taste, verdict, vote
2. array, choosing, collection, cross section, diversity, everything from…to, flexibility, freedom, gamut, group, kaleidoscope, line-up, medley, menu, mix, mixture, offering, option, portfolio, raft, range, scope, selection, smorgasbord, (broad) spectrum, spoilt for choice, variation, variety, wide range

**Choose** v., see also Decide, Specify
adopt, agonise over, appoint, assign, be at a crossroads, bite the bullet, cherry-pick, conclude, consider, curate, decide on, designate, determine, elect, embrace, favour, go for, handpick, have the ball in one's court, hem and haw/hum and haw, judge, make a call, make a choice, make a decision, make a selection, make up one's mind, narrow down, opt for, pick, pick and choose, pick one's battles, plump for, ponder, prefer, select, settle on, shortlist, single out, take a decision, um and ah, weed out, weigh, whittle down

**Circumstances** n., see also Issue
backdrop, background, climate, conditions, context, dynamics, environment, episode, events, factors, facts, footing, incident, juncture, landscape, lie of the land, life, lifestyle, matter, narrative, occurrence, outlook, position, prospects, scenario, scene, set of circumstances, setting, situation, standing, state, state of affairs, state of play, status, status quo, surroundings, territory

**Claim** v., see also Comment, Demand
affirm, allege, appeal, ask, assert, believe, call for, challenge, collect, contend, declare, hold, insist, justify, lay claim to, maintain, make a claim, make an allegation, postulate, pretend, profess, purport, receive, request, require, stake one's claim, state, take, tout, win

**Clarify** v., see also Explain, Specify
break down, clear up, crystallise, define, dispel doubts/fears/myth, detail, establish, flesh out, get down to brass tacks, get to the point, identify, illustrate, interpret, make a clarification, make (crystal) clear, make perfectly clear, make plain, pinpoint, provide details, put in context, qualify, resolve, shed/throw light on, simplify, spell out

**Classify** v., see also Describe, Distinguish
allocate, allot, alphabetise, arrange, bracket, brand, categorise, call, catalogue, class, distribute, divide into, dub, file, grade, group together, have down as,

index, label, lump together, name, number, organise, pigeonhole, put down as, put into groups, rank, sort, stereotype, systematise, tag, tar with the same brush, typecast

**Clear** adj., see also Certain, Obvious

abundantly clear, apparent, black and white, blatant, blunt, clear as day(light), clear case of, clear-cut, coherent, comprehensible, conspicuous, crystal clear, cut and dried, distinct, does what it says on the tin, emphatic, evident, explicit, express, glaring, incisive, incontrovertible, indisputable, loud and clear, lucid, manifest, no-brainer, no getting away from, open-and-shut case, overt, palpable, patent, perceptible, plain, positive, precise, prominent, resounding, self-evident, self-explanatory, simple, speaks volumes, speaks for itself, standing out like a sore thumb, stark, startling, straightforward, transparent, unambiguous, undeniable, understandable, unequivocal, vivid, with clarity

**Client** n., see also Supporter

audience, buyer, client base, clientele, consumer, customer, customer base, devotee, end customer, end user, fan, follower, lead, loyal client/customer, patron, punter, purchaser, shopper, subscriber, target audience, target group, user, valued client/customer

**Close** v., see also Complete, End

1. announce the closure, axe, bring the curtain down on, bring to a close, bring to a conclusion, bring to an end, call it a day, call time on, cancel, cease, cease trading, close the doors, come to an end, conclude, discontinue, finish, halt, knock on the head, mothball, pack up, pull the plug on, put an end to, quit, secure, shut, shut down, shutter, stop, suspend, terminate, wind up, withdraw
2. accomplish, achieve, bring about, bring off, cap, clinch, conclude, execute, land, put to bed, realise, round off, seal, wrap up

**Collaborate** v., see also Coordinate, Help

act in concert, act jointly, ally with, back up, band together, collude, combine, combine efforts, conspire, contribute, cooperate, help each other, hook up, integrate, join forces, join in, join up, learn from each other, lend a hand, link up with, make a concerted effort, participate, partner, pitch in, pool resources, pull one's weight, pull together, put heads together, share, support each other, team up, tie up, unite, work as a team, work in concert, work side by side, work together

**Collaboration** n., see also Agreement, Help
alliance, assistance, association, collaborative approach, collusion, combination, combined effort, combined resources, concert, concerted effort, conjunction, cooperation, harmony, integration, interaction, joint action, joint effort, joint project, link-up, participation, partnership, solidarity, symbiosis, synergy, tandem, teaming up, teamwork, ties, tie-up, togetherness, union, unison, unity, working together

**Collapse** n., see also Decline, Failure
bankruptcy, breakdown, breaking point, break-up, casualty, cataclysm, catastrophe, cave-in, crash, curtains, death, debacle, demise, destruction, devastation, disintegration, downfall, downward spiral, end, fall, fall from grace, falling apart, flop, folding, liquidation, meltdown, oblivion, rout, ruin, ruination, slide, slippery slope, slump, tailspin, toppling, undoing, unravelling

**Collapse** v., see also Fail, Fall
bite the dust, break apart/down/up, buckle, cave in, come crashing down, crash, crumble, crumple, disintegrate, fall apart (at the seams), fall down, flag, flatline, flop, fold, founder, give way, go belly up, go bust, go down in flames, go into a tailspin, go into reverse, go out of business, go to pieces, go to the wall, go under, go up in smoke, implode, meltdown, plummet, plunge, reach breaking point, run aground, self-destruct, shatter, slump, subside, succumb, tank, topple, unravel, weaken, wheels come off, wilt

**Collect** v., see also Meet
access, accumulate, acquire, aggregate, amass, array, assemble, bring together, build up, cluster, come together, compile, concentrate, congregate, convene, converge, corral, crowd, curate, flock, gather, get together, group, harvest, hoard, hoover up, mass, muster, obtain, pile up, pour in, rally, reap, record, rendezvous, round up, save, secure, stack up, stockpile, store, swarm, throng

**Collective** adj., see also Common, Public
aggregate, assembled, collaborative, combined, communal, community, company-wide, concerted, consolidated, cooperative, cumulative, en masse, global, in common, inclusive, joint, mass, mutual, national, nationwide, organisation-wide, pan-***** (*e.g. pan-European*), shared, social, unified, united, *****-wide, worldwide

**Combat** v., see also Oppose, Prevent
address, battle, beat, check, clamp down on, confront, conquer, contend with, contest, cope with, counter, counteract, crack down on, defeat, defend against,

disable, do battle with, engage, fight, foil, get on top off, get to grips with, go up against, knock on the head, meet head on, meet the challenge, nip in the bud, overcome, put a stop to, rectify, remedy, repel, resist, resolve, shut down, solve, stamp out, stand up to, stave off, stop the rot, tackle, take a stand against, thwart, torpedo, ward off, withstand

**Combination** n., see also Match, Merger
affiliation, alliance, amalgam, amalgamation, association, blend, blending, coalition, collaboration, combo, composite, compound, conjunction, connection, consolidation, consortium, coupling, cross between, dovetailing, equation, fusion, group, halfway house, hybrid, integration, interaction, intersection, joining, link-up, marriage, mash-up, match made in heaven, medley, meld, melding, mix, mixture, package, pairing, partnership, perfect combination, perfect storm, recipe, sequence, synergy, synthesis, team, teaming up, tie-up, together, toxic mix, unification, union, unison, winning combination

**Combine** v., see also Include, Merge
ally, amalgamate, band together, blend, bond, bring together, collaborate, collide, complement (each other), connect, converge, cooperate, coordinate, couple, dovetail, embrace, encapsulate, entwine, forge, form an alliance, fuse, gel, group, incorporate, integrate, interact, intersect, intertwine, interweave, join, join forces, knit together, link, link up, marry, meld, mingle, mix, pair, pool, put together, reconcile, share, sit well with, splice, team up, tie up with, twin, unify, unite, weave

**Comment** v., see also Say, Think
add, affirm, agree, allude to, announce, articulate, assert, claim, clarify, conclude, continue, disclose, discuss, expand on, explain, expound on, express, hint, imply, infer, insist, interject, intimate, joke, maintain, make a comment on, make a statement, make a/the point, mention, note, observe, opine, outline, point out, provide insight, put forth, quip, recount, reflect, relay, remark, report, respond, reveal, speak about, state, talk about, tell, touch on, urge, utter, voice

**Commitment** n., see also Enthusiasm, Guarantee
adherence, agreement, assurance, belief, conviction, dedication, determination, devotion, drive, duty, effort, engagement, investment, liability, loyalty, motivation, obligation, passion, pledge, promise, relish, requirement, resolve, responsibility, tenacity, undertaking, vocation, vow, word

**Committed** adj., see also Enthusiastic
active, ardent, attentive, avowed, card-carrying, conscientious, dedicated, determined, devoted, driven, duty-bound, dyed-in-the-wool, eager, earnest, energetic, enterprising, faithful, fervent, focused, hardworking, impassioned, invested in, irrepressible, keen, loyal, motivated, obliged, passionate, pledged, required, resolute, responsible, serious, single-minded, spirited, staunch, steadfast, true, unfailing, unwavering, wedded to, wholehearted

**Common** adj., see also Average, Frequent
1. accepted, banal, bog-standard, commonplace, conventional, customary, endemic, everyday, familiar, general, generic, habitual, humdrum, mainstay, mainstream, mundane, ordinary, popular, prevailing, prevalent, rank-and-file, regular, routine, run-of-the-mill, simple, standard, staple, stereotypical, ten a penny, traditional, trivial, typical, undistinguished, unexceptional, universal, usual, well-known, widespread
2. collective, combined, communal, community, joint, mutual, public, shared, social

**Communicate** v., see also Advertise, Inform
advise, advocate, announce, articulate, attest to, broadcast, claim, clarify, confer, connect, contact, convey, cut through, declare, disclose, discuss, disseminate, divulge, elaborate, enlighten, exchange ideas/views, exchange information, explain, express, get across, get through, give voice to, highlight, impart, indicate, interact, issue a statement, keep in touch, mention, make a statement, make known, note, notify, pass on, post online, point out, present, provide details, publish, put across, put forth, reach out, recount, relate, relay, report, reveal, set out, share, signal, state, tell, voice

**Communication** n., see also Information, Marketing
advice, advertising, announcement, articulation, assertion, connection, contact, conversation, correspondence, declaration, disclosure, discussion, dissemination, expression, interaction, language, link, marketing communication, media, message, messaging, news, notice, notification, publication, relations, relationship, report, revelation, statement, tone of voice, transmission, word

**Company** n., see also Business, Organisation
arm, branch, brand, business concern, concern, conglomerate, corporate entity, corporation, developer, employer, enterprise, entity, establishment, firm, group, institution, legal entity, maker, manufacturer, merchant, microbusiness, multinational, name, operation(s), operator, outfit, partnership, player,

producer, provider, retailer, service provider, setup, small business, SME, subsidiary, supplier, team, trader, unit, vendor, venture

**Compare** v., see also Contrast, Relate
analyse, assess, be in the same class as, be on a par with, bear comparison, compete with, consider, contemplate, draw parallels, equate, evaluate, find/have similarities, judge, juxtapose, liken, link, make a comparison, match (up), measure (up), measure against, mention in the same breath/sentence, put alongside/side by side, resemble, scrutinise, stack up against, study, weigh against

**Comparison** n., see also Better, Worse
allusion, analogy, analysis, assessment, benchmarking, comparability, connection, consideration, contrast, correlation, differentiation, evaluation, example, illustration, judgement, juxtaposition, likening, parallel(s), relation, relationship, resemblance, similarity, study

**Compete** v., see also Lose, Win
battle, battle it out, be close/hot on the heels of, be competitors/rivals, be in competition, be in contention, be in the hunt, be in the running, bid, breathe down someone's neck, challenge, chase down, clash, collide, contend, contest, do battle, encounter, engage, enter the fray, enter the ring, face, face off against, fight, go head to head, go toe to toe, go up against, gun for, have in one's sights, jockey (for position), jostle for position, keep pace with, knock on the door, lock horns, meet, neck and neck, oppose, participate, pit oneself against, rival, scramble for, snap at someone's heels, spar, square up, struggle, take on, throw down the gauntlet, throw one's hat in the ring, tussle, vie

**Competition** n., see also Market, Opposition
adversaries, arch-rivals, battle, bout, challenge, challengers, competitive landscape, competitive market, competitiveness, competitors, conflict, contenders, contention, contest, dog eat dog, duel, encounter, field, fierce competition, fight, game, head-to-head, match, matchup, meeting, nemesis, one-upmanship, opponents, participants, pressure, race, rivalry, rivals, stiff competition, struggle, tug-of-war, underdog, upstart, vying, war, warfare

**Competitive** adj., see also Difficult, Inexpensive
aggressive, ambitious, close-fought, combative, crowded market, cut-throat, demanding, dog-eat-dog, fair, feisty, fierce, fiercely competitive, game on, hard-fought, hard-won, highly competitive, keen, lively, motivated, opposing, relentless, rival, ruthless, stiff competition, tough, unforgiving

**Complain** v., see also Criticise, Disagree
accuse, attack, balk at, be scathing about, bemoan, bring a complaint, carp, claim, denounce, deplore, disapprove, dispute, find fault, gripe, grouse, grumble, have a bone to pick, harangue, lament, make a complaint, moan, object, oppose, protest, quibble, reject, rail against, remonstrate, take exception to, take issue with, take someone up on, whine, whinge

**Complaint** n., see also Criticism, Disagreement
accusation, backlash, bee in one's bonnet, beef, bugbear, charge, claim, discontent, dispute, dissatisfaction, grievance, gripe, grumble, grumbling, hostility, issue, lament, misgivings, moan, niggle, objection, peeve, problem, protest, protestation, qualms, quibble, rebuke, recrimination(s)

**Complement** v., see also Enhance, Support
add, add the finishing touch to, augment, be the icing on the cake, be the perfect complement to, bolster, boost, combine well with, complete, contribute to, crown, emphasise, enrich, finish, flatter, go well with, heighten, improve, lift, perfect, raise, reinforce, round off, set off, sharpen, strengthen, suit, top off

**Complete** adj., see also Comprehensive, Entire
1. across the board, all, all-in-one, all-round, all-purpose, altogether, end-to-end, exhaustive, extensive, full, full-blown, inclusive, in-depth, intact, lock stock and barrel, out-and-out, outright, root-and-branch, sweeping, thorough, total, turnkey, uncut, unedited, unlimited, versatile, whole, whole hog, works
2. accomplished, achieved, all over, completed, concluded, done, done and dusted, ended, executed, fait accompli, finalised, finished, fulfilled, implemented, over, ready, through, wrapped up
3. absolute, all-out, die-hard, downright, dyed-in-the-wool, extreme, out-and-out, outright, perfect, pure, really, sheer, total, undivided, unmitigated, unconditional, unqualified, utter, veritable

**Complete** v., see also Achieve, Finish
accomplish, bring to a conclusion, bring to completion, bring to fruition, cap, carry off, carry out, carry through, close, conclude, crown, deliver, discharge, end, execute, finalise, finish off, fulfil, get done, get done and dusted, get over the line, go through with, implement, perfect, perform, put the finishing touches to, put to bed, reach, realise, round off, seal, settle, sew up, terminate, top off, wrap up

**Completely** adv., see also Strong, Very
absolutely, comprehensively, conclusively, deeply, effectively, entirely, exhaustively, firmly, from start to finish, full-on, fully, heart and soul, in earnest, in full, lock stock and barrel, on all counts, one hundred percent, overwhelmingly, perfectly, quite, root and branch, roundly, soundly, steadfastly, thoroughly, totally, truly, unanimously, undisputedly, unquestionably, utterly, well and truly, wholeheartedly, wholly

**Complex** adj., see also Advanced, Challenging
arcane, baffling, bamboozling, bewildering, can of worms, clunky, complicated, confused, confusing, conundrum, convoluted, cryptic, difficult, elaborate, entangled, fiddly, fiendishly complex/complicated, hard to understand, head-scratcher, impenetrable, intricate, involved, knotty, labyrinthine, minefield, mixed-up, not simple, not straightforward, obscure, ornate, Pandora's box, perplexing, problematic, puzzle, puzzling, sophisticated, tangled, tortuous, tricky, unfathomable

**Complicate** v., see also Confuse, Hamper
baffle, bamboozle, be a thorn in the side, bedevil, bewilder, cloud, compound, confuse, embroil, entangle, hinder, make complex, make complicated, make difficult, make matters worse, make (more) difficult, mix up, muddle, muddy the waters, obscure, open a can of worms, open a Pandora's box, overthink, perplex, pose a problem, put a spanner in the works, snarl up, stump, unsettle, upset

**Complicated** adj., see also Advanced, Challenging
arcane, baffling, bamboozling, bewildering, can of worms, clunky, complex, confused, confusing, conundrum, convoluted, cryptic, difficult, elaborate, entangled, fiddly, fiendishly complex/complicated, hard to understand, head-scratcher, impenetrable, intricate, involved, knotty, labyrinthine, minefield, mixed-up, not simple, not straightforward, ornate, Pandora's box, perplexing, problematic, puzzle, puzzling, sophisticated, tangled, tortuous, tricky, unfathomable

**Comply** v., see also Agree, Fulfil
abide by, accede, accept, acquiesce, act in compliance with, adhere to, be aligned with, be compliant with, be in agreement with, be in harmony with, be in line with, concur, conform to, consent to, do as told, don't rock the boat, fall in line with, fall in with, fit with, follow, go along with, go with the flow, harmonise, heed, meet (requirements), obey, observe, pander to, pay lip service to, play ball, respect, satisfy, say yes, submit, toe the line, yield

**Comprehensive** adj., see also Complete, Entire
all-embracing, all-encompassing, all-in-one, all-inclusive, all-purpose, all-round, blanket, broad, catch-all, covering all bases, detailed, end-to-end, exhaustive, expansive, extensive, far-reaching, full, full-blown, general, inclusive, in-depth, lock stock and barrel, overall, overarching, root-and-branch, sweeping, thorough, turnkey, umbrella, universal, versatile, wall-to-wall, wide-ranging, whole shebang, works

**Conceal** v., see also Mislead
anonymise, belie, bury, camouflage, cloak, cover, cover up, disguise, gloss over, hide (away), hide a multitude of sins, hush up, keep hidden, keep in the dark, keep quiet, keep secret, keep under lock and key, keep under wraps, mask, masquerade, obfuscate, obscure, pull the wool over someone's eyes, put up a smokescreen, screen, shelter, shroud, squirrel away, sugar-coat, suppress, sweep under the carpet, tuck away, veil

**Concentrate On** v., see also Emphasise, Endeavour
accentuate, attend, be engrossed in, centre around, centre on, consider closely, contemplate, direct attention to, double down on, dwell on, examine, fixate on, focus on, focus attention on, give emphasis to, give priority to, highlight, increase focus on, intensify, major on, pay attention to, pinpoint, prioritise, scrutinise, showcase, spotlight, stress, underline, underscore, zero in on, zoom in on

**Concept** n., see also Idea, Innovation
aim, approach, big idea, blueprint, brainwave, brainchild, business concept, business model, conception, design, hypothesis, mentality, mindset, notion, objective, original idea, perception, philosophy, slant, strategy, tactic, take, theory, thinking, thought, view, vision

**Concern** n., see also Problem, Risk
agitation, alarm, angst, anxiety, apprehension, cause for concern, clouds on the horizon, cold feet, consideration, consternation, dismay, disquiet, distress, doubt, dread, fear, hand-wringing, interest, issue, jitters, matter of concern, misgivings, nerves, nervousness, panic, qualm, questions, reservations, scare, spectre, suspicion, trepidation, uncertainty, unease, wariness, worry

**Concern** v., see also Affect, Worry
1. apply to, be about, be connected with, be important for, be of interest to, be related to, be relevant to, cover, deal with, have a bearing on, have implications

for, have to do with, impact, involve, matter to, pertain to, refer to, regard, relate to, speak to, touch on
2. affect, aggrieve, agonise, badger, bedevil, beleaguer, bother, brood, bug, depress, distress, disturb, exercise, harry, haunt, irk, irritate, keep awake at night, nag, needle, panic, pester, perturb, plague, play on one's mind, rattle, ruffle feathers, scare, spark concern, torment, trouble, unsettle, upset, vex

**Concerned** adj., see also Cautious, Unhappy
afraid, agitated, alarmed, anxious, apprehensive, bothered, distraught, distressed, disturbed, fearful, frightened, gripped by concerns, having misgivings/reservations, ill at ease, insecure, nervous, on edge, perturbed, pessimistic, rattled, tense, troubled, twitchy, uncertain, uneasy, upset, uptight, wary, worried

**Concerning** adj., see also Serious, Uncertain
1. cause for concern, chilling, concern, daunting, disconcerting, disquieting, distressing, disturbing, fraught, of concern, perturbing, pessimistic, troublesome, troubling, unnerving, unsettling, upsetting, vexing, worrisome, worry, worrying
2. about, applying to, as regards, covering, dealing with, having a bearing on, impacting, important to, in regard to, in respect of, of interest to, pertaining to, referring to, regarding, related to, relating to, relevant to, to do with, when it comes to, with regard to, with respect to

**Conclude** v., see also Complete, Decide
1. accomplish, achieve, bring to a conclusion, bring to a close, bring to an end, bring to completion, bring about, bring the curtain down on, bring to fruition, call it a day, cease, clinch, close, come to a head, come to an end, culminate, deliver, draw to a close/conclusion, end, finalise, finish (off), put to bed, resolve, round off, settle, stop, terminate, wind up, wrap up
2. arrive at a conclusion, assume, come to a conclusion, deduce, determine, draw a conclusion, establish, find, gather, infer, judge, make a call, make up one's mind, reach a conclusion, reason, reckon, sum up, suppose, surmise, take a decision, work out

**Conclusion** n., see also Decision, End
1. accomplishment, achievement, climax, close, closure, completion, consequence, culmination, dying days, end result, endgame, ending, final chapter, final stages, finale, finish, fruition, fulfilment, home straight, outcome, realisation, resolution, result, termination, upshot

2. agreement, belief, bottom line, choice, conviction, deduction, finding, inference, judgement, opinion, position, resolution, settlement, solution, thinking, verdict

**Condition(s)** n., see also Circumstances, Terms

1. case, demeanour, fettle, fit state, health, juncture, nick, order, phase, plight, position, predicament, scenario, set of circumstances, shape, situation, stage, standing, state, state of affairs, state of health, state of play, status, status quo, way things are

2. basis, catch, caveat, clause, demand, details, fine print, limitation, must, parameters, precondition, prerequisite, provision, proviso, qualification, requirements, reservation, restriction, reservation, rider, rule, small print, specifications, stipulation, strings attached, terms and conditions, t's and c's

**Conditional** adj., see also Dependent, Related

considering, contingent, depending on, given, hinging on, in light of, in view of, limited, on condition that, on the proviso that, pending, provided that, provisional, qualified, relying on, restricted, subject to, taking account of, tentative, uncertain, with reservations, with strings attached

**Confidence** n., see also Belief, Trust

air of confidence, assertiveness, assurance, certainty, chutzpah, composure, confidence boost, conviction, cool, courage, determination, dynamism, enthusiasm, expectation, faith, fortitude, hope, hubris, inner belief/strength, mettle, nerve, optimism, overconfidence, peace of mind, poise, reassurance, reliability, resoluteness, self-assurance, self-belief, self-confidence, spirit, spring in one's step, sure-footedness, swagger, tenacity, vote of confidence

**Confident** adj., see also Certain, Optimistic

assertive, assured, believing firmly, betting on, bold, brave, brimming with confidence, bullish, buoyant, can-do, composed, convinced, cool, counting on, expectant, firm believer, having confidence, having faith, hopeful, in no doubt, overconfident, positive, satisfied, secure, self-assured, self-confident, sure, sure of one's self, sure-footed, trusting, unconcerned, unfazed, unperturbed, unruffled, upbeat, with an air of confidence

**Confidential** adj., see also Private

behind the scenes, cards close to one's chest, classified, closed, closely guarded, concealed, coy, cryptic, discreet, enigmatic, furtive, hidden, hush-hush, in confidence, inside, intimate, little-known, mysterious, not in the public domain, off the record, on a need-to-know basis, personal, restricted, secret, secretive, sensitive, shrouded in secrecy/mystery, strictly confidential, tight-lipped, top-secret, under lock and key, under wraps, undisclosed, well-kept secret

**Confirm** v., see also Agree, Approve
acknowledge, affirm, assure, attest, authenticate, authorise, back up, be confirmation of, be proof of, be testament to, bear out, cement, certify, check, double-check, endorse, establish, give the go-ahead, give the green light, give the thumbs up, make sure, okay, prove, provide confirmation, ratify, reaffirm, reassert, reinforce, rubber-stamp, sanction, seal, secure, settle, sign off on, strengthen, substantiate, support, underline, validate, verify, vindicate

**Confirmation** n., see also Approval, Evidence
admission, affirmation, agreement, attestation, authentication, clincher, consent, corroboration, credence, emphasis, endorsement, go-ahead, green light, nod, okay, proof, proof positive, ratification, recognition, reinforcing, stamp of approval, strengthening, substantiation, support, testament, testimony, thumbs up, underscoring, validation, verification, vindication

**Conflict** n., see also Difference, Disagreement
1. altercation, animosity, antagonism, at odds, bad blood, battle, battleground, beef, bickering, bloodletting, clash, collision, collision course, competition, contention, contrast of views, controversy, deadlock, difference of opinion, discord, disharmony, dispute, dissent, diverging views, divide, division, falling-out, feud, fight, fracas, fray, friction, gridlock, hostility, hue and cry, ill feeling, impasse, infighting, opposition, quarrel, revolt, rift, rivalry, row, ruckus, run-in, showdown, skirmish, sparks flying, spat, squabble, stalemate, stand-off, storm, strife, struggle, tension, tiff, tug-of-war, war, war of words, wrangle
2. at odds, contradiction, contrast, deviation, disconnect, discrepancy, disparity, divergence, variance

**Confuse** v., see also Complicate, Misunderstand
baffle, bamboozle, be a red herring, be at cross purposes, befuddle, bemuse, be none the wiser, bewilder, cloud, conflate, confound, cause confusion, confusion reigns, disorient, faze, flummox, fluster, get the wrong idea, get wires crossed, get wrong, have a misunderstanding, have someone scratching their head, jumble (up), make uncertain, mess up, mislead, mix up, muddle, muddy the waters, mystify, perplex, perturb, puzzle, rattle, send mixed messages, sow confusion, stump, throw, throw into confusion/disarray, unsettle, wreak havoc

**Congratulate** v., see also Admire, Praise
acknowledge, applaud, celebrate, commend, compliment, express appreciation, give congratulations, give credit, hand it to, hear it for, honour, laud, offer congratulations, pay homage to, pay tribute to, recognise, salute, take one's hat off to, toast, wish well

**Connect** v., see also Combine, Relate
affiliate with, ally, associate, attach, be bound up with, bind, blend, bond, bridge (the gap), bring together, correlate, couple with, dovetail, equate, hook up, integrate, interconnect, interlock, intersect, intertwine, join, join up, knit together, link, link up, marry, merge, pair, piggyback on, plug into, span, tie in with, tie up with, unite, wed

**Connection** n., see also Relationship
affiliation, affinity, alliance, association, attachment, bond, collaboration, communication, contact, cooperation, correlation, correspondence, coupling, cross-over, echoes, interaction, intersection, link, nod to, relevance, similarity, symbiosis, synergy, tie, tie-in

**Consequence** n., see also Effect, Influence
after-effect, aftermath, bearing, by-product, chain reaction, comeuppance, connotation, consequences, end result, fallout, impact, implication, knock-on effect, outcome, ramification(s), reaction, reckoning, repercussion(s), result, reverberation, shock wave, side effect, upshot, wake

**Consequently** adv., see also Consequence, Impact
accordingly, as a consequence, as a result, because of this, for that reason, hence, in that event, on account of, owing to, since, so, that is why, therefore, thus, to that end

**Consider** v., see also Analyse, Think
acknowledge, adjudge, adjust for, assess, be mindful of, be of the opinion, be of the view, bear in mind, believe, brainstorm, calculate, chew over, contemplate, countenance, deal with, deem, deliberate, determine, entertain the notion/thought, estimate, evaluate, examine, eye, factor in, feel, figure out, give consideration to, give (serious) thought to, have an opinion, interpret, judge, look at, make of, mull (over), muse, ponder, put things in/into perspective, reflect on, regard, remember, ruminate, see, speculate, study, suppose, take account of, take into account, take into consideration, take stock, think long and hard, think over, think through, toy with (the idea of), view, weigh (up)

**Consistent** adj., see also Regular, Reliable
across the board, coherent, compatible, conforming with, consistently good, constant, corresponding, dependable, even, faithful, harmonious, homogeneous, in agreement, in harmony, level, logical, matching, of consistent quality, on a level, predictable, rock-solid, same, steadfast, steady, through and through, trustworthy, unchanged, unchanging, undeviating, unfailing, uniform, unvarying

**Consult** v., see also Discuss, Enquire
ask, ask advice, brainstorm, bring in, call in, confer with, debate, deliberate, hire, liaise with, pick someone's brains, put heads together, refer to, request, review, seek advice, take advice, take counsel, talk over, turn to

**Consumer** n., see also Supporter
audience, buyer, client, client base, clientele, customer, customer base, devotee, end customer, end user, fan, follower, loyal customer, patron, purchaser, shopper, subscriber, target audience, target group, user

**Contact** v., see also Communicate, Discuss
approach, be in talks with, check with, connect with, consult, drop a line, get in contact with, get in touch with, interact with, liaise with, meet, message, network, notify, reach out to, speak to, talk to, touch base with, visit, write to

**Contain** v., see also Combine, Include
accommodate, be composed of, be infused with, be home to, be made up of, be replete with, blend, boast, bring together, comprise, consist of, constitute, count, embody, encapsulate, enclose, encompass, feature, have, have capacity for, hold, host, house, incorporate, integrate, involve, list, number, offer, provide

**Continual** adj., see also Long-term, Permanent
24/7, always, around-the-clock, ceaseless, constant, continuing, durable, endless, enduring, entrenched, eternal, for many years, forever, frequent, Groundhog Day, incessant, indefinite, interminable, lasting, long-held, long-lived, long-standing, nonstop, ongoing, perennial, perpetual, persistent, pervasive, recurrent, regular, relentless, repeated, repetitive, running, steadfast, steady, sustained, unbroken, unending, unfailing, unflinching, uninterrupted, unremitting, unstinting, unswerving

**Continue** v., see also Maintain, Sustain
battle on, be business as usual, be constantly, be permanently, build on, carry on, chip away, dwell on, continue apace, endure, extend, fight on, forge ahead, go on, keep at/on, keep calm and carry on, keep going, keep the show on the road, keep up, last, linger, not falter, never cease, perpetuate, persevere, persist, pick up the baton, plug away, press ahead, press on, proceed, prolong, pursue, push on, rage on, recommence, remain, renew, repeat, restart, resume, return to, rumble on, show no signs of fading, soldier on, stay, stay on course, stay the course, stick at/to, survive, take over from, tough it out, whittle away

**Continued** adj., see also Continual, Permanent
added, additional, another, ceaseless, constant, continuing, current, enduring, extended, further, in addition, incessant, lasting, long-held, long-lived, long-standing, long-term, maintained, more, new, ongoing, persistent, prevailing, prolonged, protracted, regular, repeated, same, steadfast, still, sustained, unchanged, undaunted, unbroken, unending, unfailing, unflinching, uninterrupted, unremitting, unstinting, unswerving, well-established

**Contract** n., see also Agreement
accord, arrangement, commitment, deal, fine print, in black and white, lease, memorandum (of understanding), obligation, pact, pledge, protocol, settlement, small print, t's and c's, terms and conditions, treaty, understanding, undertaking

**Contrast** n., see also Comparison, Difference
antidote, antithesis, at odds, chalk and cheese, conflict, contradiction, disagreement, disconnect, disparity, distinction, divergence, gulf (in difference), incompatibility, juxtaposition, million miles away from, mismatch, night and day, odd couple, opposite, opposition, polar opposite, reverse, stark contrast, strange bedfellows, world away from, worlds apart

**Contrast** v., see also Differ, Distinguish
be at odds with, be contrary to, be different from, be in opposition to, be unlike, clash, compare, conflict, contradict, depart, deviate, disagree, diverge, juxtapose, make a distinction, make strange bedfellows, not conform, oppose, run counter to, separate, set apart, stand apart, stand in contrast, stand out, vary

**Contravene** v., see also Differ, Oppose
be against, be in breach of, be in contravention of, breach, break, conflict with, contradict, defy, depart from, digress, disagree, disobey, disregard, diverge, drive a coach and horses through, encroach, flout, fly in the face of, go against,

ignore, infringe, jar with, make a mockery of, negate, not adhere to, not be in line with, not comply with, not conform to, not correspond to, not follow, not respect, overstep (the mark), run counter to, show a disregard for, spurn, transgress, violate

**Contribute** v., see Help, Support
add, aid, assist, be instrumental in, bring to the table, chip in, commit, complement, cooperate, do one's bit, donate, enrich, equip, facilitate, furnish, further, give, give support, go a long way towards, grant, have a hand in, lead to, make a contribution, pitch in, play a part in, provide, provide assistance/input/support, pull one's weight, reinforce, share, strengthen, subsidise, supply

**Control** v., see Check, Manage
1. administer, be at the helm, be in charge of, be in the driver's seat, call the shots, command, decide, determine, direct, dominate, engineer, govern, handle, harness, have charge of, have control of, head, head up, hold the reins, lead, marshal, mastermind, orchestrate, organise, oversee, own, pilot, preside over, pull the strings, regulate, rule, run, shape, stamp one's authority on, steer, supervise, tame, wield control/power
2. adjust, bring to heel, bring under control, constrain, contain, curb, get on top of, hold back, keep in check, limit, monitor, rein in, regulate, repress, restrain, restrict

**Controversial** adj., see also Challenging, Surprising
arguable, at issue, attracting criticism, bombshell, contended, contentious, contestable, courting controversy, debatable, disputable, disputed, dividing opinion, divisive, dubious, explosive, hot-button issue, hot potato, hot topic, in dispute, incendiary, love-hate, maverick, moot, much-discussed, open to debate, open to question, provocative, putting the cat among the pigeons, questionable, sensitive, shocking, toxic, under discussion, unorthodox

**Convenient** adj., see also Effective, Useful
accessible, at hand, at one's fingertips, at the press of a button, at the tap of a screen, available, beneficial, boon, clever, close at hand, comfortable, expedient, favourable, *****-friendly (*e.g. family-friendly*), functional, godsend, good, handy, helpful, ideal, intuitive, labour-saving, nearby, nifty, of benefit, of help, on tap, opportune, perfect, practical, suitable, time-saving, to your door, user-friendly, valuable, versatile, within reach

**Convince** v., see also Advise, Influence
argue, assure, bring round to, bring someone to their senses, bulldoze, cajole, coax, convert, demonstrate, enlist, entice, exhort, impress, induce, inspire, lead, make a case for, motivate, persuade, prevail upon, prompt, reassure, satisfy, seduce, sell, strong-arm, suggest, sway, talk into, talk round, twist someone's arm, urge, wage a charm offensive, wear down, win argument, win hearts and minds, win over, woo

**Cooperate** v., see also Coordinate, Help
act in concert, act jointly, ally with, back up, band together, collaborate, collude, combine, combine efforts, comply with, conspire, contribute, help each other, hook up, integrate, join forces, join in, join up, learn from each other, lend a hand, liaise, link up with, make a concerted effort, participate, partner, pitch in, pool resources, pull one's weight, pull together, put heads together, share, support each other, team up, tie up with, unite, work as a team, work in concert, work side by side, work together

**Cooperation** n., see also Agreement, Help
alliance, assistance, association, collaboration, collaborative approach, collusion, combination, combined effort, combined resources, concert, concerted effort, conjunction, harmonisation, harmony, integration, interaction, joint action, joint effort, joint project, liaison, link-up, participation, partnership, solidarity, symbiosis, synergy, tandem, teaming up, teamwork, ties, tie-up, togetherness, union, unison, unity, working together

**Coordinate** v., see also Cooperate, Organise
agree, arrange, be in charge, bring together, collaborate, combine, control, choreograph, correspond, direct, govern, group, harmonise, integrate, lead, liaise, link, link up, manage, mastermind, match, mesh, orchestrate, oversee, pair, put together, regulate, set up, supervise, synchronise, work in tandem, work together

**Cope** v., see also Handle, Succeed
bear up, carry on, come through, contend, cope admirably, deal with, endure, face, get by, get on top of, get through, hack, handle, handle the pressure, hold one's own, keep one's head above water, live with, make do, make ends meet, make the best of, manage, muddle through, muster, navigate, not succumb, overcome, ride out the storm, rise to the challenge/occasion, scrape by, see out, shrug off, struggle through, survive, weather the storm, withstand

**Copy** v., see also Correspond To, Follow
act like, ape, be a dead ringer for, be in step with, be similar to, behave like, borrow from, cannibalise, clone, conform, duplicate, echo, emulate, follow example, follow in the footsteps of, follow someone's lead, follow suit, imitate, match, mimic, mirror, model on, parallel, paraphrase, parody, parrot, pay homage to, pay tribute to, pinch, plunder, reflect, regurgitate, repeat, replicate, reproduce, rewrite, rip off, shadow, simulate, steal, swipe, take a leaf out of someone's book, take after, take inspiration from, take off

**Correct** adj., see also Accurate, Appropriate
acceptable, accepted, approved, actual, all right, apt, bang on, bingo, confirmed, consistent, dead on, done thing, due, ethical, exact, factual, faithful, faultless, fitting, flawless, impeccable, in order, legitimate, okay, on the button, on the money, perfect, precise, proper, quite right, requisite, right, right and proper, right thing to do, spot on, stacks up, suitable, true, truthful, valid

**Correspond To** v., see also Relate, Suit
accord with, agree with, apply to, balance, be consistent with, be in line with, be in sync with, be in tune with, be related to, chime with, coincide with, complement, concur with, conform with, correlate with, dovetail with, echo, equal, equate to, fit, harmonise with, have to do with, link to, live up to, match, meet (requirements), resemble, satisfy, tally with, tie in with

**Corrupt** adj., see also Unethical, Unprofessional
bogus, clandestine, criminal, crooked, deceitful, deceptive, dodgy, discredited, dishonest, exploitative, fake, false, falsified, fraudulent, illegal, irregular, misleading, nefarious, rotten, scam, shady, unacceptable, unauthorised, unfair, under the table, underhand, unlawful, unprincipled, unscrupulous, untruthful, untrustworthy, wrong

**Corruption** n., see also Failure, Unethical
abuse, abuse of one's position, abuse of power, breach of ethics, breach of trust, bribery, cheating, cooking the books, crime, discrediting, dishonesty, dodgy dealings, exploitation, fiddle, fraud, impropriety, irregularities, misdemeanour, negligence, on the take, racket, scam, shady dealings, shenanigans, skulduggery, subterfuge, unscrupulousness, wrongdoing

**Cost** n., see also Expense, Price
amount, asking price, budget, charge, damage, expenditure, fee, figure, impact, loss, outgoings, outlay, overheads, payment, price point, price tag, pricing, spend, spending, tariff, total, value, worth

**Create** v., see also Design, Produce
be the brains behind, be the creator of, breathe life into, bring about, bring into existence, bring to life, build, carve out, compose, coin, conceive, conjure (up), construct, craft, develop, devise, dream up, engineer, establish, fashion, forge, formulate, generate, give birth to, handcraft, have in the works, imagine, innovate, invent, launch, make, manufacture, mould, offer, pen, pioneer, plan, put together, realise, set up, shape, spawn, start, style, tailor, think up, work on

**Crisis** n., see also Chaos, Disaster
calamity, car crash, cataclysm, catastrophe, challenging times, crisis situation, critical situation, crossroads, danger, dilemma, dire straits, disquiet, emergency, farrago, fiasco, hot water, hot potato, imbroglio, impasse, maelstrom, mess, moment of truth, nightmare, nightmare scenario, perfect storm, peril, plight, predicament, quagmire, quandary, recipe for disaster, revelation(s), shambles, situation, storm, testing times, travails, tribulations, trouble, tumult, turbulence, turmoil, unrest, upheaval, volatility, woes

**Criticise** v., see also Complain, Disagree
accuse of, admonish, attack, bad-mouth, bash, be critical, be disparaging, be outspoken, be scathing about, be vocal, bemoan, blame, blast, brand, call out, castigate, censure, chastise, chide, condemn, decry, demonise, denigrate, denounce, deplore, deride, disapprove of, disparage, find fault, frown upon, give a dressing down, give someone stick, harangue, have a bone to pick, hit back, hit out, lambaste, lament, lash out, lay the blame at someone's door, mock, oppose, pan, pillory, point the finger, protest, quibble, rail against, rap, rebuff, rebuke, reject, reprimand, reproach, ridicule, round on, rubbish, savage, scoff at, seize upon, slam, slate, sneer at, snipe at, take a dim view of, take a swipe at, take aim at, take exception to, take issue with, take to task, tear into, trade blows, turn on, vent, vilify, villainise

**Criticism** n., see also Complaint, Opposition
accusation, animosity, attack, backlash, barrage of criticism, blistering attack, brickbats, bugbear, censure, choice words, condemnation, critical remarks, damning report, demonisation, denunciation, derision, dig, disapproval, discontent, dissent, feedback, finger-pointing, flak, frosty reception, grumbling, hatchet job, hostility, jibe, misgivings, niggle, objection, opprobrium, outcry, quibble, rebuff, rebuke, recrimination(s), rejection, reprimand, reproach, stick, swipe, under fire, vilification, vitriol

**Crucial** adj., see also Important, Key
all-important, basic, bedrock, can't do without, cardinal, chief, core, cornerstone, critical, crunch, decisive, essential, foremost, fundamental, imperative, indispensable, inherent, innate, integral, intrinsic, life-or-death, lifeblood, linchpin, lost without, main, mainstay, make-or-break, mandatory, mission-critical, must-have/read/see, necessary, needed, obligatory, of utmost importance, paramount, pivotal, prerequisite, primary, principal, required, sorely needed, urgent, vital

**Current** adj., see also Modern, New
accepted, contemporary, continuing, customary, existing, fashionable, immediate, in fashion, in progress, in use, in vogue, incumbent, latest, now, ongoing, popular, present, present-day, prevailing, prevalent, right now, today's, topical, underway, up-to-date, widespread

**Customer** n., see also Supporter
audience, buyer, client, client base, clientele, consumer, customer base, devotee, end customer, end user, fan, follower, lead, loyal client/customer, patron, punter, purchaser, shopper, subscriber, target audience, target group, user, valued client/customer

**Cut** v., see also Decrease, Remove
axe, bring down, chop, crop, cull, curb, curtail, cut back (on), cut down on, depress, discount, ditch, do away with, downsize, drive down, ease up on, eliminate, lessen, limit, lower, make cutbacks, make savings, mark down, minimise, moderate, pare, prune, push down, rationalise, reduce, rein in, restrict, scale down, sever (ties), shrink, slash, slim down, snip, take an axe to, take down, trim

# D

**Damage** v., see also Destroy, Impact Negatively
adversely affect, annihilate, batter, be costly, blemish, blight, break, bring to its knees, bruise, buffet, cause damage, corrode, cripple, damage irreparably, deal a blow, degrade, dent, derail, devastate, erode, fray, hammer, harm, hit, hurt, impact, impair, impoverish, incapacitate, inflict damage, knock, leave in tatters, mar, overwhelm, plague, play havoc with, ravage, rock, ruin, saddle, sap (energy from), scar, set back, spoil, strain, tarnish, torpedo, trash, undermine, weaken, wound, wreak havoc, wreck

**Dangerous** adj., see also Difficult, Risky
alarming, asking for trouble, critical, danger, deadly, delicate situation, exposed, fatal, flirting with danger, fraught with danger, hair-raising, hairy, hazardous, in harm's way, menacing, nasty, not without danger, on dangerous ground, on thin ice, perilous, perils, playing with fire, posing a threat, precarious, real and present danger, sailing close to the wind, serious, shaky, terminal, threatening, touch and go, treacherous, troubling, uncertain, unsafe, unsound, unstable, vulnerable

**Data** n., see also Information, News
details, documentation, documents, dossier, evidence, facts, facts and figures, figures, findings, hard data, hard facts, input, intelligence, knowledge, material, piece of information, report, results, statistics

**Debatable** adj., see also Uncertain, Undecided
advantages and disadvantages, ambiguous, ambivalent, arguable, bone of contention, contestable, costs and benefits, cuts both ways, double-edged sword, for and against, good and bad points, in two minds, inconclusive, jury is out, mixed blessing, moot, moot point, on the fence, open to debate, open to question, pluses and minuses, pros and cons, questionable, strengths and weaknesses, swings and roundabouts, trade-offs, unsettled, unsure, up for discussion

**Debt** n., see also Loan
amount borrowed/due/owed, amount outstanding, arrears, borrowing, claim, credit, credit facility, deficit, debts, dues, financial commitment, indebtedness, IOU, liabilities, liability, money borrowed/due/owed, obligation, overdraft

**Decide** v., see also Agree, Choose
action, adjudge, agonise over, arrive at a conclusion, be at a crossroads, bite the bullet, call the shots, come to a decision, come to a conclusion, conclude, consider, control, decree, deem, determine, direct, draw a conclusion, elect, establish, favour, govern, have the ball in one's court, hem and haw/hum and haw, make an assessment, make a call, make a choice, make a decision, make a determination, make the difference, make up one's mind, nail one's colours to the mast, opt, pick, pin down, plump for, reach a conclusion/decision/verdict, regulate, resolve, rule, see fit, select, settle, settle on, show one's hand, stick or twist, take a decision, take the plunge, take the view, um and ah

**Decision** n., see also Agreement, Choice
approval, assessment, call, conclusion, consensus, crossroads, decision-making, determination, evaluation, final say, finding, judgement, judgement call, make-your-mind-up time, nod, opinion, outcome, pick, position, preference, rejection, resolution, result, ruling, selection, settlement, snap decision, take, verdict, view

**Decisive** adj., see also Central, Important
1.critical, crucial, crunch, deal-breaker, defining, defining moment, definitive, fateful, fundamental, high-stakes, influential, integral, key, major, make-or-break, make-your-mind-up time, making the difference, meaningful, mission-critical, momentous, pivotal, salient, significant, telling, vital, watershed moment
2. clear, conclusive, convincing, definite, determined, firm, forthright, incisive, resolute, ruthless, strong, strong-minded

**Decline** n., see also Collapse, Decrease
abatement, blip, breakdown, contraction, crash, crumbling, curtailment, cut, cutback, death, decay, demise, dent, depreciation, depression, descent, deterioration, devaluation, dip, discount, dive, downfall, downturn, downward spiral, drop, drop-off, dwindling, ebb, erosion, fading, failure, fall, fall from grace, falling-off, fall-off, flagging, freefall, lessening, limiting, loss, lull, meltdown, narrowing, nosedive, not what it once was, on the wane, plunge, recession, reduction, retreat, rout, ruin, shadow of its former self, shrinkage, slide, slip, slippery slope, slowdown, slowing, slump, softening, tailing-off,

tailspin, tumble, undoing, unravelling, waning, weakening, withering, worsening

**Decline** v., see also Decrease, Reject
1. abate, be eroded, be in decline, be in freefall, be in retreat, be on the decline, be on the wane, become impaired, become less, become worse, bomb, buckle, collapse, contract, cool, crash, crumble, darken, depreciate, descend, deteriorate, die away, die off, diminish, dip, disintegrate, dive, drop, drop away, drop off, dry up, dwindle, ebb, edge lower, fade, fail, fall, fall apart, fall away, fall off, fare worse, flag, flatline, founder, fray, get worse, go down, go downhill, go into a tailspin, grow less, languish, lessen, nose-dive, peter out, plummet, plunge, recede, regress, retreat, rot sets in, run aground, sag, shrink, shrivel, sink, slide, slip, slow, slump, spiral down, stagnate, stumble, subside, suffer, tail off, take a hit, tank, taper off, topple, trip, tumble, turn down, unravel, wane, weaken, wilt, wither, worsen
2. abstain from, avoid, balk at, deny, dismiss, forgo, refrain from, refuse, say no, shun, spurn, turn down, veto

**Decrease** n., see also Collapse, Deterioration
abatement, blip, contraction, crash, crumbling, curtailment, cut, cutback, decline, demise, dent, depreciation, depression, descent, devaluation, dip, discount, dive, downturn, downward spiral, drop, drop-off, dwindling, easing, ebb, erosion, fall, falling-off, fall-off, flagging, freefall, lessening, limiting, loss, lull, meltdown, narrowing, nosedive, plunge, recession, reduction, retreat, rout, shortening, shrinking, slide, slip, slippery slope, slowdown, slowing, slump, softening, tailing-off, tumble, wane, waning, weakening, withering, worsening

**Decrease** v., see also Deteriorate, Lessen
abate, alleviate, be eroded, be in decline, be in freefall, be in retreat, be on the decline, be on the wane, become less, become worse, bomb, check, collapse, cool, crash, crumble, curb, curtail, cut, cut back, cut down, dampen, depreciate, depress, descend, devalue, dial down, die away, die off, diminish, dip, discount, downgrade, downsize, drop, drop off, drive down, dry up, dwindle, ease, ease off, eat into, ebb, edge lower, erode, evaporate, fade, fall off, fall off a cliff, fizzle out, flag, get worse, grow less, go downhill, hit, impair, lower, make less/lower, mark down, moderate, narrow, nosedive, pare, peter out, plummet, plunge, prune, push down, recede, reduce, rein in, retreat, scale down, shave, shorten, shrink, shrivel, sink, sink like a stone, slash, slide, slip, slow (down),

slump, soften, spiral down, subdue, subside, tail off, take a hit, take down, tank, taper off, (take a) tumble, turn down, wane, weaken, wilt, wither, worsen

**Defeat** n., see also Failure, Success
annihilation, beating, blow, capitulation, clobbering, collapse, conquest, crushing, crushing defeat, demise, demolition, destruction, disappointment, downfall, drubbing, embarrassment, fall, humiliation, loss, meltdown, overthrow, pasting, reversal, rout, setback, thrashing

**Defeat** v., see also Succeed, Win
annihilate, be victorious over, beat, beat hands down, best, blow away, blow out of the water, confound, conquer, crush, deal a blow to, demolish, destroy, edge it, fend off, foil, frustrate, gain a victory over, get the better of, hammer, have on the ropes, leave behind, leave for dead, make mincemeat of, outdo, outclass, outflank, outgun, outmanoeuvre, outperform, outplay, outrival, outsmart, outthink, outwit, overcome, overpower, overthrow, overwhelm, pip (to the post), prevail over, put to the sword, repulse, rout, run rings around, scupper, see off, steal a march on, steamroller, stymie, thrash, thwart, triumph over, trounce, upstage, vanquish, whip, wipe the floor with

**Defend** v., see also Justify, Protect
back up, champion, come to the defence of, cover, defend to the hilt, endorse, fend off, fight for, fight one's corner, guard, guard against, hold at bay, keep safe, leap to the defence of, look after, maintain, oppose, preserve, repel, resist, safeguard, save, secure, shelter, shield, speak up for, stand by, stand up for, stave off, stick up for, support, take care of, uphold, ward off, watch over

**Deficiency** n., see also Failure, Weakness
absence, Achilles heel, dearth, defect, downside, drawback, error, failing, failure, fault, flaw, frailty, gap, glitch, hole, impairment, imperfection, inadequacy, insufficiency, lack, limitation, negative, scarcity, shortage, shortcoming, shortfall, vulnerability, weak point

**Deficient** adj., see also Inadequate, Weak
ailing, amiss, bad, below par, clunky, crummy, defective, disjointed, falling short, faulty, flawed, found wanting, half-hearted, ill-equipped, impaired, ineffective, inefficient, inferior, insufficient, lacking, lacklustre, leaving a lot to be desired, low-grade, low-rent, not fit for purpose, not good enough, not up to scratch, poor, poor-quality, second-rate, shoddy, subpar, substandard, unconvincing, underperforming, unsatisfactory, unsound, wanting, woeful

**Delay** n., see also Failure, Problem
adjournment, bottleneck, deferment, deferral, disruption, distraction, downtime, foot-dragging, hiatus, hindrance, hold-up, interruption, interval, lag, limbo, logjam, lull, pause, postponement, prevarication, procrastination, standstill, stoppage, wait, waiting period

**Delay** v., see also Complicate, Trouble
adjourn, be in no hurry, beat around the bush, block, break off, buy time, cause a delay, check, defer, detain, disrupt, distract, drag one's feet, get bogged down, get in the way, get sidetracked, halt, hamper, hesitate, hinder, hold back, hold up, impede, inhibit, interrupt, keep waiting, kick into the long grass, lag, lag behind, obstruct, pause, play for time, postpone, prolong, prevaricate, put off, put on hold, put on ice, pussyfoot, put on the back burner, set back, shelve, sidetrack, slow, slow down, slow up, stall, stop, suspend, take one's time, wait

**Deliver** v., see also Complete, Transport
1. accomplish, achieve, bring about, bring to fruition, carry out, carry through, conduct, discharge, effect, execute, finish, fulfil, get something done, give, implement, make happen, perform, present, provide, realise, satisfy, see something through, supply, undertake
2. bring, carry, convey, deliver to your door, dispatch, dispense, distribute, drop off, fulfil, give, hand over, make a delivery, provide, send, ship, supply, transfer, truck

**Demand** n., see also Need, Requirement
appeal, appetite, call, claim, clamour, craving, desire, drive for, entreaty, expectation, hunger, insistence, interest, lack, market, opportunity, order, plea, pressure, request, thirst, ultimatum

**Demand** v., see also Order, Require
appeal for, ask for, beat a path to someone's door, beg, beseech, call for/on, challenge, claim, clamour for, command, compel, crave, cry out for, entail, expect, force, implore, insist, involve, look for, make demands, necessitate, need, press for, request, seek, stipulate, urge, want

**Demanding** adj., see also Difficult, Strict
ambitious, arduous, challenge, challenging, critical, discerning, discriminating, exacting, exhausting, firm, fussy, hard, hard to please, imposing, meticulous, no-nonsense, not easy, onerous, particular, picky, pressing, rigorous, scrupulous, stickler, stringent, taxing, testing, tough, trying, uncompromising, urgent, wearing, with high standards

**Demonstrate** v., see also Illustrate, Show
attest to, be testament to, bear out, clarify, confirm, describe, determine, display, establish, exemplify, exhibit, explain, expose, express, highlight, indicate, lay bare, make clear, manifest, point to, present, prove, reflect, set out, show clearly, stand testament, substantiate, (strongly) suggest, teach, testify to

**Department** n., see also Area, Division
administration, agency, area of expertise, area of interest, area of responsibility, arena, arm, branch, bureau, business, business area, capacity, discipline, domain, function, job, ministry, office, part, realm, section, sector, segment, staff, subdivision, unit

**Depend On** v., see also Relate, Require
bank on, be at the mercy of, be based on, be conditional on, be contingent on, be dependent on, be founded on, be grounded on, be influenced by, be predicated on, be reliant on, be subject to, be underpinned by, bet on, build on, count on, fall back on, hang on, hinge on, lean (heavily) on, need, pend, pivot on, relate to, rely on, rest on, rest with, revolve around, ride on, trust in, turn on

**Dependent** adj., see also Conditional, Important
banking on, contingent on, counting on, depending on, determined by, hinging on, influenced by, needing, on condition that, on the proviso that, pending, provided that, regulated by, reliant on, relying on, requiring, subject to, subordinate to

**Describe** v., see also Demonstrate, Explain
brand, call, cast, characterise, chart, chronicle, convey an image, define, depict, detail, draw, dub, elaborate, envisage, expound, express, get at, give a description of, give an opinion of, go into detail, illustrate, immortalise, label, make clear, narrate, outline, paint as, paint a picture, portray, present, recount, relate, report, represent, set out, show, sketch out, specify, spell out, sum up

**Description** n., see also Explanation
account, blow-by-blow account, characterisation, clarification, classification, commentary, definition, depiction, designation, detail(s), information, narrative, outline, picture, portrait, portrayal, presentation, report, representation, specification, summary

**Deserve** v., see also Earn, Justify
be credited with, be deserving of, be entitled to, be given credit for, be good enough, be in line for, be rewarded, be worth, be worthwhile, be worthy of,

credit where credit is due, gain, get what one deserves, get just desserts, have the right to, lay claim to, merit, richly deserve, warrant

**Design** v., see also Create, Produce
be the brains behind, breathe life into, bring to life, compose, conceive, conceptualise, craft, develop, devise, draft, dream up, endow with, engineer, envisage, fashion, foresee, formulate, imagine, innovate, intend, invent, lay out, make, mould, originate, outline, pen, plan, propose, put together, reinvent, set out, shape, style, tailor, think up, work on

**Designer** n., see also Expert, Inventor
architect, artist, author, brains behind, creative force, creative mind, creator, developer, deviser, engineer, fashion designer, founder, head of design, lead designer, maker, mastermind, originator, pioneer, producer, stylist, visionary

**Despite** prep., see also However
albeit, although, even so, even though, in spite of, in the face of, in the teeth of, irrespective of, notwithstanding, regardless of, still, though, undeterred by, whereas, while, yet

**Destroy** v., see also Damage, Spoil
annihilate, blow out of the water, break, bring to its knees, consume, corrode, cripple, crush, decimate, demolish, desolate, devastate, dismantle, eliminate, end, engulf, eradicate, erase, erode, exterminate, extinguish, flatten, gut, kill, knock out, lay waste to, level, overwhelm, pulverise, put paid to, quash, quell, ravage, raze (to the ground), ruin, shatter, sink, slay, smash, snuff out, stamp out, swallow up, sweep aside/away, tear apart, tear down, torpedo, trash, wipe out, wreck

**Detailed** adj., see also Comprehensive, Thorough
accurate, attention to detail, blow-by-blow, complete, complex, deep, elaborate, encyclopaedic, exact, exhaustive, extensive, fine print, full, granular, in elaborate detail, in (great/minute) detail, in-depth, ins and outs, into great length, intricate, itemised, lock stock and barrel, meticulous, minutiae, nuanced, nuts-and-bolts, painstaking, point-by-point, precise, profound, root-and-branch, small print, specific, technical

**Deteriorate** v., see also Decrease, Fail
abate, be eroded, be in decline, be in retreat, be on the decline, be on the wane, become impaired, become less, become worse, bomb, buckle, collapse, contract, cool, crash, crumble, darken, decay, decline, depreciate, descend, die

away, die off, diminish, dip, disintegrate, dive, drop, drop away, drop off, dry up, dwindle, ebb, edge lower, escalate (*e.g. problems/situation*), fade, fall, fall apart, fall away, fall off, fare worse, flag, flatline, founder, fray, get worse, go down, go downhill, go from bad to worse, go into a tailspin, grow less, languish, lessen, nosedive, peter out, plummet, plunge, recede, regress, retreat, rot sets in, run aground, shrink, shrivel, sink, slide, slip, slow, slump, sour, spiral down, stagnate, stumble, subside, suffer, tail off, take a hit, tank, taper off, topple, trip, tumble, turn down, turn sour, unravel, wane, weaken, wilt, wither, worsen

**Deterioration** n., see also Collapse, Decrease
abatement, blip, breakdown, contraction, corrosion, crash, crumbling, curtailment, death, decay, decline, degeneration, degradation demise, dent, depreciation, depression, descent, devaluation, dip, disintegration, dive, downfall, downturn, downward spiral, drop, drop-off, dwindling, ebb, erosion, escalation (of problems), fall, fall from grace, falling-off, fall-off, flagging, freefall, lessening, loss, lull, meltdown, narrowing, nosedive, not what it once was, on the wane, plunge, rebate, recession, reduction, retreat, rout, ruin, shadow of its former self, shrinkage, slide, slip, slippery slope, slowdown, slowing, slump, softening, souring, tailspin, tumble, undoing, unravelling, waning, weakening, withering, worsening

**Determine** v., see also Approve, Choose
action, adjudge, affect, agonise over, arrive at a conclusion, bite the bullet, call the shots, cause, come to a decision, come to a conclusion, conclude, consider, control, decide, decree, dictate, direct, draw a conclusion, elect, establish, favour, find, find out, govern, impact, make an assessment, make a call, make a choice, make a decision, make a determination, make up one's mind, nail one's colours to the mast, opt, pick, pin down, plump for, reach a conclusion, reach a decision, reach a verdict, regulate, resolve, rule, seal the fate of, see fit, select, settle, settle on, stick or twist, take a decision, take the plunge, take the view

**Develop** v., see also Happen, Invent
adapt, advance, arise, be on a journey, begin, blossom, branch out, build, build on, build up, change, come to a head, construct, craft, create, cultivate, deepen, design, devise, diversify, emerge, engineer, enlarge, ensue, establish, evolve, expand, extend, flourish, forge, form, formulate, foster, generate, get better, grow, heighten, improve, intensify, kindle, make progress, make strides, mark a turning point, materialise, mature, move on, move with the times, nurture, occur, originate, pan out, play out, prepare, produce, progress, promote,

prosper, put in place, spawn, spread, start, strengthen, take forward, take shape, thrive, transition, unfold

**Development** n., see also Change, Invention
1. advance, advancement, arc, blossoming, build-up, developing, drive, emergence, enhancement, evolving, evolution, expansion, flowering, formation, forward march, growth, improvement, incident, increase, journey, leap (forward), learning curve, maturity, move, narrative, optimisation, path, progress, progression, reinforcement, road, spread, strengthening, trajectory, transition, trend, turning point, unfolding, work in progress
2. circumstance, conclusion, event, happening, incident, materialisation, occurrence, outcome, phenomenon, situation, transition, trend, turn of events, turning point, twist, unfolding, upshot

**Deviate** v., see also Differ, Vary
be different, be distinct, be set apart from, be unusual, branch off, break from, buck the trend, contradict, contrast, depart, digress, diverge, drift, flout, fly in the face of, go against the grain, go off at a tangent, go off-piste, not conform, run counter to, tear/rip up the rule book, shift, stand apart, stand out, stray, swerve, take a turn, veer

**Device** n., see also Equipment, Machine
accessory, apparatus, appliance, component, contraption, gadget, gear, gizmo, handheld, hardware, innovation, instrument, invention, kit, mechanism, method, peripheral, system, tech, technology, tool, unit

**Differ** v., see also Deviate, Vary
be at odds, be different, be distinct, be distinguished from, be out of step, be set apart from, be unlike, be unusual, branch off, buck the trend, clash, conflict with, contradict, contrast, depart from, digress, disagree, dispute, diverge, diversify, do things differently, flout, fly in the face of, go against the grain, make strange bedfellows, not conform, not match, oppose, run counter to, stand apart, stand out, veer

**Difference** n., see also Contrast, Variation
alteration, alternative, antithesis, argument, change, clash, conflict, departure, deviation, digression, disagreement, disconnect, discord, discrepancy, disparity, dispute, distinction, distinctness, divergence, diversity, exception, far cry from, gulf (in difference), inconsistency, inequality, irregularity, nonconformity, notable exception, oddity, opposite, paradox, separation, strange bedfellows, twist, whole new ball game, world away from

**Different** adj., see also Unusual, Varied
alternative, assorted, at odds, atypical, breaking the mould, breaking the rules, breath of fresh air, conflicting, contrary, contrasting, different angle, different kettle of fish, disparate, dissimilar, distinct, distinctive, diverse, each to one's own, extraordinary, far cry from, fresh, off-piste, in (sharp) contrast to, inconsistent, individual, instead, irregular, left-field, like chalk and cheese, million miles away, mixed, modified, new, not the same, not your average/everyday, odd, oddball, odd one out, one of a kind, original, other, out of the ordinary, particular, polarised, poles apart, quirky, refreshing, refreshingly different, remarkable, separate, special, specific, standing out from the crowd, strange, unconventional, unique, unlike, unmistakable, unorthodox, various, whole new ball game, with a difference, world away, worlds apart

**Differentiate** v., see also Distinguish
categorise, contrast, denote, discern, discriminate, draw a distinction, make a distinction, pick out, separate, separate the wheat from the chaff, set apart, single out, sort, specify, spot the difference, stand apart, stand out, tell apart, weed out

**Difficult** adj., see also Challenging, Tough
ambitious, arduous, asking a lot, awkward, beset by problems, between a rock and a hard place, big ask, bruising, can of worms, complex, complicated, confusing, daunting, delicate, demanding, easier said than done, elusive, exacting, fiendishly difficult, formidable, fraught with difficulty, gruelling, hard, hard-fought, hard-going, hard-won, hard work, have one's work cut out, Herculean task, intractable, invidious, laborious, minefield, no easy task, no mean feat, no picnic, not easy, onerous, out of one's comfort zone, overwhelming, problematic, slog, strenuous, struggle, tall order, taxing, testing, thankless, thorny, time-consuming, tiresome, torrid, tricky, troublesome, trying, uncomfortable, unenviable, unmanageable, uphill (battle/task)

**Difficulty** n., see also Challenge, Problem
adversity, barrier, big ask, bind, bone of contention, bump in the road, can of worms, complexity, complication, conundrum, crisis, dilemma, disadvantage, drawback, enigma, fix, fly in the ointment, frustration, glitch, gremlin, hard nut to crack, hardship, hazard, headwind, hurdle, ill, impasse, impediment, inconvenience, in a corner, issue, misfortune, obstacle, ordeal, palaver, perfect storm, pickle, pitfall, plight, predicament, pressure, puzzle, quandary, reality check, rigmarole, setback, snag, spanner in the works, speed bump, sticking point, strain, stress, struggle, stumbling block, test, thorn in the side, tight

corner/spot, travails, trials and tribulations, tribulation, tricky situation, trouble, uphill battle, woes

**Disadvantage** n., see also Challenge, Problem
Achilles heel, blow, burden, damage, detriment, difficulty, disservice, downside, drawback, failing, flaw, fly in the ointment, glitch, harm, hindrance, impediment, inconvenience, liability, loss, millstone, minus, misfortune, negative, obstacle, on the back foot, predicament, prejudice, scourge, setback, shortcoming, snag, trouble, weak point, weakness

**Disagree** v., see also Differ, Reject
1. agree to disagree, argue, be at odds, be at loggerheads, be in conflict with, be split, beg to differ, bicker, clash, condemn, conflict, contest, contradict, contrast, criticise, cross swords, debate, depart from, deviate, dispute, diverge, fall out, feud, go toe to toe, go head to head, have a disagreement, hold differing opinions/views, lock horns, not agree, not be in agreement, not see eye to eye, object, oppose, play hardball, quarrel, question, relations sour, run counter to, spar, squabble, take issue with, trade blows, vary, wrangle
2. be at odds, clash, conflict, depart, deviate, diverge, not agree, not correspond, not match, not tally

**Disagreement** n., see also Conflict, Difference
1. altercation, animosity, antagonism, argument, bad blood, clash, contradiction, contrasting views, deadlock, debate, difference of opinion, disconnect, discord, disharmony, dispute, dissent, disunity, diverging views, division, falling-out, feud, flashpoint, friction, hostility, ill feeling, impasse, intransigence, lack of agreement, loggerheads, opposition, polarisation, quarrel, rancour, rift, run-in, showdown, spat, split, squabble, stalemate, stand-off, sticking point, stumbling block, tension, tiff, wrangle
2. contradiction, contrast, departure, deviation, disconnect, discrepancy, disparity, divergence, inconsistency, variance

**Disappear** v., see also Decrease, Lose
abandon, be a no-show, be gone, be lost, be missing in action, be no more, be nowhere to be seen, blow over, cease (to exist), depart, die out, dissipate, dissolve, drop out of sight, dry up, dwindle, ebb, end, evaporate, fade, fade away, fizzle out, go (away), go AWOL, melt away, pass, recede, retreat, sink (without a trace), vanish, vanish from the face of the earth, withdraw

**Disappointed** adj., see also Angry, Unhappy
aggrieved, aghast, bitterly disappointed, crestfallen, deflated, depressed, despondent, devastated, disconcerted, discontented, discouraged, disenchanted, disgruntled, disillusioned, displeased, dissatisfied, distressed, down, downcast, downhearted, frustrated, gutted, heartbroken, hopes dashed, let down, miffed, not impressed, saddened, short-changed, upset, underwhelmed, unimpressed

**Disappointing** adj., see also Unsuccessful, Weak
anti-climax, below expectations, below par, bitterly disappointing, bittersweet, damp squib, devastating, disappointment, disconcerting, discouraging, disheartening, dismal, dispiriting, failed, failing to satisfy, frustrating, gutting, heartbreaking, ill-judged, inadequate, ineffective, insufficient, lacklustre, lame, leaving a bad taste in the mouth, leaving much to be desired, let-down, lukewarm, mediocre, no great shakes, not impressive, not up to scratch, not what was expected, nothing to write home about, pathetic, reality check, saddening, second-rate, soul-destroying, substandard, underwhelming, unfortunate, unfulfilling, unimpressive, unsatisfactory, unspectacular, wanting, wide of the mark, woeful, worse than expected

**Disappointment** n., see also Anger, Failure
anti-climax, bad taste in the mouth, bitter disappointment, bitter pill (to swallow), bitterness, blow, chagrin, consternation, damp squib, defeat, dejection, despondency, disapproval, discontent, discouragement, disenchantment, disillusionment, disliking, dismay, displeasure, dissatisfaction, downer, false dawn, fiasco, flop, frustration, heartache, heartbreak, hopes dashed, kick in the teeth, let-down, misfortune, pyrrhic victory, reality check, regret, setback, washout

**Disaster** n., see also Crisis, Failure
accident, adversity, Armageddon, blunder, calamity, car crash, carnage, cataclysm, catastrophe, collapse, crash, debacle, destruction, devastation, disarray, downfall, emergency, fall from grace, fiasco, flop, lost cause, meltdown, mess, misadventure, misfortune, mishap, nightmare, perfect storm, recipe for disaster, rout, ruin, setback, shambles, shock, tragedy, trouble, turmoil, unmitigated disaster, upheaval, wreck

**Disastrous** adj., see also Failure, Unsuccessful
abysmal, adverse, appalling, atrocious, awful, bad, calamitous, cataclysmic, catastrophic, crisis-hit, devastating, dire, disaster, dismal, doomed, dreadful, failed, fatal, fateful, flop, floundering, fruitless, hapless, ill-fated, ill-judged,

negative, out of one's depth, shambolic, stricken, terrible, tragic, unfortunate, with disastrous consequences, woeful

**Disclose** v., see also Announce, Publish
admit, acknowledge, break the news, bring to light, clarify, communicate, confess, divulge, explain, expose, indicate, issue, lay bare, leak, let slip, make known, make public, mention, publicise, recount, relate, release, report, reveal, spill (the beans), tell, uncover, unveil

**Discount** n., see also Reduction
allowance, bargain price, cheaper, concession, cut, cut price, deal, decrease, deduction, discounted price, exemption, lower price, markdown, money off, price cut, rebate, reduced price, rollback, sale, slashing of prices, special offer

**Discover** v., see also Reveal, Understand
ascertain, bring to light, cast light on, come across, come upon, detect, devise, dig up, encounter, explore, expose, find, find out, happen on/upon, identify, invent, lay bare, learn, light upon, locate, look no further than, notice, observe, originate, perceive, realise, recognise, rediscover, rumble, see, spot, stumble upon, track down, uncover, unearth

**Discuss** v., see also Analyse, Consult
air, argue, be in dialogue, be in discussion(s), be in talks, brainstorm, chat about, chew over, communicate, conduct negotiations, confer, consider, consult with, converse, debate, deliberate, engage with, examine, exchange ideas/views on, explore, get together, go into, go over, have a conversation, have a dialogue, hold discussions, hold talks, negotiate, put heads together, review, talk about/over/through, thrash out, touch on, weigh up

**Discussion** n., see also Agreement, Meeting
airing of views, analysis, back and forth, conference, consideration, consultation, conversation, cut and thrust, debate, deliberation, dialogue, discourse, exchange, exchange of views, face-to-face talks, frank discussions, give and take, head-to-head, meeting of minds, negotiation(s), review, talk(s)

**Dislike** v., see also Criticise, Reject
abhor, balk at, be anathema to, be averse to, be cool on, be hostile towards, be loath to, be sceptical of, be wary of, begrudge, bridle at, condemn, deplore, despise, detest, disagree with, disapprove of, distance oneself from, eschew, feel uncomfortable about, frown upon, give a wide berth, give frosty reception, give the cold shoulder, hate, have a disliking of, have an aversion to, have no

time for, hold in contempt, loathe, no love lost, not be a fan of, not be enamoured with, not be happy about, not be keen on, not be to one's liking, not care for, not take kindly to, object to, resent, scorn, show hostility towards, shun, take a dim view of, take against, take exception to, take issue with

**Dismiss** v., see also Reject, Sack

1. axe, cast out, discharge, dispatch, dispense with, dispose of, drop, eject, end employment, expel, fire, force out, get rid of, give marching orders, give notice to, give the push, kick out, lay off, let go, make redundant, oust, part ways, reduce headcount/personnel/workforce, release, remove, send packing, show the door, sideline, suspend, terminate employment

2. be in denial, brush aside, decline, deny, deride, discount, disregard, give short shrift, gloss over, ignore, laugh off, pooh-pooh, pour cold water on, ridicule, take no notice of, scoff at, shrug off, take with a pinch of salt, wave away, write off

**Displease** v., see also Anger, Unpopular

alienate, annoy, antagonise, be a turn-off, disappoint, disgruntle, disgust, dissatisfy, drive away, exasperate, fail to appeal, fail to attract, fail to satisfy, fall flat, frustrate, gall, leave a bad taste in the mouth, leave much to be desired, nauseate, not be popular, not be someone's cup of tea, not be to someone's taste, offend, outrage, put off, repel, rub up the wrong way, ruffle feathers, sicken, turn off, upset, ward off

**Dispute** n., see also Argument, Disagreement

altercation, animosity, antagonism, bad blood, battle, battleground, beef, bickering, bloodletting, bone of contention, clash, collision, collision course, conflict, contention, controversy, deadlock, difference of opinion, discord, disharmony, dissent, divide, division, falling-out, feud, fight, flashpoint, fracas, fray, friction, gridlock, hostility, hue and cry, ill feeling, impasse, infighting, loggerheads, opposition, quarrel, rift, rivalry, row, run-in, showdown, skirmish, sparks flying, spat, squabble, stalemate, stand-off, storm, strife, struggle, tension, tiff, tug-of-war, war, war of words, wrangle

**Disrupt** v., see also Transform, Trouble

agitate, cause a stir, cause disruption, change, change the complexion/face of, confuse, disturb, dramatically change, interfere with, interrupt, mess up, mix up, muddle, muddy the waters, obstruct, overhaul, put the cat among the pigeons, rattle, revamp, revolutionise, rock, shake (up), sow chaos, tear/rip up the rule book, throw a spanner in the works, throw into disorder, turn upside down, unsettle, upend, upset, upset the apple cart, wreak havoc

**Distinguish** v., see also Classify, Differentiate
categorise, characterise, choose, define, denote, determine, discern, discover, discriminate, divide, draw a distinction, identify, judge, label, make a distinction, make out, mark, perceive, pick out, pinpoint, recognise, separate, separate the wheat from the chaff, set apart, single out, sort, specify, stand apart, tell apart, weed out

**Distribute** v., see also Deliver, Supply
allocate, allot, apportion, arrange, assign, be a distributor/retailer, circulate, dispense, disperse, disseminate, divide, divvy up, give, give out, hand out, issue, market, offer, present, provide, retail, sell, share, ship, split, spread, transport

**Division** n., see also Area, Dispute
1. arm, branch, business, business area, category, class, department, office, part, portion, section, sector, segment, segmentation, subdivision, unit
2. allocation, breach, breakdown, conflict, demarcation, departure, deviation, difference, disagreement, discord, distribution, divergence, divide, fault line, feud, fragmentation, gulf, partition, rift, rupture, separation, split, splitting

**Do** v., see also Implement, Undertake
accomplish, achieve, act, action, arrange, be responsible for, bring about, carry out, complete, conclude, conduct, create, deliver, deploy, develop, effect, engage in, ensure, execute, finish, forge ahead, fulfil, get on with, get something done, go about, handle, initiate, intervene, look after, make, manage, move forward, operate, perform, prepare, proceed, produce, put in place, put into action, realise, roll out, see to, set up, step up, succeed, take action/measures/steps, work

**Dominant** adj., see also Best, Leading
assertive, authoritative, bastion, best-selling, biggest, chief, commanding, controlling, first, foremost, front-runner, heavyweight, highest, influential, largest, leader, main, major, most successful, number one, outstanding, overriding, powerful, powerhouse, predominant, pre-eminent, premier, prevailing, primary, principal, prominent, reigning, ruling, standout, stellar, strongest, superior, top, world leader

**Dominate** v., see also Excel, Lead
be at the forefront, be dominant, be in control, be number one, be the leader, bestride, boss, call the shots, command, control, dictate, dwarf, eclipse, govern, have control over, have the upper hand, hold sway, influence, loom over,

manage, master, monopolise, outshine, outstrip, overshadow, preside over, prevail, reign, rule, rule the roost, stamp one's authority on, stand head and shoulders above, succeed, tower above/over

**Doubt** n., see also Uncertainty, Volatility
ambiguity, anxiety, apprehension, concern(s), confusion, disbelief, distrust, element of doubt, fear, hesitancy, hesitation, indecision, lack of certainty, lack of confidence, lack of conviction, misgiving(s), mistrust, qualms, question(s), question mark, questioning, reluctance, reservations, scepticism, suspicion, wavering

**Downturn** n., see also Decline, Recession
collapse, contraction, crash, crisis, decrease, demise, depression, deterioration, dip, downward shift/trend, drop, economic slowdown, fall, fall-off, hit, lull, meltdown, nosedive, plunge, reduction, retreat, slide, slippery slope, slowdown, slowing, slump, tumble, waning, weakening

**Drop** n., see also Collapse, Deterioration
abatement, blip, contraction, crash, crumbling, curtailment, cut, decline, decrease, demise, dent, depreciation, depression, descent, devaluation, dip, discount, dive, downfall, downturn, downward spiral, drop-off, dwindling, ebb, erosion, fall, falling-off, fall-off, flagging, freefall, hit, lessening, loss, lull, meltdown, narrowing, nosedive, plunge, recession, reduction, retreat, rout, shrinkage, slide, slip, slippery slope, slowdown, slowing, slump, softening, tumble, wane, waning, weakening, withering, worsening

**Drop** v., see also Deteriorate, Stop
1. abate, be eroded, be in decline, be in freefall, be in retreat, be on the decline, be on the wane, become less, become worse, bomb, collapse, contract, cool, crash, crumble, decline, decrease, depreciate, descend, die away, die off, diminish, dip, disintegrate, dive, drop away, drop off, dry up, dwindle, ease, ebb, edge lower, evaporate, fade, fail, fall, fall apart, fall away, fall off, fall off a cliff, fare worse, fizzle out, flag, get worse, go down, go downhill, go into reverse, lessen, lower, nosedive, peter out, plummet, plunge, recede, reduce, regress, retreat, sink, sink like a stone, shrink, shrivel, slide, slip, slump, soften, spiral down, stumble, subside, tail off, take a hit, tank, taper off, topple, tumble, turn down, wane, weaken, wilt, wither, worsen
2. abandon, axe, bin, break with, call off, can, cancel, cut, decline, desert, diminish, discontinue, dispense with, ditch, end, exclude, give up, leave, leave out, let go, omit, part with, scrap, terminate

**Due To** phr., see also Therefore
as, as a result of, attributable to, because of, caused by, by dint of, by reason of, by virtue of, given, in view of, now that, on account of, on the back of, owing to, resulting from, thanks to, through

**Durable** adj., see also Resilient, Strong
abiding, bullet-proof, constant, continual, continuing, dependable, enduring, firm, fixed, hardwearing, hardy, heavy-duty, impervious, indestructible, ironclad, lasting, long-lasting, permanent, persistent, relentless, reliable, resistant, resolute, robust, rock-solid, rugged, sound, stable, steadfast, stout, sturdy, substantial, sustained, tenacious, tough, tough as old boots, unchanging, unfaltering, unwavering

**Dynamic** adj., see also Enthusiastic, Successful
active, ambitious, animated, bold, bright, bursting with energy, can-do, changing, charismatic, compelling, eager, effective, energetic, enterprising, exciting, exuberant, fast-moving, force of nature, fluctuating, full of energy, go-ahead, go-getter, go-getting, going places, high-octane, high-powered, indefatigable, inspiring, intense, lively, motivated, on the front foot, on the move, passionate, positive, potent, powerful, productive, progressive, robust, spirited, strong, thriving, tireless, vibrant, vigorous

# E

**Earn** v., see also Deserve, Work
attain, bag, be compensated, be credited with, be deserving of, be entitled to, be in line for, be paid, be rewarded, be worthy of, bring in, draw, earn one's stripes, gain, garner, generate, get, get paid, gross, make, make a fast buck, make a living, make money, merit, net, obtain, pick up, pocket, post earnings, profit, qualify for, raise, rake in, realise, reap benefits/dividends/rewards, receive, record earnings, score, secure, take a cut, take home, trouser, warrant, win, yield

**Earnings** n., see also Profit, Wage
bottom line, compensation, cut, earnings performance, financial result(s), gain, income, money, pay, proceeds, profit margin, remuneration, results, return, revenue(s), reward, salary, take-home, yield

**Easy** adj., see also Basic, Simple
accessible, beginner's, bread and butter, breeze, child's play, cinch, clear, comfortable, convenient, couldn't be easier, dead easy, doddle, easily done, easy as anything, easy as pie, easy-peasy, easy pickings, efficient, effortless, entry-level, evident, foolproof, hassle-free, helpful, intuitive, low-hanging fruit, manageable, meat and drink, no bother, no-brainer, no problem, no sweat, no-nonsense, no trouble, not difficult, not hard, nothing to it, obvious, painless, picnic, piece of cake, plain sailing, practical, pushover, readily, seamless, simplicity, simplicity itself, smart, smooth, straightforward, trouble-free, uncomplicated, undemanding, untroubled, user-friendly, walk in the park, walkover, with ease, without a hitch

**Economy** n., see also Circumstances, Performance
1. business activity, business cycle, business sector, domestic economy, economic activity, economic conditions, economic cycle, economic performance, global economy, national economy, trade
2. austerity, care, caution, cost saving(s), cut(s), cutback, decrease, efficiencies, frugality, prudence, rationalisation, reduction, restraint, saving, scrimping (and scraping), thrift, thriftiness

**Education** n., see also Experience
apprenticeship, coaching, credentials, curriculum, development, educational background, grounding, guidance, knowledge, learning, learning curve, mentoring, nurturing, preparation, schooling, study, studying, teaching, training, tuition

**Effect** n., see also Consequence, Influence
adverse effect, after-effect, aftermath, backlash, bearing, benefit, blow, body blow, boost, brunt, burden, by-product, chain reaction, cost, development, domino effect, end result, fallout, force, fruits (of one's labour), grip, hangover, help, hit, ill effect, impact, impingement, implication, impression, knock-on effect, lasting effect/impact, legacy, negative effect, outcome, positive effect, ramification(s), reaction, repercussion(s), response, result, reverberations, shock, shock wave, side effect, significance, thrust, toll, traction, upshot, wake

**Effective** adj., see also Efficient, Strong
adequate, appropriate, beneficial, capable, come into its own, competent, constructive, convenient, does not disappoint, first-rate, fit for purpose, fruitful, functional, good, helpful, high-performance, high-performing, holding its own, impactful, impressive, instrumental, invaluable, marvellous, potent, powerful, practical, productive, proficient, proven, reliable, right, robust, sound, successful, sufficient, telling, tried-and-tested, useful, valid, valuable, well-functioning, well-proven, with aplomb, worth its salt, worthwhile

**Effectiveness** n., see also Benefit, Efficiency
advantage, beauty, beneficial effect, capability, clout, convenience, effect, efficacy, fitness, fruitfulness, functionality, impact, performance, positive effect/impact, potency, power, productiveness, productivity, results, strength, success, suitability, use, usefulness, utility, value, virtue

**Efficiency** n., see also Effectiveness, Success
1. cost-effectiveness, economy, efficacy, efficient performance, energy efficiency, frugality, fuel efficiency, low emissions, performance, productivity, reliability, sustainability, thriftiness
2. ability, adeptness, agility, benefit, capability, competence, deftness, expertise, facility, impact, know-how, performance, potency, productivity, proficiency, resourcefulness, skill, slickness, talent, value

**Efficient** adj., see also Effective, Professional
1. adept, agile, businesslike, capable, competent, convenient, experienced, expert, good at, hard-working, labour-saving, lean, like a well-oiled machine,

methodical, powerful, practised, prepared, productive, proficient, seamless, skilled, slick, smooth, streamlined, structured, successful, systematic, talented, useful, valuable, well-designed, well-organised, well-planned, well-run
2. clean, economical, energy-efficient, environmentally friendly, environmentally sustainable, frugal, high-efficiency, low-carbon, low-emissions, low-energy, low-impact, sustainable, thrifty

**Effort** n., see also Attempt, Work
achievement, application, battle, best efforts, bid, blood sweat and tears, endeavour(s), energy, enterprise, exertion(s), extra mile, grit and determination, hard graft, hard work, Herculean effort, industry, labour, labour of love, (great) lengths, level best, one's all, pains, push, slog, sterling effort/work, striving, struggle, tireless efforts/work, toil, undertaking, valiant effort, venture

**Eliminate** v., see also Cancel, Remove
abolish, annihilate, axe, banish, bin, call time on, can, cease, clamp down on, cull, curb, cut (out), delete, destroy, dismiss, dispense with, dispose of, disregard, ditch, do away with, drop, eject, end, eradicate, erase, exclude, extinguish, finish off, get rid of, jettison, knock on the head, knock out, oust, outlaw, phase out, put an end to, reject, rid, root out, rule out, scrap, shut down, shut the door on, snuff out, stamp out, stifle, take an axe to, terminate, throw out, wave goodbye to, wipe out

**Emerge** v., see also Appear, Begin
announce oneself, appear on the scene, arise, arrive, be revealed, become apparent, become established, become known, blow up, burst onto the scene, come to light, come to notice, crop up, dawn, develop, emanate, erupt, loom, make an appearance, materialise, originate, rear its head, rise, shape up, show, start, start off/out, surface, transpire, turn up

**Emphasis** n., see also Focus
accent, accentuation, attention, centre, centre stage, *****-centric, core, crux, essence, focal point, flavour, front and centre, front of mind, heart, highlighting, importance, main focus, nub, onus, oomph, pre-eminence, priority, prominence, sharp focus, significance, slant, strength, stress, thrust, urgency, weight

**Emphasise** v., see also Concentrate On, Focus On
accentuate, affirm, amplify, bring attention to, bring to the fore, call attention to, double down on, dwell on, feature, flag up, give emphasis to, give priority to, give prominence to, hammer home, heighten, highlight, impress (up)on

someone, labour the point, make clear, make much of, pinpoint, place the emphasis on, point out, press home, prioritise, put a spotlight on, put front and centre, put the accent on, reinforce, reiterate, repeat, shine a light on, showcase, single out, speak volumes, spotlight, stress, take centre stage, underline, underscore, zero in on, zone in on, zoom in on

**Employ** v., see also Appoint, Use
1. assign, bring in, bring on board, commission, engage, enlist, enrol, give someone a job, have on the payroll, hire, parachute in, recruit, retain, secure, sign up, take on, task with, use the services of, welcome
2. apply, avail oneself of, benefit from, bring to bear, deploy, exercise, exploit, leverage, make use of, operate, put to use, take advantage of, wield, utilise

**Employee** n., see also Personnel, Representative
agent, assistant, associate, colleague, co-worker, key employee, labourer, member, member of staff, member of the workforce, operator, peer, staff member, talent, wage-earner, worker

**Employment** n., see also Job, Work
appointment, business, career, career path, CV, duties, enrolment, experience, job creation, line of work, livelihood, mission, occupation, position, post, profession, recruitment, responsibility, role, service, task, trade, working life

**Enable** v., see also Allow, Help
aid, allow to get on with, authorise, drive, empower, encourage, entitle, equip, facilitate, foster, give free rein, free up, fuel, give the freedom, give the opportunity, let, make possible, open the door to, permit, power, promote, provide a platform, provide the basis, provide the means, provide the opportunity, provide the scope, support, unlock

**Encourage** v., see also Help, Promote
advocate, applaud, back, be a beacon of hope, be by someone's side, be there for someone, boost, boost morale, buoy, champion, cheer, comfort, commend, embolden, emphasise, endorse, energise, engender, excite, fire up, fortify, further, galvanise, get behind, give a boost, give full support, give hope, hearten, incentivise, incite, induce, inspire, instil, invite, lift the spirits, motivate, nurture, persuade, praise, prompt, provide encouragement/hope, push, rally, reassure, recommend, root for, spur (on), steel, stimulate, support, take heart, urge, use a carrot-and-stick approach, welcome, whip up

**End** n., see also Conclusion, Intention
achievement, cessation, climax, close, closure, completion, culmination, curtains, days are numbered, deadline, death knell, death throes, demise, discontinuation, dying days, dying embers, end in sight, end of an era, end of the line, end of the road, endgame, ending, expiry, farewell, final chapter, final nail in the coffin, final stage(s), final straw, finale, finish, fulfilment, game is up, game over, home straight, last stage(s), last straw, light at the end of the tunnel, outcome, realisation, resolution, result, swansong, tail end, termination, writing is on the wall

**End** v., see also Cancel, Conclude
abolish, abort, axe, be over, bin, block, blow over, break off, bring the curtain down on, bring to a conclusion, bring to an end, call a halt to, call it a day, call it quits, call off, call time on, can, cease, close, combat, come to a head, come to an end, come to a standstill, come to the end of the line/road, complete, crack down on, culminate, curb, curtail, cut off, cut short, desist, discontinue, ditch, draw a line in the sand, draw a line under, draw to a close, drop, dry up, dust settles, end up, eradicate, expire, fade away, finish, finish off, fizzle out, freeze, give up, halt, hinder, interrupt, kill (off), knock on the head, nip in the bud, pack it in, pan out, peter out, prevent, pull, pull the plug on, put an end to, put a stop to, put paid to, quit, reach a climax, resolve, result, round off, run its course, scotch, scrap, scupper, settle, shelve, shoot down, shut down, sign off, snuff out, stamp out, stem, stop, stop in its tracks, stop the rot, stymie, suspend, terminate, throw in the towel, thwart, torpedo, turn out, veto, wave goodbye to, wind up, withdraw, wrap up, writing is on the wall

**Endeavour** v., see also Try, Undertake
aim, aspire, attempt, be determined, bend over backwards, bid, chip away, dig deep, do one's best, exert oneself, fight tooth and nail, get stuck in, give it one's all, give it one's best shot, go for it, go the extra mile, go to town, go out of one's way, have a crack at, have a stab at, intend, labour, make a bid, make a fist of, make a foray into, make an effort, move heaven and earth, never say die, not rest on one's laurels, plug away, pull out all the stops, push, push the boat out, put one's best foot forward, put one's heart (and soul) into, put one's mind to, resort to, roll up one's sleeves, seek, step up (to the mark/plate), strain every sinew, strive, struggle, take on, take pains, take the bull by the horns, try one's hand, venture, work, work flat out, work hard, work tirelessly

**Endure** v., see also Struggle, Suffer
abide, be in the grip of, be subjected to, be victim to, bear, bear the brunt, bear the scars, brace, brave, carry on, confront, cope with, defy, encounter, experience, face, feel, get through, go through, grin and bear it, hang in there, hold out, keep going, live through, meet with, oppose, persist, prevail, put up with, remain firm, resign oneself to, resist, ride out the storm, see through, stand, stand fast, stand firm, stand one's ground, stand up to, stay strong, stick it out, stomach, survive, sustain, sweat it out, take, take on, tolerate, tough it out, undergo, weather, weather the storm, withstand

**Energy** n., see also Momentum, Power
activity, ambition, animation, boost, brio, determination, devotion, drive, dynamism, ebullience, electricity, enterprise, enthusiasm, excitement, exuberance, fire in the belly, force, fuel, get-up-and-go, intensity, life, liveliness, mojo, oomph, passion, pizzazz, potency, spirit, stamina, strength, verve, vibrancy, vigour, vim and vigour, vitality, vivacity, zeal, zest, zing, zip

**Engage** v., see also Employ, Involve
1. absorb, activate, apply, attract, become involved in, begin, captivate, capture, discuss, draw in, embark on, energise, engross, enter into, fascinate, have a dialogue, immerse, interact, interest, keep busy, join in, meet, participate, preoccupy, reach out to, tackle, take part in, take up, undertake
2. appoint, ask, bring on board, commission, contract, engage the services of, enlist, enrol, hire, recruit, request, secure (the services of), sign up, take on, task with, use (the services of)

**Enhance** v., see also Change, Update
add to, add value, advance, augment, bolster, boost, boost performance, complement, develop, ease, elevate, enrich, facelift, finesse, help, heighten, hone, improve (on), increase, intensify, lift, make better, optimise, perfect, perk up, polish, raise, reboot, refine, reform, refresh, reinforce, reinvent, reinvigorate, relaunch, restore, revamp, review, revise, revisit, revitalise, revive, sharpen, spruce up, step up, streamline, strengthen, take to the next level, tweak, up one's game, update, upgrade

**Enjoy** v., see also Like, Relax
adore, admire, appreciate, bask in, be a sucker for, be fond of, be impressed by, be in one's element, be inspired by, be keen on, be partial to, be pleased with, celebrate, delight in, experience, find pleasure in, flourish, get a kick out of, glory in, have a ball, have a good time, have fun, have the benefit of, indulge in, let one's hair down, live a little, live life to the full, love, love every minute,

marvel at, reap the benefits/dividends/rewards of, rejoice in, relish, revel in, savour, soak up, take joy/pleasure from, take satisfaction from/in, thrive, value

**Enjoyable** adj., see also Entertaining, Pleasant
agreeable, amazing, amusing, blast, blissful, brilliant, delicious, delight, delightful, endearing, engaging, for the heck of it, fun, fun-filled, good, good time, great, gripping, heaven, hoot, incredible, interesting, joy, likable, lovely, magical, memorable, nice, pleasing, refreshing, rewarding, satisfying, special, to remember, treat, uplifting, welcome, wonderful

**Enough** det., see also Adequate, Satisfactory
acceptable, agreeable, ample, aplenty, appropriate, as necessary, as required, comfortable, competent, decent, does the job, good enough, just enough, more than enough, pleasing, plentiful, plenty, proportionate, reasonable, requisite, sufficient, sufficing, suitable, that will do, tolerable, unexceptional

**Enquire** v., see also Consult, Request
angle, ascertain, ask, canvas opinion, contact, evaluate, examine, explore, inquire, inspect, investigate, look into, make enquiries, probe, query, question, quiz, research, review, scrutinise, search, seek, study, test the waters

**Enquiry** n., see also Request
analysis, application, audit, examination, exploration, evaluation, inquiry, inspection, investigation, probe, query, question, report, research, review, scrutiny, study, survey

**Ensure** v., see also Approve, Guarantee
arrange, assure, be certain, be sure, certify, check, confirm, double-check, establish, make certain, make sure, manage, organise, oversee, pledge, promise, protect, provide, put in place, safeguard, secure, see to it, set out, set up, take action, take measures, undertake

**Entertaining** adj., see also Attractive, Interesting
absorbing, amusing, barnstorming, breathtaking, bring the house down, captivating, charming, compelling, crowd-pleasing, dazzling, delightful, electrifying, enchanting, engaging, engrossing, enjoyable, enthralling, enticing, entrancing, exciting, exhilarating, fascinating, fun, funny, glitzy, glamourous, gripping, immersive, impressive, inspiring, intriguing, lively, magical, moving, must-see, not to be missed, pleasant, poignant, provocative, rip-roaring, riveting, rousing, scintillating, sensational, show-stopping, spectacular,

spellbinding, spine-tingling, stimulating, stirring, striking, thought-provoking, thrilling, unforgettable, uplifting, vibrant

**Enthusiasm** n., see also Commitment, Excitement
ambition, belief, can-do attitude, conviction, craze, dedication, determination, devotion, drive, dynamism, eagerness, energy, engagement, exuberance, fascination, fervour, flair, get-up-and-go, gusto, intensity, interest, involvement, joy, keen interest, keenness, labour of love, love, mania, mojo, motivation, obsession, passion, positivity, relish, spirit, warmth, zeal

**Enthusiastic** adj., see also Committed, Dynamic
ambitious, ardent, avid, avowed, bright-eyed and bushy-tailed, champion of, crazy about, crusader for, dedicated, desperate to, devoted, devotee of, eager, earnest, ebullient, effervescent, energetic, energised, excited, exuberant, fanatical, fascinated, fervent, fire in the belly, fired up, hungry, impassioned, indefatigable, interested, invested in, irrepressible, itching to, keen, live and breathe something, mad about, motivated, obsessed, passionate, positive, psyched, pumped(-up), raring to go, serious, single-minded, spirited, tenacious, thrilled, up for, vehement, wholehearted, zealous

**Entire** adj., see also All, Complete
absolute, all-encompassing, all-inclusive, comprehensive, consolidated, end-to-end, full, inclusive, intact, integral, outright, overall, total, thorough, unbroken, undivided, unified, uninterrupted, unmitigated, unreserved, unrestricted, utter, whole, whole hog, whole shebang, works

**Environment** n., see also Area, Sustainability
1. atmosphere, biodiversity, climate, Earth, ecology, ecosystem, great outdoors, habitat, Mother Nature, natural environment, natural resources, natural world, nature, our planet, planet, world, world around us
2. arena, atmosphere, backdrop, circumstances, climate, conditions, context, habitat, kind of place, landscape, locality, location, neighbourhood, place, scene, setting, setup, situation, surroundings, territory, work environment

**Equipment** n., see also Device, Machine
accessories, apparatus, appliances, components, facilities, fittings, gear, hardware, infrastructure, installation, instruments, kit, machinery, material, outfit, paraphernalia, peripherals, rig, setup, stuff, supplies, tech, technology, tools, trappings

**Error** n., see also Failure, Mistake
anomaly, blatant error, blunder, cardinal error, clanger, deviation, fault, fiasco, flaw, gaffe, glitch, howler, inaccuracy, inconsistency, ineptitude, howler, human error, lapse, litany of errors, miscalculation, miscue, misjudgement, mismanagement, miss, misstatement, misstep, misunderstanding, omission, oversight, schoolboy error, shambles, slip, slip-up, stumble, typo, wrong move

**Especially** adv., see Very
above all, all the more, chiefly, decidedly, distinctly, exceptionally, expressly, extraordinarily, in particular, individually, mainly, markedly, not least, notably, particularly, primarily, principally, pronounced, quintessentially, remarkably, singularly, specially, specifically, surprisingly, to say the least, tremendously, undoubtedly, uniquely, unquestionably, unusually

**Essential** adj., see also Important, Key
all-important, basic, bedrock, cannot do without, cardinal, chief, condition, core, cornerstone, critical, crucial, de rigueur, essential reading/viewing etc., fundamental, high time, imperative, indispensable, inherent, innate, integral, intrinsic, life-or-death, lifeblood, linchpin, lost without, main, mainstay, mandatory, mission-critical, must-have/read/see, necessary, necessary evil, needed, not to be missed, obligatory, of utmost importance, paramount, part and parcel, pivotal, prerequisite, primary, prime, principal, required, required reading/viewing, sorely needed, unmissable, urgent, vital

**Establish** v., see also Introduce, Launch
activate, authorise, base, begin, bring in/out, build, confirm, create, decide, demonstrate, determine, develop, enshrine, ensure, fix, form, found, get underway, green-light, implement, inaugurate, initiate, install, institute, kick-start, lay the foundations, lay the groundwork, open, organise, originate, prove, provide, put down roots, put in place, roll out, secure, set in motion, set in stone, set up, start (up), take hold, usher in, validate

**Estimate** n., see also Assessment, Forecast
analysis, appraisal, approximation, ballpark figure, best guess, calculation, conclusion, educated guess, estimation, evaluation, expectation, guess, guesstimate, gut feeling, judgement, opinion, projection, quotation, reckoning, rough calculation, rough estimate, rough idea, speculation, valuation

**Estimate** v., see also Assess, Forecast
anticipate, appraise, approximate, believe, budget, calculate approximately, calculate roughly, compute, conjecture, consider, determine, evaluate, expect,

gauge, guess, guesstimate, have a feeling/hunch, hazard a guess, judge, make an estimate, predict, project, put a value on, rate, reason, reckon, see, speculate, suppose, surmise, think, value

**Ethical** adj., see also Right, Sustainable
above board, acceptable, accountable, appropriate, conscientious, correct, decent, environmentally sustainable, equitable, ESG (environmental, social and corporate governance), ethically minded, fair, green, honest, honourable, humane, just, moral, morally acceptable, morally right, principled, professional, respectable, responsible, right-minded, right thing (to do), with a social conscience, with integrity

**Ethics** n., see also Professional, Sustainability
accountability, belief(s), conduct, conscience, core values, corporate governance, decency, ESG (environmental, social and corporate governance), ethical standards, ethos, high standards, honesty, integrity, judgement, making a difference, moral code, moral compass, morality, principles, probity, professional approach, professionalism, responsibility, rules, social conscience, standards, sustainable approach, values

**Evaluate** v., see also Analyse, Estimate
appraise, assess, calculate, check, check out, compute, conduct an assessment/evaluation, consider, decide, deduce, determine, estimate, examine, explore, explore options, figure out, forecast, gauge, grade, investigate, judge, look into, look over, make of, measure, monitor, pore over, probe, rank, rate, regard, review, screen, scrutinise, shine a light on, size up, study, take account of, test, understand, value, verify, view, weigh (up)

**Evaluation** n., see also Analysis, Forecast
appraisal, assessment, barometer, calculation, check, consideration, decision, deduction, determination, discretion, due diligence, estimate, estimation, exploration, gauge, insight, interpretation, investigation, judgement, measurement, opinion, outlook, rating, reckoning, review, scrutiny, valuation, view, weighing-up

**Event** n., see also Circumstances
accident, act, action, activity, affair, business, case, development(s), drama, engagement, episode, experience, function, incident, matter, milestone, moment, move, occasion, occurrence, phenomenon, proceeding(s), scenario, show, situation, spectacle, story

**Everywhere** adv., see also International
across, all around, all over, around, far and wide, four corners of the earth/world, globally, here and there, high and low, in all quarters, in every direction, in every place, left right and centre, near and far, omnipresent, throughout, ubiquitous, universally, wherever, wherever and whenever, wherever you go/look, world over

**Evidence** n., see also Data, Information
affirmation, attestation, authentication, borne out by, certification, clincher, clue, confirmation, corroboration, demonstration, documentation, grounds, hard evidence, hard facts, indication, manifestation, proof, proof positive, sign, smoking gun, speaks for itself, substantiation, testament, testimony, validation, verification

**Evoke** v., see also Inspire, Provoke
arouse, awaken, bring to mind, call forth, call to mind, conjure (up), elicit, evince, give rise to, ignite, induce, kindle, produce, put in mind of, recall, rekindle, rouse, spark, spring to mind, stimulate, stir (up), suggest, summon (up)

**Exact** adj., see also Accurate, Specific
absolute, bang on, careful, categorical, clear-cut, conscientious, correct, dead on, decisive, definite, detailed, distinct, explicit, faultless, limited, meticulous, on the button, on the money, on the nose, painstaking, particular, perfect, picky, precise, proper, right, rigid, rigorous, scrupulous, spot on, strict, stringent, to a T, to the letter, true, uncompromising, very, well-defined, with pinpoint accuracy

**Exaggerate** v., see also Overestimate
amplify, be a storm in a teacup, be over the top, blow out of proportion, boast, brag, build up, distort, embellish, embroider, falsify, get carried away, guild the lily, hype, inflate, lay it on thick, lay it on with a trowel, lie, magnify, make a meal of, make a mountain out of a molehill, make a song and dance out of, make too much of, misreport, misrepresent, overdo, overegg (the pudding), overemphasise, overstate, play up, romanticise

**Examine** v., see also Analyse, Explore
audit, check, check out, conduct an examination, consider, delve into, dig deeper, dig into, drill down into, get to the heart of, go over, inquire into, inspect, investigate, leave no stone unturned, lift the lid, look into, measure, ponder, pore over, probe, question, research, review, scout, screen, scrutinise,

search, seek, shine a light on, sift, size up, study, subject to analysis, survey, take stock of, test, vet, weigh up

**Example/For Example** n./phr., see also Typical
as an illustration, benchmark, by way of illustration, case, case in point, classic (case of), epitome, for instance, illustration, incarnation, instance, lesson, like, model, norm, pattern, precedent, prime example, sample, say, standard, such as, to illustrate, template, typical example, very model

**Exceed** v., see also Defeat, Grow
be better than, be greater than, be more than, be over, be superior to, beat, break [a record], better, dwarf, eclipse, go (above and) beyond, go beyond the bounds of, knock spots off, have an advantage over, have the upper hand, leapfrog, outdo, outnumber, outpace, outperform, outshine, outstrip, overshadow, overstep, overtake, pass, put in the shade, put to shame, steal a march on, surmount, surpass, top, transcend, upstage

**Excel** v., see also Specialise, Succeed
ace, be a hit, be at the forefront, be dominant, be good at, be in one's element, be master of, be on fire, be skilful, be superior, be talented, be the best, beat, bring one's A game, click, come into one's own, demonstrate skill, do well, dominate, eclipse, excel oneself, fire on all cylinders, flourish, have down to a fine art, hit one's stride, impress, lead, lead the field, outdo, outdo oneself, outperform, outrival, outshine, outstrip, predominate, pride oneself, put in the shade, put to shame, raise the bar, rise to the occasion, run rings around, set a new benchmark, set the standard, shine, show talent, stand head and shoulders above, stand out, start, surpass, take to new heights, thrive, transcend, top, wow

**Excellent** adj., see also Best, Impressive
ace, admirable, amazing, astonishing, astounding, attractive, award-winning, awe-inspiring, awesome, break-out, breathtaking, brilliant, celebrated, choice, cracking, distinguished, exceptional, exemplary, exquisite, extraordinaire, extraordinary, fab, fabulous, fantastic, fine, finest, first-class, first-rate, five-star, flagship, flawless, foremost, glorious, gorgeous, great, high-class, hit, ideal, illustrious, impeccable, incomparable, incredible, invaluable, jaw-dropping, leading, legendary, magic, magical, magnificent, mind-blowing, must-have/read/see, notable, on a roll, on fire, on form, optimal, out of this world, outstanding, peerless, phenomenal, pre-eminent, premier, premium, prestigious, priceless, remarkable, (it) rocks, second to none, sensational, smash-hit, smashing, spectacular, standout, state-of-the-art, sterling, striking, stunning, successful, superb, superior, superlative, supreme, terrific, top, top-

flight, top-notch, tremendous, ultimate, unbelievable, unequalled, unparalleled, unrivalled, unsurpassed, very best, wonderful, world-class

**Excess** adj./n., see also Large, Lots
balance, extra, extravagance, flood, glut, in excess, left over, more than enough, over, overabundance, overflow, overkill, overload, overrun, oversupply, plethora, remainder, remaining, spare, superfluous, surfeit, surplus, too much, unused, waste

**Excited** adj., see also Enthusiastic, Pleased
beside oneself (with excitement), brimming with excitement, can hardly wait, can't wait, eager, energised, exuberant, fired up, inspired, lively, looking forward to, nervous, on the edge of one's seat, passionate, psyched, raring to go, stoked, thrilled, up for, upbeat, with bated breath

**Excitement** n., see also Enthusiasm, Interest
action, activity, adventure, animation, anticipation, buzz, commotion, drama, dynamism, eagerness, elation, electricity, emotion, energy, expectancy, fanfare, fascination, feeling, fever, frenzy, frisson of excitement, fun, fuss, hubbub, hype, hysteria, inspiration, kick, magic, much ado, passion, stimulation, suspense, talk, thrill, tingle, tumult, verve

**Exciting** adj., see also Dynamic, Impressive
barnstorming, breathtaking, captivating, cliff-hanger, compelling, dazzling, dramatic, electrifying, eye-catching, exciting times, exhilarating, extravagant, fascinating, fun, fun-filled, gripping, inspiring, interesting, intoxicating, intriguing, lively, mesmerising, mind-blowing, on the edge of one's seat, overwhelming, pulsating, rip-roaring, riveting, rousing, scintillating, sensational, setting hearts/pulses racing, show-stopping, spectacular, stimulating, stirring, striking, tense, thrilling, uplifting, vibrant, vivid, wild, with flair, with panache, with verve

**Exclude** v., see also Prevent, Reject
alienate, ban, bar, block, disqualify, eject, eliminate, expel, forbid, force out, keep out, leave out, not allow, not include, not permit, not welcome, omit, ostracise, overlook, preclude, prohibit, refuse, rule out, shut out, sideline, stop, suspend

**Expand** v., see also Grow, Increase
add to, amass, augment, balloon, become bigger, become larger, beef up, bolster, boom, branch out, broaden, build up, bulk up, burgeon, conquer,

develop, diversify, enlarge, escalate, evolve, explode, explore new areas, extend, fan out, gain ground, get bigger, grow a business, grow in size, grow through acquisitions, make larger, move into, move into new areas, multiply, mushroom, open new branches, proliferate, prolong, ramp up, snowball, spread, supersize, swell, take off, widen

**Expansion** n., see also Growth, Increase
addition, augmentation, branching out, broadening, burgeoning, deepening, development, diversification, enlargement, escalation, evolution, explosion, extension, furthering, inflation, invasion, march, multiplication, mushrooming, progress, proliferation, prolongation, ramp-up, rise, scaling-up, spread, surge, widening

**Expect** v., see also Estimate, Forecast
aim, anticipate, assume, await, bank on, bargain for, be braced for, be confident, be hopeful, be prepared for, believe, bet, brace for, calculate, call for, come as no surprise, conjecture, count on, demand, envisage, factor in, fear, foresee, guess, have a feeling, have a hunch, have an expectation, have faith in, hope, hotly anticipate, imagine, insist on, look ahead, look forward, prepare for, plan for, predict, pre-empt, presume, price in, project, put money on, reckon, rely upon, require, second-guess, see, see coming, suppose, surmise, suspect, target, think likely, tip, trust, understand, wager, watch for

**Expectation** n., see also Estimate, Forecast
aim, anticipation, apprehension, assumption, belief, best guess, bet, calculation, confidence, conjecture, consensus, demand, fear, guess, guesswork, gut feeling, hope, hunch, likelihood, outlook, possibility, prediction, presumption, probability, projection, promise, prospect, requirement, sense, supposition, suspicion, view

**Expected** adj., see also Likely, Typical
according to plan, anticipated, as expected, as planned, awaited, bound to, coming, due, eagerly awaited, envisaged, factored in, feasible, forecast, foreseen, given, hardly surprising, hoped for, hotly anticipated, in store, in the offing, in the pipeline, little/small wonder, long-awaited, looked for, mooted, much-anticipated, no surprise, no wonder, odds-on, on course for, on schedule, on the cards, only natural, planned, plausible, poised, predicted, priced in, promised, proposed, scheduled, set to, slated, tipped, usual

**Expense** n., see also Cost, Price
amount, capital expenditure, charge, expenditure, fee, investment, liability, outgoings, outlay, overhead(s), payment, price tag, spend, spending, sum

**Expensive** adj., see also High-quality, Large
arm and a leg, at a premium, at a price, big-ticket item, costing a small fortune, costing over the odds, costing the earth, costly, dear, excessive, exorbitant, extravagant, eye-watering, fancy, flashy, hefty price, high-end, high-priced, lavish, luxurious, luxury, no expense spared, not cheap, opulent, outrageous, overpriced, plush, posh, pretty penny, pricey, prohibitive, prohibitively expensive, sky-high, steep, swanky, unreasonable, upmarket, upscale, valuable

**Experience** n., see also Education
1. back story, background, career, context, credibility, credentials, CV, expertise, extensive experience, familiarity, history, involvement, journey, know-how, knowledge, lesson(s), life, participation, past, pedigree, previous experience, record, story, track record, training, understanding, wisdom, work
2. adventure, contact, encounter, episode, event, exposure, foray, incident, involvement, learning experience, lesson, moment, occurrence, ordeal, salutary experience, story, taste, time

**Experience** v., see also Endure, Involve
be in the grip of, be involved in, be present, become familiar with, come up against, discover, encounter, enjoy, explore, face, gain experience, get acquainted with, get to know, go through, have experience of, have a taste of, immerse oneself, know, learn, live through, meet, partake, participate in, practise, run into, sample, see, suffer, sustain, taste, test, try, undergo

**Experienced** adj., see also Skilled, Talented
accomplished, adept, been around, been there done that, capable, competent, distinguished, expert, familiar, highly regarded, in the know, knowing one's stuff, knowing a thing or two about, knowledgeable, legendary, master, masterful, masterly, mature, no stranger to, old hand, practised, pre-eminent, professional, qualified, renowned, respected, seasoned, seen it all, skilful, trained, versed, veteran, virtuoso, well informed, well versed, wise, worldly

**Expert** n., see also Experienced, Skilled
ace, aficionado, analyst, authority, buff, commentator, connoisseur, consultant, critic, dab hand, doyen/doyenne, elite, enthusiast, evangelist, exponent, go-to person, guru, hotshot, influencer, leader, leading light, luminary, maestro, master, master of one's craft, mastermind, mine of information, mover and

shaker, old hand, past master, pro, professional, savvy, scholar, seasoned pro(fessional), specialist, supremo, thought leader, veteran, virtuoso, whizz, wizard

**Expertise** n., see also Experience, Knowledge
ability, acumen, adeptness, alacrity, calibre, capability, command, competence, craftsmanship, credentials, depth of knowledge, facility, flair, forte, grasp, in-depth knowledge, insight, involvement, judgement, knack, know-how, mastery, nous, proficiency, prowess, savvy, skilfulness, skill, skillset, talent, training, understanding, wherewithal, wisdom

**Explain** v., see also Clarify, Specify
account for, articulate, break down, clear up, comment on, communicate, contextualise, debunk, define, demonstrate, demystify, describe, disclose, dispel doubts/fears/myths, elaborate, elucidate, expound, express, flesh out, get across, get at, give details, give an explanation, give a reason, go into detail, have some explaining to do, illustrate, justify, legitimise, make a/the case for, make clear, outline, point out, put forth, put into context, put into perspective, rationalise, reveal, set out, set out one's stall, shed light on, shine a light on, simplify, spell out, tell, talk through, throw light upon, unpack, walk through

**Explanation** n., see also Description, Reason
account, answer, assessment, cause, clarification, comment, commentary, defence, details, excuse, grounds, illustration, information, insight, interpretation, justification, meaning, mitigation, motive, narrative, report, simplification, statement, why and wherefore

**Exploit** v., see also Take Advantage, Utilise
1. apply, benefit from, build on, capitalise on, cash in on, convert into, cultivate, deploy, harness, leverage, make best use of, make the most of, make use of, manage, maximise, profit from, put to use, seize the opportunity, take full advantage of, trade on, translate into, turn into, use, use to one's advantage
2. abuse, cash in on, manipulate, milk, mismanage, mistreat, misuse, prey on, profit from, profiteer, treat unfairly

**Explore** v., see also Analyse, Examine
consider, delve into, dig deeper, dig into, drill down into, get to the heart of, immerse oneself in, inquire into, inspect, investigate, leave no stone unturned, lift the lid, look into, pick over, ponder, pore over, probe, question, reflect on, research, scout, scrutinise, search, seek, shed light on, shine a light on, sift through, study, survey, unpack, weigh up

**Extensive** adj., see also Large, Many
all manner of, all-encompassing, all-inclusive, almighty, big, brimming with, broad, capacious, colossal, complete, comprehensive, considerable, covering all bases, everything from...to..., expanded, expansive, extended, far-reaching, general, generous, great, huge, in abundance, large-scale, lengthy, lots, major, massive, monumental, multiple, numerous, pervasive, plentiful, protracted, significant, sizeable, spacious, spoilt for choice, substantial, sweeping, thorough, universal, vast, voluminous, wall-to-wall, wholesale, wide-ranging, widespread

**Extent** n., see also Level, Limit
amount, area, bounds, breadth, degree, dimensions, duration, intensity, length, magnitude, measure, order, proportion(s), quantity, range, reach, scale, scope, size, spread, term, volume

**Extremely** adv., see also Completely, Especially
absolutely, achingly, acutely, all the more, all-out, ardently, awfully, brazenly, certainly, comprehensively, conclusively, considerably, decidedly, deeply, demonstrably, die-hard, downright, dramatically, drastically, eminently, emphatically, every inch, exceedingly, exceptionally, excessively, extensively, extraordinarily, firmly, full-on, genuinely, glaringly, greatly, highly, hugely, immeasurably, immensely, impossibly, in earnest, incredibly, insanely, insatiably, intensely, irretrievably, model of, monumentally, most, nothing short of, noticeably, obscenely, off the charts, off the scale, overwhelmingly, particularly, patently, profoundly, quintessentially, quite, radically, really, remarkably, resolutely, resoundingly, richly, rigorously, seriously, severely, sharply, sheer, smacks of, staunchly, steadfastly, steeped in, strongly, substantially, super-*****, supremely, surprisingly, terribly, to put it mildly, tremendously, truly, ultra*****, unanimously, unashamedly, uncompromisingly, undisputedly, undoubtedly, unequivocally, unquestionably, unusually, utmost, utterly, vehemently, veritably, very, very much, well and truly, wholeheartedly, wonderfully

# F

**Facilitate** v., see also Help, Support
aid, alleviate, allow, assist, boost, ease, empower, enable, expedite, fast-track, foster, further, help on its way, improve, make easy/easier, make life easy, make possible, oil/grease the wheels, open doors, pave the way, permit, promote, provide the means, provide the opportunity, simplify, smooth, smooth the way, speed up, streamline, underpin

**Facility** n., see also Ability, Factory
1. amenity, area, building, complex, department, equipment, infrastructure, manufacturing plant, mill, plant, premises, production plant, production unit, provision, resource(s), service, site, structure, system, unit, works
2. alacrity, aptitude, capability, competence, dexterity, ease, effectiveness, efficiency, expertise, flair, flourish, fluency, knack, mastery, opportunity, possibility, proficiency, skill, strength, talent

**Factor** n., see also Aspect, Feature
attribute, building block, cause, characteristic, circumstance, component, consideration, detail, determinant, driver, element, facet, influence, ingredient, issue, item, parameter, part, part and parcel, point, property, quality, side

**Factory** n., see also Facility, Production
assembly line, assembly plant, complex, facilities, industrial facility, laboratory, manufacturing plant, mill, plant, premises, production plant, production unit, site, unit, works, workshop

**Fail** v., see also Collapse, Decline
1. abort, backfire, be a failure, be at a low ebb, be caught napping, be dealt a blow, be defeated, be down and out, be flogging a dead horse, be found lacking, be found wanting, be in tatters, be in vain, be on one's knees, be on the back foot, be out of one's depth, be ruined, be toast, be unsuccessful, be wound up, beat a retreat, bite the dust, bite off more than one can chew, blunder, bomb, botch, break down, buckle, bungle, capitulate, cave in, collapse, come a cropper, come to nothing, come under fire, come unstuck, come up short, crash, crash and burn, crumple, deteriorate, drop the ball, end in tears, engulf, fade, fail in a bid to, fall apart (at the seams), fall by the wayside, fall flat, fall from

grace, fall on hard times, fall short, fall through, falter, fight a losing battle, fizzle out, flag, flatline, flop, flounder, founder, fold, go astray, go awry, go bankrupt, go belly up, go bust, go down in flames, go down like a lead balloon, go into a tailspin, go out of business, go pear-shaped, go to the wall, go under, go wrong, hit the buffers, implode, learn the hard way, make a pig's ear of something, make heavy weather of, meet with disaster, misfire, mishandle, mismanage, miss the boat, miss the mark, not make the grade, not succeed, reel, regress, run aground, run out of steam, shoot oneself in the foot, stagnate, stall, struggle, stutter, succumb, suffer, suffer a blow/hammer blow, take one's eye off the ball, tank, teeter, tread water, turn sour, unravel, wheels come off
2. disappoint, forget, ignore, let down, miss an opportunity, neglect, not do, omit, overlook

**Failure** n., see also Collapse, Defeat
adversity, also-ran, anti-climax, bad day at the office, bankruptcy, blip, blunder, breakdown, breaking point, car crash, casualty, closure, collapse, crash, curtains, dead-end, death, debacle, decline, demise, deterioration, disarray, disaster, downfall, downward spiral, drubbing, failing, fall, fall from grace, fiasco, flop, game over, has-been, inaction, ineptitude, insolvency, lack of success, lead balloon, liquidation, lost cause, malaise, meltdown, mess, misadventure, miscalculation, misfire, mishandling, mismanagement, missed opportunity, misstep, neglect, non-starter, oblivion, own goal, rout, ruin, setback, shadow of its former self, shambles, shortcoming, slide, slippery slope, slump, struggle, tumble, turkey, undoing, unravelling, waning, washout, white elephant, winding up, wobble, wreck

**Fair** adj., see also Ethical, Honest
above board, acceptable, according to the rules, by the rules, correct, decent, disinterested, dispassionate, equal, equitable, even-handed, fair-minded, honourable, impartial, just, justified, lawful, legitimate, level playing field, neutral, objective, only fair, principled, proper, reasonable, respectable, responsible, right, right thing (to do), satisfactory, sincere, trustworthy, unbiased, uncorrupted, unprejudiced, without fear or favour

**Fall** n., see also Collapse, Deterioration
abatement, blip, contraction, crash, crumbling, curtailment, cut, cutback, decline, decrease, demise, dent, depreciation, depression, descent, devaluation, dip, dive, downfall, downturn, downward spiral, drop, drop-off, dwindling, ebb, erosion, falling-off, fall-off, flagging, freefall, lessening, loss, lull, meltdown, narrowing, nosedive, plunge, recession, reduction, retreat, rout,

shrinkage, slide, slip, slippery slope, slowdown, slowing, slump, softening, tailspin, tumble, wane, waning, weakening, withering, worsening

**Fall** v., see also Decrease
abate, be eroded, be in decline, be in freefall, be in retreat, be on the decline, be on the wane, become less, become worse, bomb, collapse, contract, cool, crash, crumble, decline, decrease, depreciate, descend, deteriorate, die away, die off, diminish, dip, disintegrate, dive, drop, drop away, drop off, dry up, dwindle, ease, ebb, edge down/lower, evaporate, fade, fail, fall apart, fall away, fall off, fall off a cliff, fare worse, fizzle out, flag, get worse, go down, go downhill, go into reverse, lessen, lower, nosedive, peter out, plummet, plunge, recede, reduce, regress, retreat, sink, sink like a stone, shrink, shrivel, slide, slip, slump, soften, spiral down, stumble, subside, tail off, take a hit, tank, taper off, topple, trip, tumble, turn down, wane, weaken, wilt, wither, worsen

**False** adj., see also Corrupt, Incorrect
artificial, baseless, bogus, cooked-up, counterfeit, covering up, deceitful, deceptive, dishonest, disloyal, dissembling, distorted, dummy, erroneous, fabricated, fake, fallacious, fallacy, falsehood, fanciful, feigned, fictitious, fishy, flawed, forged, fraudulent, hollow, imprecise, improper, inaccurate, inconsistent, insincere, invalid, lie, lying, made-up, misleading, mistaken, myth, not true, nothing could be further from the truth, phoney, ringing hollow, sham, spurious, trumped-up, two-faced, unfair, unfaithful, unfounded, unreal, unreliable, unsound, untrue, untrustworthy, untruthful, wrong

**Famous** adj., see also Popular
acclaimed, all-star, best-known, big, big name, blockbuster, box-office, catapulted to fame, celebrated, celebrity, distinguished, eminent, esteemed, fabled, famed, familiar, famous face, feted, foremost, great and the good, hallowed, high-profile, hit, honoured, household name, iconic, illustrious, in the limelight, in the spotlight, in the public eye, infamous, influential, known, leading, legend, legendary, megastar, memorable, much-discussed, name on everyone's lips, national treasure, needing no introduction, notable, noted, noteworthy, notorious, of note, pre-eminent, prominent, public, recognised, renowned, reputable, respected, revered, rising star, rock-star, star, star-studded, stellar, stuff of legend, superstar, talked about, VIP, well-known, widely known, widely respected, world-famous

**Fast** adj./adv., see also Agile, Brief
abrupt, accelerated, all of a sudden, animated, apace, at a blistering pace, at full tilt, at pace, at speed, before you know it, blistering, breakneck, brisk, bustling,

double-quick (time), energetic, ephemeral, express, fast-changing, fast-paced, fast-growing, fast-growth, fast-moving, flat out, fleet, fleet of foot, fleeting, full speed ahead, full throttle, furious, hasty, headlong, hell for leather, high-speed, hurried, immediate, in a flash, in a jiffy, in an instant, in no time, in the blink of an eye, instant(ly), instantaneous, keen, lightning-quick, like a bat out of hell, like a flash, like a rocket, like a shot, like (greased) lightning, lively, meteoric, momentary, nimble, nippy, no slouch, overnight, post-haste, promptly, quick, quick as a flash, quick-and-dirty, rapid, short-lived, short-term, snappy, speedy, sprightly, sudden, supersonic, swift, unhesitating, urgent, whirlwind, zippy

**Favour** v., see also Help, Support

1. advance, aid, assist, be good for, benefit, bolster, boost, capitalise, contribute to, do good, do (the world of) good, empower, enhance, facilitate, further, gain, improve, make possible, promote, provide an advantage, reinforce, serve, strengthen
2. advocate, appreciate, approve of, back, be in favour of, believe in, champion, encourage, incline towards, lean towards, like, opt for, prefer, value

**Favourable** adj., see also Effective, Good

advantageous, agreeable, appropriate, auspicious, beneficial, benign, constructive, convenient, encouraging, fortunate, helpful, ideal, invaluable, kind, lucky, manna from heaven, music to one's ears, of benefit, of help, opportune, optimum, perfect, pleasing, positive, productive, promising, reassuring, sound, suitable, supportive, timely, useful, valuable, welcome

**Fear** n., see also Problem, Risk

agitation, alarm, angst, anxiety, apprehension, cold feet, concern, consideration, consternation, dismay, disquiet, distress, doubt, dread, hand-wringing, horror, issue, jitters, misgivings, nerves, nervousness, panic, paranoia, qualm, questions, reservations, scare, spectre, suspicion, trepidation, uncertainty, unease, wariness, worry, worst nightmare

**Fear** v., see also Expect, Worry

anticipate, be afraid, be alarmed, be anxious, be apprehensive, be concerned, be fearful, be frightened, be gripped by fear, be nervous, be scared, be terrified, be uncertain, be wary, be worried, doubt, dread, feel uneasy, foresee, fret, have concerns, have qualms, shrink from, shudder at, suspect, take fright, tremble at

**Feature** n., see also Advantage, Characteristic

accent, aspect, attribute, bells and whistles, benefit, component, detail, distinction, distinguishing feature, DNA, element, facet, facility, factor, forte, function, hallmark, ingredient, innovation, merit, nice touch, party piece, pièce de résistance, peculiarity, point, property, quality, selling point, signature, slant, special feature, speciality, strength, strong point, strong suit, take, trait, trump card, twist, uniqueness, USP, virtue, wow factor, X factor

**Feature** v., see also Contain, Include
accentuate, add, advertise, be dominated by, be equipped with, be home to, be infused with, be peppered with, boast, brim with, call attention to, combine, come with, deliver, emphasise, encompass, enjoy, entail, give, grace, have, highlight, involve, number, offer, ooze, present, provide, scream, showcase, sport, spotlight, stress, underline, underscore

**Feeling** n., see also Effect, Idea
awareness, belief, concern, conviction, emotion, gut feeling, hunch, impression, inkling, instinct, intuition, judgement, opinion, outlook, perception, point of view, reaction, response, sensation, sense, sentiment, suspicion, take, takeaway, taste, thought(s), vibe, view

**Few** det., see also Absence, Small
almost no, dearth of, deficiency of, distinct lack of, few and far between, handful, hardly any, in short supply, insufficient, lack, limited, little, meagre, measly, mere, modest, negligible, not many, not much (in the way of), paltry, paucity, piffling, precious little, rare, scant, scarce, scarcely any, scarcity, short, short of, short on, slender, slight, slim, slim pickings, small number of, smattering of, sparing, sparse, sprinkling of, thin, thin on the ground, trifling

**Final** adj., see also Complete, Finally
clinching, closing, completed, concluding, conclusive, crowning, decisive, definite, definitive, dying, eleventh hour, end, eventual, finished, irrevocable, last, last but not least, last-ditch, last-gasp, last-minute, latest, latter, settled, terminal, valedictory, very last

**Finally** adv., see also Complete, Ultimately
at last, at long last, at the end of the day, conclusively, decisively, definitively, eventually, for all time, forever, for good, in conclusion, in the end, in the final analysis, in the fullness of time, in the long run, irrevocably, last but not least, lastly, once and for all, permanently, sooner or later, when all is said and done

**Finance** v., see also Invest, Pay
back, bail out, bankroll, champion, contribute to, fund, inject capital/money, invest in, lend money, pay for, pick up the tab, pour money into, provide

financing, provide financial support, provide funds, provide money, put up money, sponsor, stump up the cash, subsidise, support, support financially, throw money at, underwrite

**Financing** n., see also Investment, Money
backing, bankrolling, capital injection, contribution, credit, finance, financial backing, financial support, funding, funds, lending, loan, money, support, underwriting

**Find** v., see also Believe, Identify
arrive at, attain, become aware of, bring to light, chance upon, come across, come by, come up with, come upon, detect, dig out, dig up, discover, encounter, experience, expose, happen on/upon, hit the nail on the head, hit upon, lay bare, learn, light upon, locate, look no further than, meet, note, notice, observe, perceive, pinpoint, put one's finger on, reach, recognise, reveal, rumble, source, spot, stumble upon, trace, track down, uncover, unearth

**Finish** v., see also Achieve, Complete
accomplish, be done with, be over, bow out, bring to a close, bring to a conclusion, bring to fruition, call time on, cap, carry through, cease, close, come to a head, conclude, culminate, cut short, defeat, discontinue, dispose of, draw a line under, end, exhaust, expend, finalise, finish off, fulfil, get done, get over the line, lay to rest, move on, perfect, polish off, put an end to, put the finishing touches to, put to bed, quit, reach the end, round off, settle, sew up, sign off, stop, terminate, top off, use up, wave goodbye to, wind up, wrap up

**Fire** v., see also Dismiss, Remove
axe, can, call for someone's head, cast out, dispense with, drop, eject, eliminate, exclude, expel, force out, get rid of, give marching orders, give notice, give the boot, give the elbow, give the heave-ho, give the push, kick out, lay off, let go, make redundant, oust, part company with, part ways, reduce headcount/personnel/workforce, release, replace, sack, send packing, show the door, strip of, terminate employment

**First** adj., see also Best, New
1. early, basic, beginner's, debut, earliest, early, early adopter, first mover, first of its kind, first out of the blocks, fundamental, groundbreaking, inaugural, initial, introductory, maiden, oldest, opening, original, pioneering, rookie, seminal, trailblazing, uncharted, unprecedented, very first, world's first
2. best-selling, cardinal, champion, chief, dominant, finest, first-class, first-rate, foremost, front-runner, greatest, head, highest, in pole position, key, leader,

leading, main, most successful, number one, outstanding, overriding, paramount, predominant, premier, primary, principal, supreme, top, winning

**Fix** v., see also Address, Resolve
1. adjust, amend, correct, counter, debug, get to grips with, maintain, make good, mend, nip in the bud, overcome, overhaul, patch up, put back together, put in order, put right, rebuild, recalibrate, recover, rectify, refurbish, remedy, renovate, repair, restore, revamp, revise, revisit, revive, service, solve, sort, sort out, stabilise, stop the rot, tackle, tinker with, troubleshoot, turn around, tweak, upgrade, work around, work out
2. agree on, appoint, arrange, cement, conclude, confirm, decide, define, determine, embed, establish, organise, resolve, secure, set, settle, specify

**Flexibility** n., see also Choice, Scope
adaptability, adjustability, agility, alternatives, amenability, buffer, cooperation, flexible approach, free rein, freedom, give (and take), headroom, helpfulness, leeway, luxury, openness, options, preparedness, responsiveness, room for manoeuvre, support, understanding, versatility, wiggle room, willingness

**Flexible** adj., see also Agile, Resilient
accommodating, adaptable, adjustable, all-round, amendable, compliant, cooperative, deft, easy-going, fluid, give-and-take, helpful, offering a choice, offering the freedom to, open, open-minded, receptive, responsive, supportive, understanding, versatile, willing

**Focus** n., see also Centre, Emphasis
accent, all eyes on, central point, centre of attention, centrepiece, centre stage, *****-centric, clarity, concentration, core, crux, essence, focal area, focal point, front and centre, front of mind, haven, heart, hub, kernel, laser focus, lightning rod, limelight, mecca, nerve centre, nub, obsession, onus, priority, sharp focus, single-mindedness, spotlight, stress, target, thrust, weight

**Focus On** v., see also Emphasise
accentuate, aim, be fixated/obsessed with, be focused on, bring attention to, bring into focus, centre on, channel, concentrate, converge, direct attention at/on, direct efforts at/towards, double down on, dwell on, fix (one's attention) on, fixate, focus attention, highlight, home in on, major on, make a priority, obsess over, pinpoint, prioritise, put a spotlight on, put centre stage, put front and centre, refocus, set one's sights on, sharpen, shine a light on, showcase,

single out, spotlight, stress, tap into, turn attention to, underline, underscore, work on, zero in on, zoom in

**Follow** v., see also Comply, Monitor
1. come after, come next, copy, ensue, follow in the footsteps, follow on from, follow suit, pursue, replace, result, succeed, supersede, take the place of
2. accompany, come with, dog, escort, go after, haunt, hound, keep pace with, keep up with, overshadow, persecute, plague, pursue, stalk, track, trail
3. adhere to, adopt, agree to, conform, fall in line with, follow rules, follow suit, harmonise, heed, keep to, obey, observe, pander to, respect, take after, toe the line

**Force** v., see also Demand, Persuade
bring pressure to bear upon, bulldoze, bully, cajole, coerce, command, compel, drive, enforce, exact, exert pressure on, foist, force someone's hand, hold someone's feet to the fire, hold to ransom, impose, impress upon, insist, lean on, make, oblige, order, pressure, put pressure on, push, railroad, require, strong-arm, turn the screw, urge, twist someone's arm

**Forecast** n., see also Estimate, Expectation
analysis, anticipation, assumption, best guess, bet, big call, budget, calculation, call, consensus, crystal ball, estimation, feeling, foresight, forewarning, guess, guesstimate, gut feeling, hope, hunch, outlook, planning, prediction, prognosis, projection, smart money, speculation, suspicion, tip

**Forecast** v., see also Assess, Estimate
anticipate, augur, be confident, be hopeful, believe, bet, bode, call it, come as no surprise, conjecture, count on, expect, foresee, foreshadow, foretell, forewarn, gauge, guess, have a feeling, have a hunch, hazard a guess, herald, hint, hope for, infer, intimate, look ahead to, look forward to, plan on, predict, pre-empt, prepare for, presage, project, prophesy, reason, second-guess, see, see coming, speculate, take a guess, think likely, tip, watch for

**Forthcoming** adj., see also Potential
anticipated, approaching, around the corner, awaited, close at hand, ensuing, expected, fast-approaching, future, imminent, impending, in prospect, in store, in the making, in the pipeline, in the offing, in the works, in waiting, inevitable, intended, later, long-awaited, looming, next, on the horizon, pending, promising, prospective, rising, subsequent, to come, up-and-coming, upcoming

**Fortunate** adj., see also Favourable, Successful
advantageous, as luck would have it, auspicious, beneficial, blessed, charmed, coincidental, coming up roses, encouraging, everything clicking, falling into place, falling on one's feet, fluky, fortuitous, golden, helpful, jammy, lucky, on a roll, on a winning streak, opportune, prosperous, prospering, right place right time, serendipitous, timely, unplanned

**Frequent** adj., see also Common, Regular
all the time, at the drop of a hat, commonplace, constant, continual, customary, endemic, everyday, expected, familiar, habitual, incessant, mainstay, normal, numerous, often, periodic, persistent, pervasive, prevalent, prolific, recurrent, recurring, repeated, standard, ubiquitous, usual, widespread

**Frustrating** adj., see also Disappointing, Worrying
aggravating, annoying, at one's wits' end, confusing, disconcerting, discouraging, disheartening, disquieting, dissatisfying, driving mad, exasperating, infuriating, irksome, irritating, maddening, nagging, niggling, nuisance, source of frustration, testing, troublesome, trying, worrisome

**Fulfil** v., see also Achieve, Succeed
abide by, accomplish, address, adhere to, answer, attain, bring about, bring to completion, bring to fruition, carry off, complete, comply with, conclude, conform to, correspond to, deliver, discharge, do, effect, execute, finish, get something done, hit a target, honour (a commitment), implement, live up to, manage, match, meet (requirements), obey, observe, perfect, perform, realise, respect, respond to, satisfy

**Function** v., see also Operate, Work
act, adopt a role, be deployed, be employed, be in operation, be used as, behave, carry out, conduct, do, fulfil a function, handle, have the role of, make for, perform, play a part, provide, run, serve, take care of, work well

**Fund** v., see also Invest, Pay
back, bail out, bankroll, champion, contribute to, finance, fork out, inject capital/money, invest in, lend money, pay for, pick up the tab, pour money into, provide financial backing/support, provide funding/funds, provide money, sponsor, stump up the money, subsidise, support, support financially, throw money at, underwrite

**Funding** n., see also Investment, Money
backing, bankrolling, capital injection, contribution, credit, finance, financial backing, financial support, financing, funds, lending, loan, money, support, underwriting

**Future** adj., see also Potential
anticipated, approaching, around the corner, aspiring, awaited, budding, ensuing, eventual, expected, fast-approaching, for future generations, for posterity, forthcoming, future-proof, future-ready, having the makings of, imminent, impending, in due course, in prospect, in store, in the making, in the pipeline, in the offing, in the works, in waiting, inevitable, intended, later, looming, next, next-generation, on the horizon, pending, promising, prospective, rising, subsequent, to come, up-and-coming, upcoming

# G

**Gain** n., see also Profit, Success
achievement, acquisition, addition, advance, advantage, appreciation, benefit, boost, earnings, growth, improvement, income, increase, proceeds, progress, receipts, return, revenue, rise, upsurge, upturn, value, yield

**Gain** v., see also Achieve, Acquire
access, advance, amass, appreciate, attain, bag, benefit, bring about, bring in, build up, capture, collect, earn, expand, extend, fetch, fulfil, garner, generate, get, glean, gross, improve, increase, intensify, make, make gains, net, obtain, pick up, procure, profit, prosper, pull off, rack up, raise, reach, realise, reap benefits/dividends/rewards, rise, secure, win, yield

**Gather** v., see also Meet
access, accumulate, acquire, aggregate, amass, array, assemble, bring together, build up, cluster, collect, come together, compile, concentrate, congregate, convene, converge, corral, crowd, curate, flock, get together, group, harvest, hoard, hoover up, mass, muster, obtain, pile up, pour in, rally, reap, record, rendezvous, round up, save, secure, stack up, stockpile, store, swarm, throng, unite

**General(ly)** adj./adv., see also Broad, Varied
accepted, across-the-board, all things considered, all-embracing, all-purpose, all-round, approximately, as a whole, blanket, broad-based, broad-brush, by and large, catch-all, collective, common, commonplace, complete, comprehensive, everyday, extensive, far-reaching, generic, habitual, in the grand scheme of things, in the main, in the round, largely, miscellaneous, on the whole, ordinary, overall, overarching, prevailing, public, regular, run-of-the-mill, sweeping, total, umbrella, universal, unspecific, vague, wholesale, wide-ranging, widespread

**Generate** v., see also Create, Produce
achieve, attract, breed, bring about, bring in, cause, develop, drum up, engender, fetch (a price), form, fuel, gain, garner, give birth to, give rise to, induce, initiate, lead to, make, muster, net, obtain, occasion, power, provoke, raise, reap benefits/dividends/rewards, result in, spark, spawn, whip up, yield

**Genuine** adj., see also Real
accurate, actual, attested, authentic, authoritative, bona fide, confirmed, convincing, certified, credible, earnest, faithful, frank, heartfelt, honest, honest-to-goodness, kosher, legitimate, natural, official, original, proper, pure, real deal, real McCoy, real-life, reliable, signed-up, sincere, true, true colours, true-to-life, trusted, trustworthy, truthful, undisputed, unmistakeable, unquestionable, valid, verified, veritable

**Global** adj., see also Comprehensive, Everywhere
abroad, across/around the globe/planet/world, all corners of the world, all-encompassing, all-round, cosmopolitan, diverse, far afield, far and wide, foreign, general, globalised, globetrotting, intercontinental, international, multinational, overall, overseas, spanning the globe, the world over, universal, world, worldwide

**Goal** n., see also Aim, Objective
ambition, aspiration, desire, destination, determination, dream, end, end goal, expectation, express aim, focus, holy grail, hope, horizons, idea, intent, intention, mission, plan, point, purpose, stated aim, target, ultimate objective, vision

**Good** adj., see also Effective, Excellent
able, acceptable, accomplished, adept, adequate, admirable, advantageous, agreeable, ample, appropriate, approved, attractive, award-winning, beneficial, boding well, capable, celebrated, commendable, competent, constructive, convenient, correct, decent, dependable, does not disappoint, efficient, enjoyable, exceptional, exemplary, favourable, feel-good, fine, first-class, first-rate, fit for purpose, fitting, gem, good news, go-to, great, healthy, ideal, impressive, in a good place, in good shape, laudable, lovely, nice, no bad thing, of benefit, pleasant, positive, productive, proficient, proper, reliable, respectable, rewarding, right, robust, satisfactory, solid, sound, sterling, strong, successful, sufficient, suitable, superior, terrific, top, useful, valid, valuable, viable, welcome, well worth, worth its salt, worthwhile, worthy

**Govern** v., see also Control, Manage
administer, affect, be at the head of, be at the helm, be in charge, be in power, be responsible, call the shots, captain, command, conduct, decide, determine, dictate, direct, exercise authority, exercise control, guide, have an impact on, head, head up, hold office, hold power, hold sway over, influence, lead, master, orchestrate, order, oversee, pilot, preside over, pull the strings, regulate, reign

over, rule, run, shepherd, spearhead, steer, steward, stipulate, supervise, take care of, take charge of, watch over, wield power

**Gradual** adj., see also Moderate, Slow
bit by bit, by degrees, by increments, by stealth, cautious, continual, continuous, creeping, even, gentle, graded, imperceptible, incremental, insidious, on a sliding scale, phased, piecemeal, progressive, regular, sequential, slowly but surely, staggered, steady, step by step, successive

**Group** n., see also Category, Team
alliance, association, band, batch, bevy, body, bracket, bunch, camp, circle, class, clique, clump, cluster, cohort, collective, combination, community, company, contingent, crop, crowd, delegation, demographic, ensemble, faction, family, fold, force, fraternity, gang, lobby, organisation, pack, set, society, squad, stable, taskforce, tier, troop, unit

**Grow** v., see also Expand, Increase
abound, accelerate, accumulate, add to, advance, appreciate, ascend, balloon, become, be on the increase, be on the rise, be on the up, become larger, boom, branch out, breed, build, build up, burgeon, climb, creep up, cultivate, develop, edge higher, emerge, enlarge, escalate, evolve, explode, extend, flourish, gain, gain ground, gather pace, get bigger, go through the roof, go up, grow in size, heighten, hot up, improve, intensify, jump, leap, mature, mount, move up, multiply, mushroom, nurture, outstrip, pick up, progress, proliferate, prosper, rise, rocket, shoot up, show growth, skyrocket, snowball, soar, spike, spread, sprout, stack up, strengthen, surge, swell, take off, thrive, widen, zoom

**Growth** n., see also Boost, Expansion
acceleration, accretion, accumulation, addition, advance, augmentation, blossoming, boom, bounce, branching out, broadening, build-up, burgeoning, climb, cultivation, development, elevation, enlargement, escalation, evolution, explosion, extension, gain, groundswell, growing, growth spurt, hike, improvement, increase, increment, inflation, intensification, jump, leap, meteoric rise, multiplication, mushrooming, pick-up, progress, proliferation, rally, ramp-up, rebound, rise, scaling-up, snowball effect, spike, spread, spurt, success, surge, swell, upsurge, upswing, uptake, uptick, upturn, widening

**Guarantee** n., see also Commitment, Confirmation
affirmation, agreement, assurance, certainty, certificate, certification, clause, collateral, confidence, contract, deposit, insurance, obligation, peace of mind,

pledge, promise, security, testament, undertaking, verification, vow, warranty, word, word of honour

**Guarantee** v., see also Certify, Promise
affirm, assert, assure, attest, commit, confirm, endorse, ensure, give a guarantee, give one's word, insist, maintain, make a commitment, make certain, make a pledge, make sure, pledge, provide a guarantee, ratify, reassure, secure, swear, testify, undertake, underwrite, verify, vouch, vow

**Guide** v., see also Advise, Lead
accompany, be at the helm, be by someone's side, be there for someone, brief, conduct, control, counsel, direct, educate, encourage, escort, explain, facilitate, give advice, govern, head up, help, indicate, influence, instruct, lead the way, manage, marshal, mastermind, mentor, navigate, orchestrate, organise, oversee, pave the way, pilot, point the way, provide guidance, shepherd, show the way, spearhead, steer, steward, supervise, support, take charge, take the helm, train, tutor, watch over

# H

**Hamper** v., see also Obstruct, Prevent
be a hindrance, block, check, curb, cut short, delay, depress, dog, doom, encumber, fetter, foil, frustrate, get in the way, hamstring, hinder, hobble, hold back, hold up, impede, inconvenience, inhibit, interfere, interrupt, restrain, restrict, scupper, shackle, slow down, stand in the way, stifle, stop, stymie, subdue, throw a spanner in the works, thwart, tie hands, trouble, weigh on

**Handle** v., see also Manage, Treat
act towards, address, administer, approach, behave towards, care for, cater for, contend with, control, cope with, deal in, deal with, engage with, get on top of, get to grips with, look after, navigate, operate, process, react, regard, resolve, respond to, undertake, use, utilise, work with

**Happen** v., see also Appear
arise, arrive, be afoot, be present, be met with, befall, come about, come into being, come to pass, crop up, develop, emerge, ensure, feature, follow, go down, go on, manifest, materialise, occur, pan out, pass, play out, proceed, result, see happening, strike, take effect, take place, transpire, turn out, unfold

**Happy** adj., see also Positive
all smiles, blessed, cheerful, can't complain, comfortable, content, contented, delighted, ecstatic, elated, euphoric, glad, gleeful, have a spring in one's step, heartened, in seventh heaven, in high spirits, jubilant, more than happy, on cloud nine, on top of the world, over the moon, overjoyed, pleased, proud, satisfied, thankful, thrilled, tickled pink, upbeat, walking on air

**Hard** adj., see also Challenging, Tough
ambitious, arduous, asking a lot, awkward, beset by problems, big ask, bruising, can of worms, complex, complicated, confusing, daunting, delicate, demanding, difficult, easier said than done, elusive, exacting, formidable, fraught with difficulty, gruelling, hard-fought, hard-won, hard work, have one's work cut out, Herculean task, intractable, invidious, laborious, minefield, no mean feat, no picnic, not easy, onerous, out of one's comfort zone, overwhelming, problematic, slog, strenuous, struggle, tall order, taxing, testing,

thankless, thorny, time-consuming, tiresome, torrid, tough, tricky, troublesome, trying, uncomfortable, unenviable, unmanageable, uphill (battle/task)

**Have** v., see also Contain, Include
be faced with, be home to, be the owner of, bear, boast, carry, comprise, consist of, embody, embrace, encompass, enjoy, experience, feature, have at one's disposal, hold, incorporate, involve, keep, list, number, occupy, offer, own, possess, provide, retain, suffer, supply, sustain, undergo, use

**Help** n., see also Advice, Support
aid, assistance, backing, benefit, blessing, boon, boost, break, care, contribution, cooperation, empowerment, encouragement, favour, godsend, guidance, hand, helping hand, input, lifeline, lifesaver, lift, means, moral support, reinforcement, relief, service

**Help** v., see also Advise, Enable
accommodate, advocate, aid, alleviate, allow, assist, back, be a help, be a lifeline/lifesaver, be by someone's side, be there for someone, bend over backwards (to help), benefit, bolster, boost, champion, come to someone's aid, contribute, cooperate, do (the world of) good, do one's bit, do wonders for, ease, empower, encourage, endorse, facilitate, foster, further, get behind, give a leg up, go a long way towards, have someone covered, have someone's back, help out, intervene, lend a (helping) hand, improve, make life easy/easier, make possible, nurture, oil/grease the wheels, open the door to, partner, pitch in, promote, provide help, provide the means, provide the opportunity, pull one's weight, rally behind/round, reinforce, rescue, save, simplify, smooth the path/way, solve, stand by someone, streamline, support, sustain, take under one's wing, throw a lifeline, underpin

**Hide** v., see also Mislead
anonymise, bury, camouflage, cloak, conceal, cover, cover up, disguise, gloss over, hide a multitude of sins, hide away, hush up, keep hidden, keep in the dark, keep quiet, keep secret, keep to oneself, keep under lock and key, keep under one's hat, keep under wraps, mask, masquerade, obfuscate, obscure, pull the wool over someone's eyes, put up a smokescreen, screen, shelter, squirrel away, suppress, sweep under the carpet, tuck away, veil

**Highlight** v., see also Emphasise, Focus On
accent, accentuate, bring attention to, bring to the fore, call attention to, demonstrate, draw attention to, expose, feature, flag up, focus attention on, give centre stage to, give priority to, give prominence to, illustrate, intensify, lay

bare, make a lot of, pinpoint, place emphasis on, point out, put front and centre, put centre stage, reinforce, reiterate, set off, shine a light on, showcase, single out, spotlight, stress, underline, underscore, zero in on, zone in on, zoom in on

**High-quality** adj., see also Effective, Expensive
acclaimed, admirable, award-winning, best, blue-chip, choice, class act, classy, coveted, cream of the crop, deluxe, excellent, exceptional, exclusive, expertly built/created/engineered/made, exquisite, fine, finest, first-rate, five-star, flagship, foremost, good, handpicked, high-class, high-end, high standard, illustrious, luxury, no expense spared, of exceptional quality, of high quality, of the highest quality, oozing class, outstanding, plush, posh, premium, prestigious, prime, quality, refined, renowned, select, standout, state-of-the-art, stellar, superior, top, top-flight, top-notch, top-of-the-range, top-quality, ultimate, upmarket, upscale, very best, well-built, well-made, world-class

**High-tech** adj., see also Advanced, Automated
ahead of its time, ahead of the curve, AI, all-singing all-dancing, breakthrough, complex, connected, cutting-edge, digital, future-proof, future-ready, game-changing, groundbreaking, innovative, intelligent, latest thing, leading-edge, modern, next-generation, online, pioneering, remote, revolutionary, smart, sophisticated, specialised, specialist, state-of-the-art, technical, technological, latest, ultramodern, up-to-date, very latest, (technical) wizardry

**Hinder** v., see also Obstruct, Prevent
be a hindrance, block, check, curb, cut short, delay, depress, dog, encumber, fetter, foil, frustrate, get in the way, hamper, hamstring, hobble, hold back, hold up, impede, inconvenience, inhibit, interfere, interrupt, restrain, restrict, scupper, shackle, slow down, stand in the way, stifle, stop, stymie, subdue, throw a spanner in the works, thwart, tie hands, trouble, weigh on

**History** n., see also Past
account, ancient history, ancient times, annals, antiquity, background, back in the day, back story, biography, bygone days/times/years, chronicle(s), days of old, days of yore, dim and distant past, experience(s), good old days, heritage, hindsight, historical events, history books, long ago, looking back, narrative, old days, olden days, past events, past times, record books, record(s), story, tale, times past, yesterday, yesteryear

**Honest** adj., see also Ethical, Fair
above board, authentic, bona fide, brutally honest, candid, come clean, conscientious, decent, fair and square, forthright, frank, from the heart,

genuine, hand on heart, hard-hitting, heartfelt, honest-to-goodness, honourable, impartial, in one's heart of hearts, like it is, naked truth, no-holds-barred, objective, open, outspoken, principled, reliable, reputable, respectable, revealing, scrupulous, sincere, straight, straight-talking, straight-shooting, straightforward, transparent, trustworthy, truthful, true, true to one's word, unvarnished, upfront, warts-and-all

**Hope** v., see also Expect, Want
aim for, anticipate, aspire, assume, be hopeful, be keen to, be prepared for, believe, cling to, count on, contemplate, cross fingers, desire, dream, envisage, foresee, have faith, have high hopes, have hope, hope and pray, hope for the best, keep one's fingers crossed, long for, look ahead to, look for, look forward to, look to the future, pin hopes on, plan, pray, presume, rely, sincerely hope, speculate, target, trust, wish

**However** adv., see also Despite
admittedly, albeit, all the same, although, anyhow, anyway, be that as it may, but, conversely, even so, even though, having said that, in contrast, in spite of, irrespective, leaving aside, meanwhile, mind you, nevertheless, nonetheless, notwithstanding, on the flip side, on the other hand, putting this to one side, regardless, still, this aside, though, while, yet

**Hurry** v., see also Pressure, Quick
accelerate, act fast, be in a hurry, be in a rush, be pushed for time, be quick, bustle, catch up, crack on, dart, dash, expedite, fast-track, fly, gallop, get a move on, get cracking, get one's skates on, hasten, hotfoot it, hurry up, hurtle, lose no time, make a beeline, make haste, make short work of, move quickly, nip, pick up the pace, play catch-up, precipitate, press on, race, race against the clock/time, rattle through, run, rush, scramble, scurry, speed, speed up, spring, step on it, surge, take swift/urgent action, waste no time, whisk, whizz, zip

# I

**Idea** n., see also Concept, Innovation
aim, approach, belief, big idea, blueprint, brainchild, brainwave, breakthrough, bright idea, business concept, conclusion, conviction, design, epiphany, eureka moment, flash of inspiration, germ of an idea, goal, hunch, impression, initiative, intention, interpretation, invention, judgement, lightbulb moment, meaning, mentality, method, notion, object, objective, opinion, original idea, perception, perspective, plan, point, position, principle, proposal, purpose, reason, recommendation, scheme, sense, solution, strategy, suggestion, tactic, teaching, theory, thinking, thought, understanding, view, viewpoint, vision, way of thinking

**Identify** v., see also Find, Understand
analyse, ascertain, become aware, bring to light, catalogue, classify, confirm, decipher, deduce, describe, detect, determine, discover, distinguish, establish, flag, flag up, get to the heart of, glean, heed, hit the nail on the head, hit upon, label, locate, notice, pick out, pinpoint, put one's finger on, recognise, select, shine a light on, single out, spot, spy, target, trace, uncover, unearth

**Ignore** v., see also Refuse, Reject
avoid, be impervious to, be (wilfully) ignorant, be in denial, be oblivious to, bin, brush aside/off, bury one's head in the sand, discount, disdain, disobey, disregard, evade, fail, fall on deaf ears, flout, forget, give the cold shoulder, gloss over, leave aside, look the other way, neglect, not consider, omit, overlook, pass over, pay no attention to, pooh-pooh, scorn, shrug off, shun, shut one's eyes to, sideline, skip, sleepwalk, slight, snub, switch off, take no notice, take with a pinch of salt, turn a blind eye to, turn a deaf ear to, turn one's back on, write off

**Illogical** adj., see also Ridiculous, Unlikely
absurd, bonkers, crazy, false, groundless, half-baked, implausible, impossible, inconsistent, incorrect, invalid, irrational, mad, making no sense, meaningless, nonsense, nonsensical, not holding water, not sensible, not stacking up, not thought through, perverse, preposterous, senseless, unreasonable, unsound, untenable, without basis/foundation, wrongheaded

**Illustrate** v., see also Demonstrate, Reflect
bear out, bring home, clarify, depict, embody, emphasise, encapsulate, epitomise, exemplify, exhibit, explain, expose, get across, highlight, interpret, lay bare, make clear, make plain, mirror, outline, personify, present, provide an example, represent, reveal, set out, show, spotlight, sum up, summarise, symbolise, typify, underline, underscore

**Image** n., see also Brand, Reputation
1. appearance, brand values, cachet, concept, ethos, face, feel, idea, imagery, impression, look, marketing, message, opinion, optics, perception, portrayal, public relations, representation, standing, values, vibe, view, vision
2. copy, figure, illustration, imagery, likeness, photo, photograph, photography, picture, representation

**Immediate/Immediately** adj./adv., see also Quick, Sudden
acute, at a stroke, at once, at present, close, critical, direct(ly), forthwith, here and now, instant, instantaneous, knee-jerk, nearest, next, now, on demand, on hand, on the spot, present, pressing, prompt(ly), pronto, rapid(ly), right away, right now, speedy, split-second, straight away, swift(ly), there and then, unhesitating, unthinking, urgent, with immediate effect, without delay

**Impact** n., see also Consequence, Influence
adverse effect, after-effect, aftermath, backlash, bearing, beneficial impact, benefit, blow, body blow, brunt, burden, by-product, chain reaction, clash, contact, cost, effect, domino effect, end result, fallout, force, fruits (of one's labour), grip, hangover, hit, ill effect, impingement, implication, impression, jolt, knock-on effect, lasting effect/impact, legacy, negative effect, outcome, positive effect, ramification(s), reaction, repercussion, response, result, reverberations, scars, shock, shock wave, side effect, significance, thrust, toll, traction, upshot, wake

**Impact** v., see also Cause, Impact Negatively
act on, affect, affect deeply, alter, be at play/work, bear upon, bite, change, concern, drive, exert influence, fuel, gain traction, grip, have a bearing on, have an effect on, have an impact on, have an influence on, have implications for, impinge on, influence, involve, kick in, leave one's mark, make a change, make a difference, make an impact, make waves, modify, move the needle, permeate, prompt, provoke, regard, relate to, shake, shape, spark, spur, stimulate, take effect, touch, transform, trigger

**Impact Negatively** v., see also Damage, Hinder
adversely affect, affect negatively, afflict, assail, be costly for, blight, blindside, bring to one's knees, bruise, buffet, cripple, deal a (body/hammer) blow, dent, derail, detract from, devastate, diminish, disrupt, disturb, doom, embroil, engulf, hammer, hamper, have a negative effect/impact/influence on, have on the ropes, hit, hit hard, hobble, hound, hurt, impair, imperil, impoverish, incapacitate, inflict damage, inhibit, knock, knock for six, leave in tatters, mar, overwhelm, plague, poleaxe, put on the back foot, put under pressure, rock, rock to one's core, scupper, send into meltdown, send reeling, set back, shackle, shake, spell trouble for, strain, strike, take a toll on, throw a spanner in the works, trouble, undermine, upset, weaken, weigh on, wound, wreck

**Implement** v., see also Deliver, Perform
accomplish, achieve, action, apply, bring about, carry out, carry through, complete, conduct, deploy, discharge, do, effect, enable, enforce, establish, execute, exercise, fulfil, get on with, get something done, invoke, make possible, make things happen, move forward, produce, put into action, put in place, put into effect, put into practice, realise, roll out, start, step up, take action, take measures, take steps, transact, undertake

**Implementation** n., see also Achievement, Action
accomplishment, application, completion, conduct, delivery, deployment, enforcement, establishment, execution, fulfilment, intervention, measure, operation, performance, practice, production, realisation, roll-out, undertaking, use, utilisation

**Imply** v., see also Indicate, Suggest
allude to, be a sign, be a symbol, connote, convey, denote, entail, evidence, hint at, illustrate, implication being, infer, insinuate, intimate, involve, mean, mention, point to, presuppose, refer, reflect, reveal, signal, signify, strongly suggest, symbolise

**Importance** n., see also Emphasis, Focus
authority, bearing, bottom line, concern, connotation, consequence, crux, distinction, essence, force, gravity, heart of the matter, impact, implication, import, influence, key element, magnitude, matter, meaning, poignancy, power, prestige, principle, priority, prominence, ramifications, relevance, role, seriousness, significance, standing, status, strength, substance, usefulness, value, weight, worth

**Important** adj., see also Main, Principal
1. all-important, at the heart of, be all and end all, bedrock, big, big deal, cardinal, central, chief, coming to the fore, considerable, core, cornerstone, critical, crucial, crunch, decisive, defining, distinctive, dominant, essential, far-reaching, foremost, front-line, fundamental, game-changer, game-changing, going to the heart of, grave, heart of the matter, high-profile, high-stakes, historic, imperative, indispensable, influential, integral, it matters, key, landmark, lifeblood, linchpin, looming large, mainstay, major, material, meaningful, mission-critical, momentous, necessary, notable, noteworthy, of (great) importance, of note, of significance, paramount, pertinent, pivotal, poignant, pressing, primary, prime, priority, prominent, red-letter day, relevant, salient, seismic, seminal, serious, signal, significant, special, strategic, substantial, substantive, telling, to the fore, topping the agenda, urgent, valuable, valued, vital, watershed moment
2. acclaimed, authoritative, big deal, distinguished, eminent, high-level, high-profile, high-ranking, influential, leading, notable, noteworthy, powerful, prominent, remarkable, special, valued, VIP

**Impossible** adj., see also Difficult, Unlikely
absurd, beyond the bounds of possibility, cannot be done, contrary to reason, fanciful, futile, hopeless, illogical, implausible, impractical, in vain, inaccessible, inconceivable, insurmountable, irreparable, irretrievable, million to one chance, no way, nonstarter, not a cat in hell's chance, not a chance, not a hope, not a prayer, not doable, not happening, not possible, not remotely possible, no-win, out of the question, unacceptable, unachievable, unattainable, unfeasible, unimaginable, unobtainable, unthinkable, unworkable

**Impress** v., see also Attract, Surprise
astonish, awe, be a hit, be memorable, blow away, bowl over, dazzle, delight, electrify, enthuse, excite, get through to, influence, inspire, interest, knock someone off their feet, knock someone's socks off, knock out, leave its mark, leave speechless, light up, make a splash, make an impression, make headlines, move, overawe, overwhelm, prove a hit, provoke, rock, set alight, show off, silence one's critics, steal the headlines/show, stick in the mind, stimulate, stir, strike, stun, sway, thrill, touch, wow

**Impression** n., see also Idea, Opinion
air, aura, conclusion, conviction, deep impression, distinct impression, effect, emotion, feeling, first impression, gut feeling, hunch, image, impact, inkling, instinct, intuition, judgement, lasting impression, outlook, perception, point of

view, reaction, recollection, response, sensation, sense, sentiment snapshot, suspicion, take, takeaway, thought(s), vibe, view

**Impressive** adj., see also Attractive, Effective

absorbing, admirable, amazing, attention-grabbing, awe-inspiring, breathtaking, captivating, class act, commendable, delightful, dramatic, drawing headlines, emphatic, evocative, excellent, exceptional, exemplary, exciting, extraordinary, eye-catching, fascinating, fine, first-class, five-star, formidable, glorious, good, grand, great, gripping, having the wow factor, iconic, impactful, imposing, influential, inspiring, intense, interesting, jaw-dropping, lavish, leaving a lasting impression, luxurious, magical, majestic, making a deep impression, marvellous, masterclass, masterstroke, memorable, mind-blowing, monumental, moving, must-have/read/see, notable, outstanding, phenomenal, poignant, powerful, profound, remarkable, rousing, spectacular, splendid, standout, stirring, striking, strong, stunning, superb, superlative, thrilling, touching, tour de force, unforgettable, wonderful, world-class

**Improve** v., see also Strengthen, Update

add to, advance, augment, be on the up, become better, beef up, better, blossom, bolster, boost, boost performance, brighten, build on, change (for the better), come on leaps and bounds, complement, correct, develop, ease, elevate, enhance, enrich, facelift, fare better, gain ground, gain strength, get better, go from strength to strength, grow, heighten, help, hone, improve on, increase, kick on, lift, look up, make better, make strides, move in the right direction, move on, move up a gear, optimise, perfect, perk up, pick up, polish, progress, promote, raise, raise one's game, raise the bar, rally, reboot, recover, refine, reform, refresh, reinvent, reinvigorate, relaunch, restore, revamp, review, revise, revisit, revitalise, revive, sharpen, shore up, spruce up, step it up, step up, streamline, take a turn for the better, take to the next level, transform, turn around, turn the corner, turn the tide, tweak, up one's game, upgrade

**Improvement** n., see also Development, Recovery

advance, advancement, amendment, augmentation, boost, change for the better, comeback, complement, correction, easing, elevation, enhancement, enrichment, facelift, gain, green shoots, growth, improved performance, increase, leap forward, learning curve, marked improvement, modernisation, modification, move in the right direction, next level, optimisation, overhaul, positive development, progress, progression, rally, reboot, reform, regeneration, relaunch, renovation, return to form, revamp, revision, revitalisation, rise, shake-up, step-up, strengthening, turnaround, tweak, update, upgrade, upswing, vast improvement

**Inadequate** adj., see also Deficient, Inferior
below expectations, below par, defective, disappointing, faulty, feeble, found wanting, imperfect, inappropriate, incompetent, incomplete, ineffective, inefficient, inferior, insubstantial, insufficient, lacking, lacklustre, leaving a lot to be desired, let-down, meagre, mean, mediocre, miserly, not enough, not fit for purpose, not good enough, not up to scratch, pathetic, poor, sketchy, second-rate, shoddy, short on, subpar, substandard, too little (too late), unacceptable, underperforming, unsatisfactory, unspectacular, unsuccessful, unsuitable, unsuited, weak

**Inappropriate** adj., see also Inadequate, Unacceptable
1. bad, disproportionate, ill-judged, ill-suited, ill-timed, inapplicable, inauspicious, incompatible, incongruous, incorrect, inopportune, irrelevant, not appropriate, not fit for purpose, not ideal, not (quite) right, not suitable, not up to scratch, out of place, poor, shoddy, sloppy, undue, unfit, unsatisfactory, unsuitable, unsuited, untimely, wrong
2. ill-judged, ill-suited, ill-timed, improper, not on, offensive, out of line, out of order, out of place, regrettable, tactless, unbecoming, unbefitting, uncalled for, unfortunate, unpleasant, unprofessional, wrong

**Include** v., see also Combine, Contain
add, adjust for, allow for, amalgamate, be composed of, be full of, be made up of, be part and parcel of, be replete with, bear in mind, blend, boast, bring together, come with, comprise, consist of, constitute, count, cover, embed, embody, embrace, encapsulate, encompass, entail, factor in, feature, go hand in hand with, have, implicate, incorporate, inject, insert, integrate, involve, merge, number, number among, offer, pervade, price in, provide, reflect, span, straddle, take account of, take into account

**Income** n., see also Profit, Sales
cash flow, commission, compensation, earnings, earnings performance, income generated, livelihood, money, pay, proceeds, receipts, remuneration, return(s), revenue(s), revenue generated, revenue stream, salary, sales revenue, takings, turnover, wage

**Inconsistent** adj., see also Volatile, Weak
arbitrary, at odds, capricious, changeable, chequered, conflicting, contradictory, contrary, erratic, fitful, haphazard, hit and miss, in conflict, in fits and starts,

incoherent, incompatible, incongruent, incongruous, intermittent, irreconcilable, irregular, lumpy, not consistent, not the same, out of kilter, out of step, patchy, sporadic, stop and start, temperamental, uncertain, uneven, unpredictable, unreliable, unstable, up and down, variable

**Incorrect** adj., see also Negative, Wrong
erroneous, false, faulty, flawed, imprecise, improper, inaccurate, inappropriate, inexact, misinformed, misleading, mistaken, not accurate, not correct, not right, not true, unreliable, unsound, unsuitable, untrue, way off, wide of the mark

**Increase** n., see also Boost, Expansion
acceleration, accretion, accumulation, addition, advance, amplification, appreciation, augmentation, bolstering, boom, bounce, broadening, build-up, burgeoning, climb, development, elevation, enhancement, enlargement, escalation, evolution, explosion, extension, flowering, fuelling, gain, groundswell, growing, growth, growth spurt, heightening, hike, improvement, increment, inflation, intensification, jump, leap, magnification, meteoric rise, multiplication, mushrooming, pick-up, progress, proliferation, raising, rally, ramp-up, rebound, recovery, rise, rising tide, scaling-up, snowball effect, spike, spread, spurt, step-up, strengthening, surge, swell, turbocharging, upgrade, upping, upsurge, upswing, uptake, uptick, upturn, widening

**Increase** v., see also Grow, Raise
accelerate, accumulate, add fuel to the fire, add to, advance, amplify, appreciate, augment, balloon, be on the increase, be on the rise, be on the up, be up, become larger, become more, boom, boost, broaden, build, build up, bump up, climb, crank up, creep up, deepen, develop, dial up, do more, double-down on, drive (up), edge higher, elevate, enhance, enlarge, enrich, escalate, expand, explode, extend, extend gains, fan the flames, fuel, further, gain ground, gather pace, get bigger, go through the roof, grow more, heat up, heighten, hot up, improve, inflate, intensify, jump, leap, lengthen, make larger, magnify, make bigger, make more, mount, multiply, mushroom, notch up, outstrip, pick up, pile up, proliferate, prolong, promote, put up, ramp up, ratchet up, redouble, reinforce, rise, rocket, scale up, send through the roof, shoot up, skyrocket, snowball, soar, spike, spiral, spread, spur, step up, stoke, strengthen, supercharge, supersize, surge, swell, take off, take the number to, tick up, turbocharge, up, upgrade, widen, zoom

**Independent** adj., see also Fair, Separate
autonomous, contracted, external, free, freethinking, going it alone, impartial, individualistic, neutral, nonaligned, nonpartisan, non-proprietary, not

dependent, on one's own, open-minded, outside, outsourced, private, self-confident, self-contained, self-governing, self-reliant, self-sufficient, self-supporting, sovereign, stand-alone, third-party, unaffiliated, unaided, unbiased, unconnected, uncontrolled, unfettered, unprejudiced, unrelated

**Indicate** v., see also Demonstrate, Show

allude to, announce, be a harbinger of, be a sign, communicate, denote, designate, display, evidence, exhibit, express, flag up, give a foretaste, give an indication, herald, highlight, hint, illustrate, imply, infer, insinuate, intimate, mark, outline, pinpoint, point out, point to, presage, present, prove, record, report, reveal, showcase, signal, signify, specify, (strongly) suggest, symbolise, testify to

**Indication** n., see also Forecast, Warning

barometer, bellwether, bright spot, canary in the coal mine, caution, clue, cue, encouraging sign, evidence, flag, foreboding, foretaste, forewarning, gauge, glimmer, guide, harbinger, herald, hint, index, indicator, mark, marker, measure, milestone, omen, pointer, precursor, prediction, proof, reminder, sign, signal, signpost, suggestion, symbol, symptom, taster, temperature, tip of the iceberg, trace, wake-up call, writing on the wall

**Industry** n., see also Activity, Market

area, area of activity, arena, bracket, branch of industry, business, category, commerce, commercial enterprise, cottage industry, domain, enterprise, field, game, industrial production, landscape, line, line of business, line of work, practice, production, profession, sector, segment, space, sphere, trade, world of

**Inefficient** adj., see also Inferior, Weak

afterthought, awkward, bungling, careless, clunky, confusing, crude, cumbersome, decidedly average, disorganised, dysfunctional, falling short, far from perfect, found wanting, half-hearted, in need of improvement, incapable, incompetent, ineffective, ineffectual, inept, inexpert, lacklustre, lumbering, mediocre, not fit for purpose, not great, not ideal, not inspiring confidence, not perfect, not up to scratch, not (very) good, not working well, old-fashioned, poor, poorly designed/run etc., room/scope for improvement, second-rate, shambolic, shoddy, slipshod, sloppy, slow, substandard, time-consuming, underachieving, underperforming, uneconomical, unfit, unimpressive, uninspiring, unprepared, unrefined, unsatisfactory, unsuccessful, wanting, wasteful, with a low level of efficiency

**Inexpensive** adj., see also Few, Small
affordable, attractively priced, bargain, bargain-basement, budget, budget-friendly, cheap, cheap and nasty, cheap as chips, competitive, competitively priced, cost-effective, cut-price, cut-rate, dime a dozen, dirt-cheap, discounted, economical, economy, fair, good value, going for a song, keenly priced, knock-down, low-cost, low-priced, low-rent, marked down, moderate, moderately priced, next to nothing, not expensive, on sale, peanuts, pittance, reasonable, reduced, rock-bottom, shoestring, slashed, snip, song, steal, thrifty, uncostly, value for money, won't break the bank

**Inferior** adj., see also Deficient, Weak
below par, can't hold a candle to, can't keep up with, can't match, can't touch, cheap, crummy, decidedly average, disappointing, eclipsed, falling behind, falling short, flawed, found wanting, half-hearted, inadequate, ineffective, insufficient, lacking, lacklustre, lagging behind, leaving a lot to be desired, less, less effective, limited, low-grade, low-quality, mediocre, negative, no match for, not a patch on, not as good as, not fit for purpose, not good enough, not in the same class/league as, not up to scratch/standard, ordinary, outclassed, outperformed, outshone, overshadowed, paling in comparison with, poor, poor-quality, retrograde, second-rate, shoddy, smaller, subpar, substandard, trailing, unconvincing, unsatisfactory, upstaged, wanting, weaker, woeful, worse

**Influence** n., see also Authority, Effect
balance of power, bearing, charm offensive, clout, connections, control, diplomacy, dominance, esteem, force, friends in high places, grip, guidance, hold, impact, importance, impression, imprint, in thrall to, knock-on effect, leverage, magnetism, mark, orbit, power, predominance, pressure, prestige, prominence, reputation, say, say-so, significance, soft power, sphere of influence, supremacy, sway, weight

**Influence** v., see also Affect, Persuade
act on, bear upon, bring about, bring one's influence to bear, bring pressure to bear, carry weight, cast a (long) shadow, cause, coax, colour, compel, control, convince, counsel, determine, direct, dominate, elicit, empower, entice, evoke, exert an influence, feed into, guide, have a bearing on, have an effect on, have an impact on, have an influence on, hold sway, hold the balance of power, impact, impinge upon, impress, incite, induce, inform, leave one's mark on, make an impact, make one's mark on, make one's presence felt, permeate, pervade, plant/sow a seed, play a part, prejudice, pressure, prevail upon, prompt, provoke, pull strings, put pressure on, rub off on, seduce, set the tone,

shape, spark, spin, spur, stimulate, sway, urge, wage a charm offensive, win hearts and minds

**Inform** v., see also Communicate
acquaint, advise, alert, apprise, articulate, brief, bring up to speed, caution, convey, declare, disclose, divulge, enlighten, explain, express, familiarise, feed back, fill in, forewarn, get across, give notification, hint, imply, instruct, invite, issue a statement, keep in the loop, keep posted, let someone in on, let know, make known, mention, notify, outline, provide details, put across, relate, relay, remind, report, reveal, set out, state, suggest, tell, tip off, update, warn

**Information** n., see also Communication, News
advice, announcement, article, briefing, bulletin, data, details, disclosure, documentation, dossier, facts, facts and figures, feedback, hard data, hard facts, heads-up, info, ins and outs, inside story, insight, intelligence, knowledge, latest information/news, lowdown, material, message, notice, notification, presentation, report, revelation(s), statement, statistics, story

**Infrequent** adj., see also Few, Unusual
abnormal, almost never, atypical, exceptional, few and far between, hardly ever, irregular, isolated, limited, little, not common, not often, occasional, once in a blue moon, out of the ordinary, outlier, rare, scant, scarce, seldom, sparse, special, sporadic, strange, surprising, thin on the ground, uncommon, unexpected, unfamiliar, unlikely

**Inhibit** v., see also Hamper, Reduce
arrest, check, choke, constrain, control, cool, curb, dampen, depress, discourage, drag down, encumber, foil, frustrate, get in the way, hinder, hold back, hold down, impede, moderate, obstruct, prevent, prohibit, put the brakes on, restrict, sap, slow (down), stem, stifle, stop, stunt, stymie, subdue, suppress, thwart, weigh on, withhold

**Initiate** v., see also Introduce, Launch
activate, be a catalyst for, begin, blaze a trail, break new ground, bring about, broach, cause, commence, conceive, debut, embark on, enter upon, establish, fire the starting gun, found, get cracking, get going, get the ball rolling, get underway, give birth to, give rise to, herald, inaugurate, innovate, inspire, install, instigate, institute, jump-start, kick off, kick-start, kindle, lay the foundations, lay the groundwork, light the fuse, make a start, mount, open, originate, pioneer, precipitate, premier, proceed, provoke, roll out, set about, set in, set in motion, set to, set up, sow the seed(s), spark, spawn, start, start off,

start out, start up, stimulate, take the initiative, trigger, undertake, unleash, unveil, usher in

**Initiative** n., see also Action, Idea
1. approach, campaign, concept, crusade, drive, effort(s), endeavour(s), gambit, measure, move, plan, platform, programme, project, proposal, push, response, scheme, step, strategy, stunt, undertaking, venture, work
2. ambition, drive, dynamism, eagerness, energy, enterprise, enthusiasm, get-up-and-go, inspiration, inventiveness, leadership, resourcefulness, spirit, vigour, wherewithal

**Innovate** v., see also Launch, Pioneer
be at the forefront, be in the vanguard, be the first, begin, be creative, be inventive, blaze a trail, break new ground, break through, brim with ideas, bring about, bring in, change the face of, change the game, coin, conceive, create, develop, discover, embark on, establish, evolve, fizz with ideas, found, hatch, inaugurate, initiate, institute, introduce, invent, lay the foundations, lead the way, mark a breakthrough/revolution etc., modernise, originate, pave the way, plan, premier, produce, push the envelope, reinvent, rewrite the rule book, set up, show the way, spark, spawn, start, take a different/new approach, think outside the box, think up, unveil, usher in

**Innovation** n., see also Idea, Start
addition, brainchild, brainwave, breakthrough, bright idea, change, concept, creativity, cutting edge, departure, eureka moment, freshness, game-changer, inception, ingenuity, introduction, invention, latest thing, leading edge, lightbulb moment, modernisation, modification, new approach, new concept, new feature, new idea, new way, originality, paradigm shift, quantum leap, revolution, sea change, shift, thinking outside the box, transformation, vision

**Innovative** adj., see also New
breaking new ground, breakthrough, changing the face of, clever, contemporary, creative, cutting-edge, departure, different, fresh, game-changing, groundbreaking, ingenious, inventive, latest, latest word in, leading-edge, modern, new-fangled, next-generation, original, pioneering, radically different, refreshing, revolutionary, rewriting the rule book, state-of-the-art, taking a new approach, trailblazing, transformational, transformative, ultramodern, unconventional, unorthodox, unusual, up-to-date

**Inquire** v., see also Consult, Request
angle, ascertain, ask, canvas opinion, contact, enquire, evaluate, examine, explore, inspect, investigate, look into, make inquiries, probe, query, question, quiz, research, review, scrutinise, search, seek, study, test the waters

**Inquiry** n., see also Request
analysis, application, assessment, audit, enquiry, evaluation, examination, exploration, inspection, investigation, probe, query, question, report, research, review, scrutiny, study, survey

**Insignificant** adj., see also Irrelevant, Small
drop in the ocean, forgettable, futile, immaterial, inconsequential, inconsiderable, infinitesimal, little, meagre, meaningless, minimal, minor, minuscule, negligible, no skin off one's nose, nonessential, not important, not significant, of no account, of no consequence/importance/relevance, on the periphery, paltry, petty, pointless, secondary, senseless, small fry, small potatoes, trifling, trivial, unimportant, unimpressive, vanishingly small, worthless

**Insist** v., see also Demand, Maintain
assert, assert oneself, badger, be adamant, be assertive, be clear, be firm, be insistent, claim, contend, declare, dictate, dig one's heels in, double down on, emphasise, entreat, expect, hold, not take no for an answer, order, persist, put one's foot down, reiterate, repeat, require, stand by, stand firm, stand one's ground, stick to one's guns, stipulate, stress, swear, take a stand, underscore, urge, vow

**Inspiration** n., see also Concept, Influence
approach, awakening, brainstorm, catalyst, creativity, encouragement, enthusiasm, flash of inspiration, forerunner, genius, good idea, idea, imagination, impulse, incentive, ingenuity, innovation, insight, interest, inventiveness, launch pad, motivation, notion, originality, precursor, role model, source of inspiration, spark, springboard, spur, stimulation, stimulus, thought, thinking outside the box, trigger, vision

**Inspire** v., see also Cause, Influence
arouse, awaken, challenge, electrify, encourage, energise, enthuse, evoke, excite, fire up, galvanise, generate inspiration, get someone inspired, give an idea, give impetus, give inspiration, give rise to, ignite, impress, inform, infuse, instil, interest, kindle, lay the foundations, motivate, move, pave the way, pique interest, plant/sow a seed, produce, prompt, provide inspiration, provoke, result

in, shape, spark ideas/inspiration, spawn, spring to mind, spur, start, stimulate, stir, strike with inspiration, support, trigger, unleash, urge

**Instability** n., see also Chaos, Uncertainty
changeability, combustibility, confusion, disarray, disorder, disquiet, doubt, fluctuation, fluidity, fragility, frailty, imbalance, inconsistency, insecurity, lack of certainty, lack of stability, precariousness, rollercoaster ride, shakiness, uneasiness, unpredictability, unreliability, ups and downs, variability, volatility, vulnerability, weakness

**Instruct** v., see also Order, Teach
1. advise, brief, call for, charge, command, communicate, counsel, demand, disclose, enjoin, guide, inform, instil, mandate, notify, require, stipulate, tell, urge
2. coach, drill, educate, give lessons, guide, impart knowledge, instil, lecture, mentor, prepare, provide instruction/teaching, show how, show the ropes, train, tutor

**Instructions** n., see also Advice, Requirement
authorisation, brief, briefing, coaching, command, counsel, demand, direction(s), directive, guidance, guidelines, information, lesson, mandate, order, recommendations, remit, specifications, stipulations, teaching, training

**Insufficient** adj., see also Few, Small
deficient, devoid, disappointing, found wanting, in short supply, inadequate, incomplete, infrequent, insubstantial, lack of, lacking, let-down, limited, meagre, measly, miserly, not enough, paltry, poor, rare, scant, scarce, short of, shy, thin, thin on the ground, too little (too late), unsatisfactory, wanting, weak

**Intelligent** adj., see also Skilled, Smart
able, analytical, astute, brains, bright, brilliant, calculating, canny, capable, clever, far-sighted, enlightened, gifted, incisive, ingenious, innovative, insightful, intellectual, inventive, knowledgeable, on the ball, perceptive, quick on the uptake, quick-witted, rational, resourceful, savvy, sharp, shrewd, switched on, talented, thinking, thoughtful, understanding, well-informed, wise, with it

**Intend** v., see also Aim, Hope
anticipate, aspire, be determined, be hell-bent on, be hopeful, be minded to, be resolved to, contemplate, count on, determine, endeavour, envisage, expect, foresee, have designs on, have in mind, have the intention, look ahead to, look

forward to, look to, mean, plan, plot, propose, pursue, resolve, see, seek, set one's sights on, strive, target, think, try, venture, want, work towards

**Intention** n., see also Aim, Purpose
ambition, anticipation, aspiration, design(s), desire, determination, dream, goal, hope, idea, intent, mission, motivation, motive, objective, plan, resolve, sights, statement of intent, target, vision, wish

**Interest** n., see also Attraction, Investment
1. activity, affection, affinity, appetite, attention, attentiveness, benefit, care, concern, curiosity, engagement, enthusiasm, excitement, fascination, flair, focus, fondness, hobby, importance, inquisitiveness, involvement, liking, love, passion, pastime, penchant, preoccupation, regard, relevance, significance, value
2. claim, holding, involvement, ownership, participation, percentage, shareholding, stake

**Interesting** adj., see also Attractive, Entertaining
absorbing, alluring, appealing, arresting, captivating, compelling, engaging, engrossing, enjoyable, enlightening, enthralling, entrancing, exceptional, exciting, eye-catching, fascinating, gripping, imaginative, impressive, insightful, intriguing, inviting, mesmerising, must-see, of interest, refreshing, relevant, riveting, spellbinding, stimulating, striking, tantalising, tempting, thought-provoking, thrilling, unusual, whetting one's appetite, worth noting

**International** adj., see also Everywhere
abroad, across/around the globe/planet/world, all corners of the earth/world, cosmopolitan, diverse, far afield, far and wide, foreign, global, globalised, globetrotting, intercontinental, multinational, overseas, spanning the globe, the world over, world, worldwide

**Intervene** v., see also Engage, Involve
arbitrate, become involved, chip in, contribute, get caught up in, get involved, give one's opinion, intercede, interfere, interrupt, make one's voice heard, meddle, mediate, muscle in, participate, reach out, step in, take a stand, take action, wade into, weigh in on

**Introduce** v., see also Initiate, Launch
add, announce, begin, break new ground, bring in, bring into being, bring out, bring to market, create, debut, embark, establish, familiarise, get going, get the ball rolling, get things rolling, get underway, herald, inaugurate, include,

infuse, inject, innovate, instigate, instil, institute, invent, kick off, lead to, open, originate, pave the way, premier, present, propose, put forward, put in place, put together, release, reveal, roll out, set up, start, submit, take the wraps off, unleash, unveil, usher in

**Introduction** n., see also Beginning, Initiative
acquaintance, addition, advent, announcement, appearance, big reveal, breakthrough, commencement, debut, encounter, entry, establishment, familiarisation, first encounter, first taste, inauguration, inception, induction, initiation, injection, institution, issue, launch, launch pad, lead-in, onset, opening, outset, overture, preamble, preface, prelude, premiere, presentation, proposal, release, roll-out, run-up, start, start-up, unveiling, ushering in

**Invent** v., see also Create, Innovate
be creative, be inventive, break new ground, breathe life into, bring into being, change the game, coin, come up with, conceive, concoct, conjure up, cook up, craft, design, develop, devise, discover, dream up, engineer, envisage, establish, fabricate, fashion, formulate, give birth to, hatch, have a brainwave, have an idea, hit upon, imagine, initiate, introduce, originate, pen, pioneer, plan, produce, push the envelope, put together, reinvent, think outside the box, think up, unveil

**Invention** n., see also Innovation
brainchild, brainwave, breakthrough, bright idea, concept, creation, creativity, design, development, discovery, eureka moment, forerunner, game-changer, genius, idea, imagination, ingenuity, inventiveness, lightbulb moment, modernisation, new product, original idea, pioneering, resourcefulness, revolution, vision

**Inventor** n., see also Designer, Expert
architect, author, brains behind, creator, developer, discoverer, entrepreneur, founder, genius, innovator, leader, maker, mastermind, originator, pioneer, visionary

**Invest** v., see also Acquire, Buy
back, bankroll, become an owner/shareholder, bet on, buy a stake in, buy into, buy out, buy shares/stock, buy up, co-own, finance, fund, hold, inject money into, invest money, make an acquisition, make an investment, own, pay for, plough money into, prop up, provide, purchase, put money into, put one's money where one's mouth is, sink money into, spend, splash the cash, support, take a stake in, throw money at

**Investigate** v., see also Analyse, Assess
check out, conduct an investigation, conduct an enquiry/inquiry/investigation, consider, delve into, dig, dissect, drill down into, enquire, evaluate, examine, explore, inquire, inspect, judge, lift the lid on, look at in detail, look into, make enquiries/inquiries, pick over, pore over, probe, question, research, review, scour, scrutinise, search, shine a light on, sift, study, subject to investigation, verify, weigh up

**Investigation** n., see also Analysis, Review
assessment, case, check, delving into, dossier, enquiry, evaluation, examination, exploration, fact-finding, inquiry, inquisition, insight, inspection, judgement, look, probe, quizzing, report, research, scrutiny, search, study, testing, verification

**Investment** n., see also Acquisition, Asset
backing, bet, buy-out, buy-up, capital injection, capital investment, financial backing/support, financing, funding, gamble, holding, injection of capital, interest, investing, investment decision, ownership, participation, project, property, purchase, shares, shareholding, stake, takeover, transaction, venture

**Investor** n., see also Owner
backer, bondholder, buyer, financial backer, financial stakeholder, financial supporter, financier, institutional investor, partner, private investor, provider of finance, shareholder, stockholder, vested interest

**Involve** v., see also Concern, Include
affect, afflict, apply to, associate, be a factor, be about, be associated with, become involved, bring together, call for, comprise, come into play, cover, demand, depend on, draw in, embrace, embroil, encompass, engage, engulf, enshrine, entail, entangle, feature, get involved, get mixed up, have to do with, hinge on, implicate, imply, incorporate, link, mire, mix up, number, play a part/role, occasion, refer to, relate, require, rope in, span, stem, take in

**Involvement** n., see also Commitment
activity, affiliation, alliance, association, attachment, concern, connection, contribution, embroilment, engagement, enthusiasm, entanglement, implication, inclusion, interaction, interest, intervention, link, part, participation, preoccupation, relationship, responsibility, role, support, ties

**Irrelevant** adj., see also Insignificant
beside the point, by the by, distraction, futile, immaterial, inapplicable, inappropriate, incidental, inconsequential, neither here nor there, not connected with, not important, not relevant, nothing to do with, off-topic, of no consequence/importance, of no relevance, pointless, trivial, unconnected, unimportant, unnecessary, unrelated, unsuitable

**Issue** n., see also Circumstances, Problem
affair, argument, battleground, bone of contention, business, case, concern, controversy, debate, difficulty, discussion, elephant in the room, episode, fact, factor, flashpoint, focus, food for thought, gist, heart of the matter, issue at hand, key issue, matter, matter at hand, million-dollar question, nub of the problem, paradox, point in question, predicament, quandary, question, question mark, significance, situation, subject, subject matter, substance, talking point, theme, topic

# J

**Jeopardise** v., see also Risk, Threaten
endanger, expose, gamble, imperil, menace, pose a risk, put at risk, put at stake, put in danger, put in jeopardy, put on the line, put under pressure, raise the stakes, risk, run the risk of, spell danger, subject to danger, tempt fate

**Job** n., see also Employment, Work
activity, appointment, assignment, brief, calling, capacity, career, commission, craft, duties/duty, function, gig, job description, line of work, livelihood, mantle, mission, occupation, office, portfolio, position, post, profession, project, remit, responsibility, role, sideline, task, trade, vocation

**Join** v., see also Cooperate, Start
affiliate with, align, band together, become a member of, become involved with, begin, collaborate with, come on board, commence, cooperate, enrol, enter, get the gig, join forces, join together with, join the ranks, participate, partner with, sign up, start a job, take a job with, take part in, take up a position, take up a role, team up with, tie up with

**Judge** v., see also Assess, Estimate
adjudge, analyse, appraise, believe, calculate, conclude, consider, criticise, decide, deem, determine, discern, estimate, evaluate, examine, find, gauge, give one's opinion, grade, make a judgement call, make of, measure, put to the test, rank, rate, reckon, review, rule, scrutinise, size up, test, value, weigh (up)

**Judgement** n., see also Analysis, Assessment
acumen, appraisal, astuteness, belief, call, choice, common sense, consideration, conviction, decision, deduction, discretion, estimate, estimation, evaluation, examination, expertise, finding, gauge, grasp, insight, interpretation, intuition, judgement call, measurement, observation, opinion, perception, prudence, reason, reasoning, result, review, ruling, scrutiny, shrewdness, study, understanding, valuation, verdict, view, wisdom

**Justify** v., see also Defend, Deserve

advocate, argue, back up, bear out, clarify, condone, confirm, excuse, exonerate, explain, explain away, forgive, give an excuse for, give grounds for, give reason for, legitimise, maintain, make a case for, merit, provide a justification, provide an explanation, rationalise, square, stand by, stand up for, substantiate, support, validate, verify, vindicate, warrant

# K

**Keep** v., see also Continue, Sustain
accumulate, amass, be in charge of, be responsible for, care for, cherish, conserve, contain, control, defend, keep control of, keep hold off, keep under lock and key, keep possession of, keep up, hang on to, have, have charge of, hoard, hog, hold, hold back, hold onto, look after, maintain, manage, nurture, oversee, own, preserve, protect, reserve, retain, run, safeguard, save, store, support, withhold

**Key** adj., see also Essential, Important
all-important, basic, bedrock, cardinal, central, chief, core, cornerstone, critical, crucial, crunch, decisive, foremost, front-line, fundamental, headline, imperative, indispensable, instrumental, integral, keynote, leading, main, major, material, must-have/read/see, of key importance, of utmost importance, paramount, pertinent, pivotal, primary, prime, principal, relevant, top-of-mind, vital

**Kind** n., see also Category, Group
character, class, classification, description, designation, family, form, genre, ilk, like, nature, persuasion, sort, standard, style, type, variant, variety, version

**Know** v., see also Realise, Understand
appreciate, be acquainted, be (well) aware, be certain, be common knowledge, be conscious of, be conversant, be familiar with, be informed, be knowledgeable about, be up on, be versed in, comprehend, experience, have confidence, have experience, have knowledge of, have no doubt, know a thing or two about, know back to front, know inside out, know like the back of one's hand, know the ropes, know (full/very) well, learn, recognise, see, trust

**Knowledge** n., see also Expertise, Information
ability, acquaintance, awareness, capability, competence, comprehension, credentials, education, experience, facts, familiarity, grasp, information, inside story, insight, intelligence, judgement, know-how, learning, lesson, mastery, news, perception, proficiency, sense, skill, skillset, training, understanding, wisdom

# L

**Lack** n., see also Few, Small
absence, almost no, bereft, conspicuous absence, dearth, deficiency, devoid, distinct lack, few and far between, gone, inadequacy, inadequate, in short supply, insufficient, need, no, no real, none, nonexistence, omission, paucity, precious little, scarcity, short of/on, short supply, shortage, shortfall, sparsity, thin on the ground, unavailability, vacuum, virtually no, want, zero

**Large** adj., see also Extensive, Many
abundant, almighty, ample, aplenty, astronomical, awesome, behemoth, big, blockbuster, boundless, bountiful, broad, bulky, bumper, capacious, colossal, colossus, comprehensive, considerable, copious, dominating, enormous, epic, expansive, exponential, eye-watering, formidable, gargantuan, generous, giant, gigantic, ginormous, goliath, grand, great, heavy, hefty, Herculean, huge, humungous, immeasurable, immense, imposing, impressive, in force, innumerable, jumbo, king-size, large-scale, largish, legion, leviathan, limitless, major, mammoth, massive, mighty, monumental, monster, monstrous, mountain, of epic proportions, of huge proportions, omnipresent, outsize(d), oversize(d), overwhelming, plentiful, prodigious, roomy, seismic, significant, sizeable, spacious, staggering, strong, substantial, supersize(d), sweeping, swingeing, thumping, titanic, towering, tremendous, vast, voluminous, whacking (great), whopping, wide, wide-ranging, widespread

**Launch** v., see also Innovate, Introduce
announce, begin, bring out, bring to market, come out with, commence, debut, embark upon, establish, found, get the ball rolling, get the show on the road, get underway, herald, inaugurate, initiate, instigate, institute, issue, kick off, mark the launch/start of, open, open its doors, open up, originate, pioneer, premier, present, raise the curtain, release, reveal, roll out, set in motion, set up, start, take the wraps off, throw open the doors, unleash, unveil, usher in, welcome

**Lead** v., see also Manage, Pioneer
1. be at the head of, be at the helm of, be in charge of, be responsible, call the shots, captain, command, control, direct, drive (forward), govern, guide, head,

head up, influence, inspire, lead by example, lead from the front, lead the charge, lead the way, marshal, mastermind, mobilise, orchestrate, organise, oversee, pave the way, pilot, point the way, preside over, rule, run, shepherd, show the way, skipper, spearhead, stamp one's authority on, steer, steward, supervise, take forward, take the helm, take the lead, watch over

2. be ahead, be at the cutting edge, be at the forefront, be first, be in pole position, be in the lead, be in the vanguard, be number one, be out in front, be the leader in, blaze a trail, defeat, dominate, lead the field, lead the pack, leave behind, outdo, outperform, outrival, outshine, outstrip, surpass, take the lead, top

**Lead To** v., see also Cause, Start

be the cause of, breed, bring, bring about, conclude in, contribute to, create, culminate in, drive, end in, engender, ensure, evoke, fan (the flames), fuel, generate, give rise to, incite, influence, kick-start, kindle, lay the ground for, make for, pave the way, precipitate, produce, prompt, provoke, result in, see, sow the seeds, spark, spawn, stoke, trigger, unleash

**Leader** n., see also Best, Management

1. big beast, big cheese, big shot, bigwig, boss, captain, chief, chief executive (officer), commander, director, executive, expert, figurehead, founder, frontman/frontwoman, guru, head, head honcho, luminary, manager, mover and shaker, number one, officer, person in charge, premier, president, ruler, senior executive/manager, skipper, standard-bearer, strategist, superior, supervisor, supremo, talisman, top brass, visionary

2. best-seller, big hitter, big gun, big name, biggest, champion, dominant business/player etc., frontrunner, greatest, largest, leading exponent, most successful, number one, outstanding, pioneer, powerhouse, premium brand, role model, second to none, standard-bearer, standout performer, titan, top dog, trailblazer, trendsetter, very best

**Leadership** n., see also Authority, Management

1. administration, at the helm, captaincy, command, control, decision-making, direction, domination, governance, guidance, influence, lead, leadership skills, leading role, power, premiership, reign, rule, stewardship, supervision, tenure, time in charge, vision

2. administration, chiefs, decision-makers, executive(s), government, hierarchy, leaders, officialdom, officials, senior management, those in charge/power, top brass

**Leading** adj., see also Best, Dominant
best-known, best-selling, biggest, cardinal, champion, chief, class-leading, famous, first, foremost, front-runner, greatest, heavyweight, high-profile, in pole position, key, largest, lead, leader, main, most successful, notable, noted, number one, outstanding, popular, predominant, pre-eminent, premier, premium, primary, prime, principal, prominent, respected, ruling, standout, stellar, strong, superior, top, unrivalled, very best, well-known

**Learn** v., see also Analyse, Understand
absorb, acquire, ascertain, be informed, be on a learning curve, be taught, be trained, become able, become aware, become versed, brush up on, comprehend, cut one's teeth, discern, discover, drink in, explore, face a (steep) learning curve, familiarise oneself with, find one's feet, find out, gain knowledge, gather, get the hang of, get the knack of, get up to speed, grasp, identify, learn a lesson, learn the ropes, master, pick someone's brains, pick up, pore over, prepare, read up on, receive information, soak up, study, take in, uncover

**Leave** v., see also Resign
abandon, abstain from, bail out, beat a (hasty) retreat, bid farewell, bow out, cease, depart, desert, disappear, discontinue, ditch, drop, drop out, escape, exit, fall on one's sword, flee, forsake, give up, go away, hand over (the reins) to, jump ship, leave behind, move on (to pastures new), part company with, part ways, pull out, quit, refrain, relinquish, renounce, retire, retreat, say goodbye, sever ties with, step down, stop, vacate, vanish, walk away from, walk out, wash one's hands of, withdraw

**Lessen** v., see also Decrease, Mitigate
abate, allay, alleviate, assuage, calm, cancel out, contract, counter, curb, curtail, cushion, cut, cut back, dampen, decline, depress, dial back on, dial down, die down, dilute, diminish, dwindle, eat into, ease, erode, grow less, lighten, lower, make less, minimise, moderate, mollify, narrow, offset, provide relief, quell, rebalance, recede, reduce, rein in, relieve, shrink, slash, slow, slow down, soften, soothe, stabilise, stem, subdue, tail off, take the edge off, take the heat out of, take the sting out of, taper (off), temper, tone down, undermine, weaken, weigh on

**Level** n., see also Amount, Extent
achievement, degree, depth, grade, height, measure, pace, part, percentage, portion, position, proportion, quality, rank, ranking, rate, rating, ratio, result, scale, score, stage, standard, standing, status, value

**Like** conj./prep., see also Related
à la, akin, alike, along the same lines, analogous, chiming with, close to, comparable to, corresponding to, cut from the same cloth, dead ringer for, déjà vu, echoing, equivalent to, *****esque, following in the footsteps of, having an affinity with, having echoes of, having shades of, identical to, in keeping with, in line with, in step with, in the vein of, in tune with, indistinguishable from, kindred (spirit), like-minded, matching, much of a muchness, much the same, not a million miles away from, not dissimilar to, not unlike, on a par with, owing a debt to, parallel, rehash, reminiscent of, resembling, resonating with, similar, taking inspiration from, tantamount to

**Like** v., see also Admire, Praise
adore, appreciate, approve, be a sucker for, be crazy about, be drawn to, be fond of, be keen on, be partial to, be pleased by, be wild about, cherish, delight in, embrace, endorse, enjoy, fall (head over heels) for, fall in love with, find appealing, get a kick out of, have a liking for, have a preference for, have a soft spot for, have a weakness for, have affection for, hold dear, hold in high esteem, incline towards, lap up, love, prefer, prize, rejoice in, relish, revel in, savour, take a shine to, take delight in, take satisfaction in, take to, think a lot of, think highly of, treasure, value, warm to, welcome

**Likely** adj., see also Future, Potential
achievable, anticipated, apparent, believable, bound to happen, chances are, conceivable, convincing, credible, every chance, expected, feasible, foregone conclusion, hopeful, in all likelihood, in all probability, in the offing, inclined, liable, most likely, odds-on, on the cards, on the verge of, plausible, poised, possible, predictable, predicted, presumable, probable, promising, prone, reasonable, safe bet, seemingly, set to, slated, thinkable, tipped, unsurprising

**Limit** n., see also Extent
border, bound, boundary, breaking point, cap, ceiling, check, confines, constraint, control, curb, curtailment, cut-off point, deadline, demarcation, edge, end point, extremity, limitation, limits, margin, maximum, minimum, most, outer limit, perimeter, periphery, red line, regulation, reservation, restraint, restriction, rule, stipulation, threshold, tipping point, tops, upper limit

**Limit** v., see also Prevent, Reduce
cap, check, circumscribe, confine, constrain, constrict, contain, control, curb, curtail, define, delimit, demarcate, diminish, draw the line, fence in, fix, hamper, hamstring, hem in, hinder, hold back, hold in check, impede, inhibit, keep a lid on, keep within limits, lessen, lock down, minimise, moderate,

narrow, prescribe, put a brake on, put a limit on, ration, regulate, rein in, restrain, restrict, set a limit, specify, stop, temper, thwart, tie, tighten

**Link** n., see also Combination, Relationship
affiliation, affinity, alliance, association, attachment, bond, collaboration, communication, connection, contact, cooperation, correlation, correspondence, coupling, cross-over, echo, interaction, nod, pairing, relevance, similarity, symbiosis, synergy, tie, tie-in

**Link** v., see also Combine, Relate
ally, associate, attach, be bound up with, bind, blend, bond, bridge (the gap), connect, correlate, couple with, dovetail, equate, fuse, hook up, integrate, interconnect, interlock, intersect, intertwine, join, join up, knit together, marry, merge, piggyback on, pair, plug into, span, splice, tie, tie in, tie up with, unite, wed

**Little** adj./det., see also Few, Lack
almost no, baby, barely, bite-size(d), brief, compact, concise, deficiency, diminutive, dinky, few and far between, fleeting, fun-size(d), hardly any, humble, immaterial, imperceptible, in short supply, inadequate, inappreciable, inconsequential, inconsiderable, infrequent, insignificant, insufficient, junior, lesser, light, limited, meagre, measly, mere, microscopic, mini, miniature, minnow, minor, minuscule, minute, miserly, modest, muted, narrow, negligible, next to nothing, not large, not many, not much, paltry, paucity of, piffling, pint-size(d), pocket-size(d), portable, potted, precious little, rare, reduced, scaled-down, scant, scarcely, scarcity, short, short of/on, short-lived, slender, slight, slightly, slim, small, small but perfectly formed, small fry, smallish, small-scale, small-time, smattering, smidgeon, sparse, subdued, succinct, tad, teeny, thin on the ground, tiny, trifling, trivial, undersize(d), ungenerous, unsatisfactory, vanishingly small, virtually no, wanting, wee

**Loan** n., see also Debt
advance, allowance, amount borrowed/due/lent/owed/outstanding, bailout, borrowing, credit, credit facility, financing, funding, IOU, lending, liability, lifeline, line of credit, money borrowed/due/lent/owed/outstanding

**Location** n., see also Area
bearings, district, environment, geographical position, locale, locality, neck of the woods, neighbourhood, place, point, position, property, region, scene, section, setting, site, situation, spot, territory, venue, vicinity, whereabouts, zone

**Logical** adj., see also Obvious, Sensible
appropriate, clear, clear-eyed, coherent, common-sense, consistent, convincing, fair, fitting, holds water, intelligent, judicious, justifiable, legitimate, level-headed, makes (complete) sense, methodical, natural, necessary, perfect sense, plausible, probable, prudent, rational, realistic, reasonable, reasoned, relevant, sound, stacks up, stands to reason, structured, suitable, systematic, understandable, valid, well-reasoned, well-thought-out, wise

**Long-term** adj., see also Continual, Permanent
abiding, constant, continued, continuing, continuous, deep-rooted, durable, endless, enduring, established, eternal, for many years, for the long haul, forever, in the long run, in the long term, incessant, indefinite, indelible, inexhaustible, lasting, lifelong, long-established, long-held, long-lasting, long-lived, long-maintained, long-standing, long-time, marathon not a sprint, perennial, perpetual, persisting, prolonged, standing the test of time, sustainable, sustained, time-honoured, unceasing, unremitting, unstinting

**Look For** v., see also Explore
cast about, chase after, check, comb, delve into, enquire, examine, go in quest of, go in search of, go through, go through with a fine-tooth comb, hunt, inquire, inspect, investigate, leave no stone unturned, look everywhere, look high and low, pore over, probe, prospect, pursue, research, scan, scour, scout, scrutinise, search, seek, sift, study, track down, trawl

**Lose** v., see also Disappear, Fail
1. be beaten, be defeated, be humbled, be toast, be unsuccessful, beat a retreat, bite the dust, capitulate, come a cropper, come to grief, come up short, crash, disappoint, elude, fade, fail in a bid to, fall by the wayside, fall short, lose ground to, lose out, miss out on, struggle, succumb, suffer, suffer defeat, surrender, take a beating/hammering/thrashing, yield
2. alienate, be deprived of, be dispossessed of, be without, fail to keep, fall through the cracks, haemorrhage, miss, no longer have, part company with, part with, pass up, relinquish, sacrifice, slip through the net, squander, surrender, use up, waste

**Lots** n., see also Extensive, Large
a lot, abounding, abundance, abundant, acres, all manner, ample, aplenty, array, awash, back to back, bags, boundless, bountiful, brimming, bristling, buckets of, bundles, bursting, by the truckload, chock-a-block, chock-full, colossal amount, considerable, copious, countless, crammed with, deluge, deluged, depth, dizzying (amounts of), dozens, droves, embarrassment, en masse,

endless, excess, exuding, fair few, feast, ***** fest, filled with, flood, flurry, frequent, full of, galore, glut, goldmine, good deal, great amount, great deal, host, huge quantity, hundreds, in abundance, in force, in numbers, in spades, influx, innumerable, inundated, jam-packed, kaleidoscope, large amount, large numbers, lashings, legion, loaded with, loads, many, many a, masses, millions, mine of, more than enough, mountain, multiple, multitude, myriad, no end, no shortage, number, numerous, oodles, oozing, packed with, panoply, plentiful, plenty, plethora, profuse, profusion, proliferation, quantities, raft, range, reams, rich vein of, rife, scores, series of, slew, spades, spate, spoilt for choice, stacks, stream, string, succession, surfeit, swathes, teeming, thick and fast, thousands, tonnes, torrent, treasure trove, umpteen, untold (amounts of), wall-to-wall, wave, wealth, whole host, wholesale, wide range, widespread

**Low** n., see also Decrease, Weakness
all-time low, base, bottom, depths, foot, low point, lowest level, lowest point, minimum, nadir, record low, rock bottom, trough, very bottom

**Lower** v., see also Decrease, Deteriorate
alleviate, bring down, check, cool, curb, curtail, cut, cut back (on), cut down, dampen, de-escalate, depress, devalue, devaluate, dial down, dilute, discount, downgrade, downsize, drag down, drive down, ease, eat into, erode, have a negative impact on, impair, lessen, make less, make lower, make worse, mark down, minimise, moderate, pare, prune, push down, rationalise, reduce, rein in, sap, scale back, scale down, shave, shrink, slash, slow (down), subdue, take down, taper, tighten, tone down, trim, turn down, undermine, weaken, weigh on, whittle down

**Luck** n., see also Opportunity, Success
accident, advantage, as luck would have it, bad luck, big break, blessing, break, chance, coincidence, destiny, fate, fluke, fortune, godsend, good fortune, good luck, good timing, happenstance, karma, Lady Luck, lucky hap, lucky break, lucky stars, meant to be, providence, pure coincidence, right place right time, rub of the green, serendipity, stars (aligning), stroke of luck, synchronicity, talisman, twist of fate, winning streak

**Lucky** adj., see also Favourable, Successful
advantageous, as luck would have it, auspicious, beneficial, blessed, charmed, coincidental, coming up roses, everything going for someone, falling into place, falling on one's feet, fluky, fortuitous, fortunate, good fortune, jammy, lucky break, on a roll, on a winning streak, opportune, prosperous, prospering, right place right time, serendipitous, timely, unplanned

# M

**Machine** n., see also Device, Equipment
apparatus, appliance, automation, computer, contraption, facility, gadget, gizmo, hardware, implement, innovation, instrument, invention, kit, machinery, mechanism, robot, setup, system, tech, technology, tool, unit

**Main** adj., see also Important, Key
all-important, basic, biggest, cardinal, central, central plank, chief, core, cornerstone, critical, crucial, defining, definitive, dominant, essential, first and foremost, flagship, foremost, fundamental, go-to, head, instrumental, integral, keynote, landmark, largest, leading, linchpin, mainstay, major, most important, necessary, outstanding, overriding, paramount, predominant, pre-eminent, premier, prevailing, primary, prime, principal, priority, seminal, significant, standout, star, strongest, top, underlying

**Maintain** v., see also Continue, Keep
1. carry on, dwell on, keep going, keep on, keep up, manage, nurture, perpetuate, persevere, persist, plough on, plug away, press ahead, prolong, renew, retain, save, stick at, support, sustain, uphold
2. care for, conserve, cultivate, extend the life of, guard, keep up, look after, manage, nurture, preserve, prolong, protect, repair, retain, safeguard, save, service, support, sustain, take care of
3. advocate, affirm, argue, assert, claim, declare, defend, insist, reaffirm, reassert, say, state, stress

**Make** v., see also Force, Manufacture
accomplish, achieve, arrange, assemble, breathe life into, bring about, bring to life, build, carry out, cause, churn out, compose, conceive, conduct, conjure (up), construct, craft, create, deliver, design, develop, devise, do, effect, engineer, establish, fashion, forge, form, generate, give rise to, hatch, have in the works, implement, lead to, mass-produce, occasion, originate, organise, prepare, produce, provoke, put together, render, shape, secure, shape, tailor

**Manage** v., see also Lead, Resolve
1. administer, arrange, be at the head of, be at the helm of, be head of, be in charge of, be in control of, be manager of, be responsible for, bring about, call

the shots, captain, command, conduct, control, direct, engineer, get a handle on, get on top of, govern, guide, handle, head, head up, influence, instruct, juggle, look after, maintain, marshal, mastermind, micromanage, officiate, operate, orchestrate, organise, oversee, pilot, preside over, regulate, respond to, rule, run, shape, shepherd, spearhead, steer, steward, supervise, tackle, take care of, take charge of, take ownership of, take the lead, undertake, watch over
2. accomplish, achieve, bear up, carry on, contend with, cope, cope admirably, endure, get by, get on top of, get through, hack, handle, handle the pressure, hold one's own, make the best of, muddle through, muster, overcome, scrape by, shrug off, struggle through, succeed in, survive, weather, withstand

**Management** n., see also Authority, Leadership
1. administration, care, command, conduct, control, decision-making, governance, guidance, handling, management style, marshalling, micromanagement, operation, orchestration, organisation, oversight, regulation, running, spearheading, stewardship, supervision, tenure
2. administration, administrators, board of directors, bosses, control, corridors of power, decision-makers, directors, executives, executive management, heads, hierarchy, key people, key players, management group, management team, managers, officials, those in charge/power, top brass

**Mandatory** adj., see also Essential
binding, compulsory, de rigueur, familiar, fundamental, imperative, indispensable, integral, invaluable, matter of course, much-needed, necessary, needed, normal, obliged, obligatory, required, requisite, standard, unavoidable, vital

**Manufacture** v., see also Create, Produce
assemble, build, churn out, complete, construct, craft, custom-make, devise, engineer, fabricate, fashion, forge, handcraft, handmake, have in the works, make, mass-produce, oversee the manufacture/production of, precision-build, process, produce on an industrial/large scale, pump out, put together, roll off the production line, scale up production, supply, tailor, turn out

**Many** det., see also Extensive, Large
a lot of, abounding, abundance of, abundant, acres of, all manner of, ample, aplenty, array, awash with, back to back, bags of, boundless, bountiful, brimming with, bristling with, buckets of, bundles of, bursting, by the truckload, chock-a-block, chock-full of, colossal amount of, considerable, copious, countless, crammed with, deluge of, deluged with, depth of, dizzying (amounts of), dozens of, droves of, embarrassment of, en masse, endless,

excess of, exuding, fair few of, feast, ***** fest, filled with, flood of, flurry of, full of, galore, glut of, goldmine, good deal of, great amount of, great deal of, host of, huge quantity of, hundreds of, in abundance, in force, in numbers, in spades, influx of, innumerable, inundated with, jam-packed with, kaleidoscope, large amount of, large numbers of, lashings of, legion, loaded with, loads of, lots of, many a, masses of, millions of, mine of, more than enough, mountain of, multiple, multitude of, myriad, no end of, no shortage of, number of, numerous, oodles of, oozing with, packed with, panoply of, plentiful, plenty, plethora of, profuse, profusion of, proliferation of, quantities, raft of, range of, reams of, rich vein of, rife with, scores of, series of, slew of, spades, spate of, spoilt for choice, stacks of, stream of, string of, succession of, surfeit of, swathes of, teeming with, thousands of, tonnes of, torrent of, treasure trove of, umpteen, untold (amounts of), wall-to-wall, wave of, wealth of, whole host of, wide range of, widespread

**Market** n., see also Industry
area, arena, business, buyers, commerce, competition, competitive landscape, customers, demand, field, gap in the market, landscape, market conditions, market opportunities, marketplace, niche market, sales market, scene, sector, segment, space, target market, trade

**Marketing** n., see also Advertising, Communication
announcement, claims, coverage, endorsement, hard sell, highlighting, hype, marketing blitz/push, marketing blurb, marketing communication, mass marketing, pitch, plug, positioning, presentation, promotion, public relations, publicity, sale, showcase

**Match** v., see also Combine, Correspond
accord, agree, be a good fit/match, be a match made in heaven, be compatible, be consistent, be identical, be in line, be related, be similar, be the perfect match, be the same, blend with, chime, coincide, compare (favourably), complement, concur, conform, coordinate, copy, correlate, echo, equal, equate, fit (with), go together/with, harmonise, go well with, join, link up, make a pair, match perfectly, pair, reciprocate, resemble, resonate with, sit well with, synchronise, tally, tie in with, unite

**Matter** n., see also Concern, Problem
affair, argument, bone of contention, business, case, controversy, debate, discussion, elephant in the room, episode, event, fact, factor, focus, incident, issue, issue at hand, matter at hand, million-dollar question, nub of the problem, point in question, predicament, quandary, question, question mark,

significance, situation, subject, subject matter, substance, talking point, theme, topic

**Measure** n., see also Action, Initiative

1. achievement, activity, course (of action), delivery, deployment, effort, endeavour(s), execution, exertion, gambit, idea, implementation, intervention, manoeuvre, means, move, procedure, proposal, roll-out, scheme, step, strategy, undertaking, work
2. acid test, amount, barometer, benchmark, capacity, criteria, criterion, extent, gauge, guide, indicator, litmus test, magnitude, metric, model, percentage, proportion, quantity, range, reference, scale, scope, share, standard, size, test, touchstone, yardstick

**Measure** v., see also Assess, Value

adjudge, appraise, calculate, check, compute, consider, count, determine, estimate, evaluate, gauge, grade, judge, monitor, quantify, rank, rate, size up, survey, take a measurement, take account of, test, track, verify, weigh (up)

**Media** n., see also Information, News

broadcast media, channel, column inches, commentary, commentators, coverage, journalism, mass media, media coverage, media glare, media outlets, media reporting, news outlets, press, press coverage, reporting, social media, wall-to-wall coverage, written media

**Meet** v., see also Discuss, Satisfy

1. assemble, bring together, collect, come face to face, come together, congregate, consult, convene, convene a meeting, converge, encounter, engage in dialogue, gather, get together, go head to head, have a conversation, have a meeting, hobnob, hold a meeting, hold talks, hook up with, join up, meet face to face, meet in person, meet up, negotiate, network, rendezvous, rub shoulders with
2. address, answer, be in line with, be sufficient, come up to, comply with, conform to, correspond, equal, fit, fulfil, get to grips with, live up to, match, meet head on, meet the challenge, measure up to, meet requirements, perform, reach, respond to, rise to the challenge, suffice, suit, tackle, withstand

**Meeting** n., see also Discussion

assembly, audience, conference, conflict, confrontation, congress, contest, convention, dialogue, encounter, engagement, face time, gathering, get-together, head-to-head, negotiations, reunion, roundtable (meeting), session, showdown, talks

**Mention** v., see also Say
acknowledge, allude to, bring up, broach, cite, comment on, detail, disclose, draw attention to, hint at, indicate, introduce, make mention, make reference to, name, namecheck, observe, point out, recount, refer to, reference, remark on, report, reveal, speak about, specify, touch on/upon

**Merge** v., see also Combine, Include
absorb, ally with, amalgamate, assimilate, be absorbed, be subsumed, be swallowed up, become partners, blend, bring together, centralise, come together, concentrate, consolidate, converge, couple, dovetail, fuse, hook up with, incorporate, integrate, join (together/up with), join forces, link up, marry, meld, mingle, mix, pool, share, take over, team up, tie in, tie up, unify, unite

**Merger** n., see also Acquisition, Combination
alliance, amalgamation, coalition, collaboration, combined entity, combining, consolidation, cooperation, corporate merger, coupling, fusion, hook-up, inclusion, incorporation, joining, link-up, marriage, merged entity, merging, team-up, tie-up, unification, union, unison

**Method** n., see also Approach, Strategy
arrangement, art, basis, craft, craftsmanship, execution, fashion, form, format, formula, instrument, lever, manner, means, mechanism, methodology, modus operandi, path, plan, practice, procedure, proceeding, process, route, routine, scheme, skill, structure, style, system, tack, tactic(s), take, technique, touch, way, workmanship

**Mislead** v., see also Conceal
be a red herring, belie, betray, bluff, cheat, cook the books, create a smokescreen, create the illusion, deceive, delude, distract, divert attention, double-cross, dress up, dupe, fiddle, fool, fudge, give the wrong idea/impression, hoax, hoodwink, keep in the dark, kid, lead astray, lead up the garden path, lie, lull into a false sense of security, masquerade, misdirect, misguide, misinform, misrepresent, pretend, pull the wool over someone's eyes, rewrite (history), rip off, scam, spin, sugar-coat, take for a ride, take in, throw off the scent, trick, whitewash

**Mistake** n., see also Error, Failure
blip, blunder, bungle, cardinal error, clanger, confusion, false step, fault, fiasco, gaffe, howler, inaccuracy, lapse, litany of errors, miscalculation, misconception, misconduct, miscue, misjudgement, misstatement, misstep,

misunderstanding, muddle, neglect, omission, oversight, schoolboy error, screw-up, shambles, slip, slip-up, stumble, trip, typo, wrong move

**Misunderstand** v., see also Complicate, Confuse
be at cross purposes, be confused, be out of touch, confuse, get muddled, get the wrong end of the stick, get the wrong idea, get the wrong impression, get things back to front, get wires crossed, get wrong, have a misunderstanding, make a mistake, misapply, misapprehend, miscalculate, miscomprehend, misconstrue, misinterpret, misjudge, misread, miss, miss the point, mistake, mix up, muddle up, not be on the same page, not get the memo, not understand, take wrongly

**Mitigate** v., see also Balance, Lessen
allay, alleviate, appease, assuage, balance out, blunt, calm, cancel out, check, compensate (for), cool, counter, counteract, counterbalance, curb, cushion, dampen, diffuse, dilute, diminish, dull, ease, even out, lighten, make milder, make up for, moderate, mollify, negate, neutralise, offset, outweigh, pacify, placate, provide relief, rebalance, redress, reduce, reduce the force of, relieve, soften, subdue, take the edge off, take the heat out of, temper, tone down, weaken

**Moderate** adj., see also Average, Little
balanced, calm, careful, cautious, compromising, conservative, considered, controlled, fair, gentle, inconsequential, intermediate, limited, low-key, measured, mediocre, medium, middle-of-the-road, middling, midway, mild, modest, muted, normal, not excessive, ordinary, passable, reasonable, reserved, restrained, slight, sober, somewhat, steady, subdued, unexceptional

**Modern** adj., see also Innovative, New
advanced, avant-garde, bang up to date, contemporary, current, cutting-edge, emerging, forward-looking, fresh, future-proof, game-changing, groundbreaking, in vogue, latest, latest word in, leading-edge, modernised, new-fangled, new-look, next-generation, novel, now, on-trend, pioneering, present, present-day, progressive, recent, revolutionary, state-of-the-art, today, twenty-first-century, ultra-modern, up-to-date, up-to-the-minute

**Modify** v., see also Adjust, Improve
adapt, alter, amend, calibrate, change, convert, correct, customise, develop, edit, enhance, facelift, fine-tune, fix, hone, freshen up, make a change, make a modification, make an amendment, optimise, overhaul, put right, recalibrate, reconfigure, rectify, redesign, refine, reform, refresh, rejig, remedy, remodel,

renew, reorganise, repair, reshape, rethink, revise, revisit, rework, ring the changes, shake up, switch up, transform, tweak, update, upgrade

**Momentum** n., see also Energy, Success
boost, critical mass, direction of travel, drive, dynamism, force, forward motion, gaining traction, gathering pace, groundswell, impetus, impulse, moment, popularity, power, progress, purple patch, push, spotlight, strength, swell, support, surge, traction

**Money** n., see also Investment, Wealth
affluence, assets, bank balance, big bucks, billions, bread, capital, cash, coffers, currency, deep pockets, dough, earnings, finances, financial clout, financial muscle, financial resources, fortune, funds, hard-earned cash, kitty, means, millions, money in the bank, prosperity, readies, ready money, resources, riches, savings, wherewithal

**Monitor** v., see also Analyse, Check
assess, audit, be across, catalogue, confirm, control, ensure, evaluate, examine, follow, follow up (on), gauge, keep abreast of, keep an eye on, keep tabs on, keep track of, keep under review, keep up on/with, make sure, observe, oversee, record, scan, screen, study, supervise, survey, track, verify, watch

**More** adv./det., see also And, Better
added, additional, all the more, another, augmented, besides, better, by a country mile, deeper, enhanced, even more, expanded, extended, extra, far more, further, greater, heightened, higher, improved, in addition, increased, increasingly, larger, more besides, more broadly, much more, other, over and above, renewed, so much more, spare, supplementary, to a greater extent

**Motivate** v., see also Encourage, Inspire
animate, be passionate about, boost morale, buoy, cause, compel, convince, drive, energise, excite, fan, fire up, foster, fuel, galvanise, give a kick up the backside, get behind, give a prod, give a reason, give an incentive, give support, have a dream, impel, incentivise, incite, induce, influence, lead to, light the fuse, make someone tick, move, nurture, pass on one's enthusiasm/love/passion, persuade, prompt, provide inspiration, provoke, push, put on the path, rouse, set on a path, spark, spur (on), stimulate, support, trigger, urge, whet appetite

**Motivation** n., see also Enthusiasm, Purpose
ambition, belief, carrot and stick, catalyst, compulsion, desire, dream, drive, driving force, encouragement, fire, get-up-and-go, goal, hunger, impetus, impulse, incentive, inclination, inducement, inspiration, interest, keenness, kick, mojo, motive, objective, passion, rationale, reason, spirit, spur, thirst, stimulus, vested interest, wish

**Must** v., see also Need, Require
be bound to, be compelled, be driven, be essential, be forced, be obliged, be required, be vital, call for, could do with, could use, got to, had better, have a need, have no choice, have to, necessitate, ought, resort to, should, supposed to

# N

**Nearly** adv., see also Approximate, Similar
about, about to, all but, almost, approaching, approximately, around, as good as, bordering on, borderline, close, close but no cigar, de facto, essentially, hair's breadth, in effect, in the vicinity of, just about, just shy of, near-*****, nigh on, not far from/off, not quite, on the brink of, on the cusp of, on the point of, on the verge of, practically, roughly, substantially, to all intents and purposes, very nearly, virtually, well-nigh, within grasp, within reach, within sight, within touching distance

**Necessary** adj., see also Essential, Important
all-important, basic, can't do without, central, chief, compelling, compulsory, core, critical, crucial, de rigueur, decisive, elementary, fundamental, imperative, indispensable, inescapable, integral, key, linchpin, lost without, mainstay, mandatory, mission-critical, much-needed, must-have/read/see, necessary evil, needed, obligatory, paramount, prerequisite, pressing, principal, required, requisite, significant, sorely needed, unavoidable, urgent, vital

**Necessity** n., see also Need, Requirement
basics, basic element, compulsion, core component, core requirement, demand, duty, essential(s), essential element, fundamental requirement, imperative, importance, key component, key element, mainstay, must, must-have, necessary evil, no choice, obligation, precondition, prerequisite, stipulation, urgency, vital element

**Need** n., see also Demand, Necessity
call for, claim, clamour for, compulsion, condition, deficiency, desire, desperate need, dire need, duty, fundamental requirement, imperative, inadequacy, lack, must, obligation, paucity, precondition, prerequisite, real need, requirement, shortage, specification, stipulation, urge, urgency, want

**Need** v., see also Must, Want
ask, be crying out for, be essential, be in (desperate) need of, be incumbent on, be obliged, be short of, behove, call for, call upon, claim, could do with, could use, crave, demand, depend on, expect, got to, had better, have call for, have

need of, have to, insist on, involve, lack, look for, necessitate, occasion, ought to, push for, require, resort to, take

**Negative** adj., see also Bad, Pessimistic
adverse, against, bearish, counterproductive, cynical, damaging, defeatist, depressed, detrimental, disappointing, disapproving, down on, downbeat, dubious, gloomy, ineffective, inferior, lacklustre, negativity, not boding well, not hopeful, not in a good place, opposing, rejecting, resigned, subpar, substandard, uncooperative, unenthusiastic, unfavourable, unwilling, weak

**Negatively Affected** adj., see also Fail, Impact
adversely affected, afflicted by, ailing, at risk, at sixes and sevens, beleaguered, beset by, blighted, blindsided, buffeted by, crisis-hit, crisis-stricken, damaged, dealt a blow, devastated, doomed, embattled, embroiled in, engulfed by, facing difficulties, falling foul of, floundering, foundering, hard-hit, hard-pressed, hit, hit hard, ill-fated, impacted, imperilled, in danger, in distress, in crisis, in tatters, in trouble, knocked for six, laid low, negatively impacted, on the back foot, on the ropes, paying the price, poleaxed, reeling, rocked, shaken, stricken, struggling, suffering, threatened, troubled, under fire, under pressure, under scrutiny, undermined

**Negotiate** v., see also Discuss, Meet
accommodate, agree, agree terms, arbitrate, arrange, bargain, be in negotiations, broker, confer, consult, cut a deal, deal, debate, drive a bargain, engage in brinkmanship, engage in negotiations, engage in horse-trading, enter into negotiations, give and take, haggle, hammer out a deal, handle, hold talks, make a deal, make an offer, mediate, play hardball, settle, thrash out, work out

**New** adj., see also Different, Innovative
all-new, advanced, bang up to date, box-fresh, brand-new, brave new world of, breakthrough, breath of fresh air, burgeoning, contemporary, current, cutting-edge, emerging, fashionable, first of its kind, fledgling, fresh, game-changing, groundbreaking, hot off the press, improved, inaugural, initial, just out, latest, latest word in, modern, nascent, never before seen, new and improved, newcomer, new-fangled, new-found, new kid on the block, new-look, newly minted, next-generation, novel, original, pioneering, previously unknown, recent, redesigned, refreshed, refreshing, revolutionary, rookie, shiny new, state-of-the-art, topical, trailblazing, trendy, ultra-modern, unparalleled, unprecedented, untapped, up-to-date, very latest, without parallel, without precedent, young

**News** n., see also Communication, Information
account, announcement, article, bad news, breaking news, buzz, column inches, communiqué, coverage, disclosure, dispatch, exposé, front-page news, good news, gossip, headlines, intelligence, knowledge, latest (news), lowdown, media glare, media reports, news bulletin, press coverage, reporting, report(s), revelation(s), rumour, scoop, statement, story, word

**Nice** adj., see also Enjoyable, Good
acceptable, admirable, agreeable, amiable, attractive, brilliant, charming, commendable, considerate, cordial, courteous, decent, delightful, endearing, engaging, entertaining, fab, favourable, fine, friendly, genial, gorgeous, great, heart-warming, helpful, inviting, kind, likeable, lovely, pleasant, pleasing, pleasurable, satisfactory, welcome

**Normal** adj., see also Average, Common
accepted, accustomed, banal, bog-standard, bread and butter, business as usual, classic, common-or-garden, commonplace, conventional, customary, default, established, everyday, expected, familiar, general, habitual, mainstream, meat and drink, moderate, natural, no great shakes, not bad, nothing special, off-the-peg, ordinary, orthodox, par for the course, plain, plain-vanilla, prevalent, prevailing, rank-and-file, regular, routine, run-of-the-mill, simple, standard, standard-issue, staple, stock, traditional, typical, undistinguished, uneventful, unexceptional, uninspiring, unremarkable, usual, widespread, workaday

**Notable** adj., see also Important, Special
celebrated, conspicuous, defining, definitive, distinct, distinctive, distinguished, eminent, exceptional, extraordinary, famous, great, high-profile, illustrious, impressive, landmark, marked, memorable, momentous, no ordinary, noteworthy, not your average, original, outstanding, particular, pre-eminent, prominent, pronounced, remarkable, renowned, salient, singular, specialist, speciality, specific, standout, striking, uncommon, unique, unusual, well-known

**Nothing** pron., see also Few, Lack
absence, absolutely no, big fat zero, blank, emptiness, empty-handed, from scratch, nil, none, nonexistence, not one (single), nothing to show (for one's efforts), nought, omission, pointless, unavailability, vacuum, virtually no, zero, zilch, zip

**Notice** v., see also Discover, Identify
acknowledge, be aware, clock, detect, discern, feel, find, get the feeling, get the impression, get the sense, heed, make out, note, observe, pay attention to, perceive, pick up on, point out, realise, recognise, regard, register, remark, see, sense, spot, spy, (sit up and) take notice, twig, witness

**Notify** v., see also Communicate
acquaint, advise, alert, apprise, articulate, brief, bring up to speed, caution, convey, declare, disclose, divulge, enlighten, explain, express, familiarise, feed back, fill in, forewarn, get across, give notification, hint, imply, inform, instruct, invite, issue a statement, keep in the loop, keep posted, let someone in on, let know, make known, mention, outline, provide details, put across, relate, relay, remind, report, reveal, set out, state, suggest, tell, tip off, update, warn

**Now** adv., see also Current, Urgent
as soon as possible, at once, at present, at the moment, at the time of writing, at this moment in time, at the present, at the present moment, at this time, currently, here and now, in this day and age, in today's world, immediately, instantly, just now, now more than ever, nowadays, presently, promptly, right here right now, right now, straight away, these days, today

# O

**Objective** n., see also Ambition, Goal
aim, aspiration, desire, destination, determination, dream, end, end goal, endeavour, expectation, focus, hope, horizons, idea, intent, intention, mission, object, plan, point, purpose, sights, stated aim, target, vision, wish

**Obligation** n., see also Requirement, Responsibility
accountability, agreement, commitment, compulsion, constraint, contract, demand, duty, engagement, expectation, imperative, liability, must, necessity, need, onus, pledge, prerequisite, promise, stipulation, undertaking

**Obligatory** adj., see Essential
binding, compulsory, de rigueur, familiar, fundamental, imperative, indispensable, integral, invaluable, mandatory, matter of course, must, necessary, needed, obliged, required, requisite, standard, traditional, unavoidable, vital

**Obsolete** adj., see also Old, Previous
abandoned, anachronistic, ancient, antiquated, antique, archaic, behind the times, bygone, dated, defunct, dinosaur, discarded, discontinued, disused, extinct, has-been, no longer in use/needed, old-fashioned, old-hat, old-school, outmoded, out-of-date, out of fashion, out of style, over the hill, passé, past it, past its prime, replaced, superseded, surplus to requirements, thing of the past, time-worn, unfashionable, useless

**Obstacle** n., see also Challenge, Problem
bar, barrier, block, catch, deterrent, difficulty, disadvantage, disincentive, downside, drawback, encumbrance, hard nut to crack, hindrance, hitch, hurdle, impediment, mountain to climb, obstruction, setback, snag, stumbling block, tall order, test, trial, trouble, uphill battle/task

**Obstruct** v., see also Hamper, Prevent
bar, be a hindrance, block, check, curb, encumber, foil, frustrate, get in the way, hamstring, hobble, hold back, hold up, impede, inhibit, interfere, restrain, restrict, scupper, shackle, slow down, stand in the way of, stifle, stop, stymie, throw a spanner in the works, thwart, tie hands, veto, weigh down

**Obtain** v., see also Acquire, Purchase
access, accomplish, achieve, attain, bag, bring, capture, collect, come by, earn, elicit, extract, fetch, gain, garner, gather, generate, get, get hands on, get hold of, glean, grab, have, nab, net, pick up, procure, reach, reap, receive, recover, retrieve, score, scrape together, secure, seize, source, take, take delivery of, take possession of, welcome, win

**Obvious** adj., see also Clear, Of Course
anyone can see, apparent, black and white, blatant, blatantly obvious, blindingly obvious, blunt, clear as day(light), clear-cut, conclusive, conspicuous, crystal clear, discernible, distinct, distinguishable, does what it says on the tin, elephant in the room, evident, explicit, flagrant, glaring, go-to, impossible to miss, in evidence, incontrovertible, indisputable, inescapable, it goes without saying, manifest, natural, needless to say, no-brainer, noticeable, only natural, open-and-shut case, overt, palpable, patent, plain, plain to see, pronounced, resounding, self-evident, self-explanatory, speaks for itself, standing out like a sore thumb, stark, straightforward, telltale, transparent, undeniable, undisguised, unequivocal, unmistakable, unquestionable, visible

**Occur** v., see also Appear
arise, arrive, be afoot, be present, befall, come about, come into being, come to pass, crop up, develop, emerge, ensue, erupt, feature, follow (on from), go down, go on, happen, manifest itself, materialise, pan out, pass, present itself, proceed, rear its head, result, see happening, take effect, take place, transpire, turn out, turn up, unfold

**Of Course** adv./phr., see also Obvious
absolutely, as expected, as is well known, as you (may) know, assuredly, by all means, certainly, clearly, definitely, indeed, indubitably, it goes without saying, it is clear, it is true, naturally, needless to say, obviously, sure, surely, there can be no doubt, to state the obvious, undoubtedly, unquestionably, without (a) doubt, yes indeed

**Offer** n., see also Offering, Proposal
arrangement, attempt, bid, bidding, commitment, endeavour, offer on the table, overture, package, pitch, presentation, promise, proposition, quote, recommendation, submission, suggestion, tender, terms, value proposition

**Offer** v., see also Propose, Supply
accord, advance, advise, afford, allow, bid, bring, cite, come forward, come up with, comprise, contain, enable, extend, feature, furnish, give, give the

opportunity, grant, hand, include, introduce, make an offer, make a pitch, make available, make an offer, market, pitch, place at one's disposal, present, provide, put forth, put forward, put on the market, put on the table, recommend, sell, set out, show, submit, suggest, tender, volunteer

**Offering** n., see also Assortment, Range
business concept, collection, concept, market offering, market proposition, package, pitch, product range, proposal, proposition, provision, range of services, sales pitch, selection, USP, value proposition

**Offset** v., see also Balance, Lessen
allay, alleviate, appease, assuage, balance out, blunt, calm, cancel out, check, compensate (for), cool, counter, counteract, counterbalance, curb, cushion, dampen, diffuse, dilute, diminish, dull, ease, even out, lighten, make milder, make up for, mitigate, moderate, mollify, negate, neutralise, outweigh, pacify, placate, provide relief, rebalance, redress, reduce, reduce the force of, relieve, soften, subdue, take the edge off, take the heat out of, temper, tone down, weaken

**Old** adj., see also Obsolete, Previous
advanced in years, aged, ageing, age-old, ancient, antiquated, antique, archaic, behind the times, bygone, crumbling, dated, decayed, decrepit, dinosaur, elderly, enduring, established, experienced, extinct, familiar, feeling one's age, former, getting on (in years), hackneyed, has-been, legacy, lifelong, long-established, long in the tooth, long-lasting, long-standing, many moons ago, mature, no spring chicken, not new, not young, of long standing, of old, of yore, old as the hills, old-fashioned, old-hat, old guard, old-school, old-time, out of style, outdated, outmoded, out-of-date, over the hill, passé, past, past it, past its best, past one's prime, past its sell-by date, perennial, relic, rusty, seasoned, seen better days, senior, showing its age, sometime, stale, steeped in history, thing of the past, time-honoured, time-worn, tired, traditional, tried-and-tested, unfashionable, venerable, veteran, vintage, way back when, well-worn, wise, worn-out

**Online** adj., see also High-tech
app-based, at the tap/touch of a button/screen, at one's fingertips, cloud-based, connected, cyber, digital, digitalised, e-commerce, intelligent, interconnected, linked, mobile, networked, on social media, on the internet, on the web, on your phone, smart, streaming, virtual, web-based

**Operate** v., see also Manage, Work
act, administer, apply, be in business, be in charge, behave, bring about, carry out, conduct, control, deploy, direct, do, engage, exercise, function, handle, implement, organise, oversee, perform, proceed, produce, put into effect, put into operation, put in place, roll out, run, serve, supervise, take action, take measures, trade, undertake, use, utilise

**Operation(s)** n., see also Activity, Business
1. business activity, business operations, company, concern, corporation, dealings, enterprise, establishment, event, firm, industry, organisation, outfit, performance, procedure, proceeding(s), process, production, project, service, setup, undertaking, venture
2. administration, arrangements, command, control, deployment, exercise, implementation, management, organisation, roll-out, running, supervision

**Opinion** n., see also Approach, Belief
analysis, angle, appraisal, argument, assessment, attitude, comment, conclusion, consensus, considered opinion, consideration, conviction, estimation, feeling, idea, impression, in one's book, judgement, matter of opinion, mindset, notion, outlook, perception, perspective, philosophy, point of view, position, reaction, school of thought, sentiment, slant, stance, standpoint, supposition, take, theory, thinking, thought, vantage point, verdict, view, viewpoint, way of thinking

**Opportunity** n., see also Ability, Possibility
big moment, break, chance, circumstances, convenience, event, excuse, favourable circumstances/conditions, fighting chance, freedom, golden opportunity, good fortune, luck, lucky break, means, moment, occasion, opening, potential, promise, prospect, right time, room, scope, shot, space, stab, time, window of opportunity

**Oppose** v., see also Criticise, Reject
argue, attack, bar, battle, balk at, be an opponent of, be averse to, be hostile to, be opposed to, block, challenge, check, clash over, combat, confront, contest, contradict, counter, debate, defy, deny, disagree, disapprove, dislike, dispute, face down, fight, fight one's corner, go toe to toe, go head to head, hinder, object to, obstruct, prevent, protest, push back against/on, quarrel with, rebuff, resist, speak out against, square up to, stand in opposition to, stand in the way, stand up to, stifle, struggle against, stymie, take a stand against, take issue with, take on, thwart, veto, withstand

**Opposite** adj., see also Contrast, Different
antithesis, at odds, chalk and cheese, complete opposite, conflicting, contradiction, contradictory, contrary, contrasting, converse, counter, diametrically opposed, differing, dissimilar, flip side, hostile, incompatible, irreconcilable, night and day, odd bedfellows, odd couple, opposed, opposing, paradoxical, polar opposite, poles apart, reverse, rival, stark contrast, unlike, very opposite, world away from

**Opposition** n., see also Competition, Conflict
1. animosity, antagonism, argument, aversion, backlash, clash, combat, contention, deadlock, disagreement, disapproval, dislike, dismissal, dispute, feud, frosty reception, gripe, grumbles, hostility, impasse, misgivings, obstruction, outcry, prevention, rebellion, rejection, resentment, resistance, revolt, skirmish, struggle, tension(s), uproar, wrangle
2. adversary, arch-rival, competitor, contender, detractors, enemy, fierce rival, foe, nemesis, opponent, participant, rival, rivalry, sworn enemy

**Optimise** v., see also Develop, Improve
advance, amend, augment, beef up, boost, calibrate, correct, edit, elevate, enhance, get right, hone, improve on, increase, maximise, overhaul, perfect, polish, raise, raise one's game, reboot, reconfigure, rectify, refine, reform, restore, revamp, review, revise, revisit, sharpen, step up, straighten out, strengthen, switch up, take to the next level, tighten up, turn around, tweak, update, upgrade

**Optimistic** adj., see also Confident, Positive
assured, boding well, bold, bright, bright-eyed and bushy-tailed, brimming with optimism, bullish, buoyant, can-do, cheerful, encouraged, encouraging, enthusiastic, expectant, focusing on the positives, glass half full, glimmer of hope, having cause for optimism, heartened, heartening, hopeful, keeping the faith, light at the end of the tunnel, looking forward, looking on the bright side, promising, raring to go, rosy, silver lining, sky's the limit, sunny, sounding a note of optimism, taking a favourable view, upbeat, with rose-tinted glasses

**Optimum** adj., see also Best, Good
choice, choicest, elite, excellent, exceptional, finest, first-class, first-rate, flawless, foremost, greatest, highest, ideal, impeccable, incomparable, leading, matchless, maximum, most favourable, of choice, optimal, optimised, outstanding, peak, peerless, perfect, pinnacle, pre-eminent, premium, second to none, select, stellar, strongest, superlative, supreme, top, top-flight, ultimate,

unmatched, unparalleled, unrivalled, unsurpassed, utmost, very best, world-class, world-leading

**Option** n., see also Choice, Flexibility
add-on, advantage, alternative, another, assortment, avenue, backup, benefit, contingency, diversity, entitlement, equivalent, flip side, offering, opportunity, other options, plan B, possibility, preference, range of options, replacement, right, scope, selection, substitute, variety

**Order** v., see also Buy, Instruct
1. apply for, arrange, ask for, book, call for, demand, obtain, organise, place an order, purchase, request, require, reserve, secure, select, sort, specify, stipulate
2. authorise, call for, charge, command, commission, compel, demand, dictate, direct, enact, enjoin, mandate, mobilise, organise, prescribe, require, rule, stipulate, tell

**Ordinary** adj., see also Regular, Standard
accepted, accustomed, banal, bog-standard, bread and butter, business as usual, classic, common-or-garden, commonplace, conventional, customary, default, established, everyday, expected, familiar, general, habitual, mainstream, meat and drink, moderate, natural, no great shakes, normal, not bad, nothing special, orthodox, par for the course, pedestrian, plain, plain-vanilla, prevalent, prevailing, rank-and-file, routine, run-of-the-mill, simple, standard-issue, staple, stock, traditional, typical, undistinguished, unexceptional, uninspiring, unremarkable, usual, widespread, workaday

**Organisation** n., see also Business, Company
1. alliance, association, body, club, coalition, concern, configuration, corporation, employer, enterprise, entity, establishment, federation, firm, group, institution, operator, outfit, setup, structure, unit
2. arrangement, assembly, categorisation, classification, composition, configuration, coordination, design, establishment, format, formation, framework, grouping, hierarchy, logistics, make-up, management, operation, order, organisational structure, organising, planning, regulation, setup, structure, system, unity

**Organise** v., see also Lead, Manage
administer, allocate, arrange, be responsible for, bring together, call the shots, catalogue, choreograph, classify, command, compose, construct, control, coordinate, create, devise, engineer, ensure, establish, formulate, get together, guide, handle, harmonise, index, institute, juggle, line up, look after, marshal,

mastermind, mobilise, officiate, operate, orchestrate, oversee, pilot, prepare, put in order, put in place, put on, put together, rally, regulate, run, schedule, see to, set up, shape, shepherd, steer, steward, supervise, systematise, take care of, take charge, watch over, whip into shape

**Outcome** n., see also Effect, Performance
after-effect, aftermath, benefit, bottom line, by-product, chain reaction, conclusion, consequence, culmination, development, end, end product, end result, event, fallout, finding(s), fruit(s), fruition, impact, implication(s), influence, knock-on effect, payback, pay-off, product, ramifications, reaction, repercussion, result, return, reverberations, side effect, significance, thrust, upshot, verdict, wake

**Outlook** n., see also Attitude, Forecast
1. anticipation, assumption, estimate, estimation, expectation(s), forecast, future, future prospects, hope, indications, lie of the land, likelihood, possibility, potential, prediction, probability, prognosis, projection, promise, prospect(s), scenario, signs, spectre, speculation
2. approach, belief, culture, direction, disposition, ethos, frame of mind, ideology, mentality, mindset, perspective, point of view, position, scope, stance, standpoint, take, values, viewpoint, vision, way of thinking, world view

**Outstanding** adj., see also Impressive, Successful
ace, admirable, amazing, astonishing, astounding, attractive, award-winning, awe-inspiring, awesome, beacon of, best, break-out, breathtaking, brilliant, celebrated, choice, cracking, distinguished, excellent, exceptional, exemplary, exquisite, extraordinaire, extraordinary, fab, fabulous, fantastic, fine, finest, first-class, first-rate, five-star, flagship, flawless, foremost, formidable, glorious, gorgeous, great, high-class, hit, ideal, illustrious, impeccable, incomparable, invaluable, jaw-dropping, leading, legendary, magic, magical, magnificent, mind-blowing, must-have/read/see, notable, on a roll, on fire, on form, optimal, out of this world, peerless, phenomenal, pre-eminent, premier, premium, prestigious, priceless, remarkable, (it) rocks, second to none, sensational, smash-hit, smashing, spectacular, standout, state-of-the-art, stellar, sterling, striking, stunning, superb, superior, superlative, supreme, terrific, top, top-flight, top-notch, ultimate, unequalled, unparalleled, unrivalled, unsurpassed, very best, wonderful, world-class

**Overestimate** v., see also Exaggerate
aggrandise, blow out of proportion, boost, distort, dramatise, embellish, embroider, expect too much of, get carried away, get wrong, go overboard, go

too far, hype, inflate, magnify, make too much of, miscalculate, misconstrue, misinterpret, misjudge, mislead, misread, overcook, overdo, overemphasise, overplay, overrate, oversell, overstate, overvalue, place too much emphasis on, rate too highly

**Owing To** phr., see also Therefore

as, as a result of, attributable to, because of, caused by, by dint of, by reason of, by virtue of, courtesy of, driven by, due to, for that reason, fuelled by, given, in light of, in view of, now that, on account of, on the back of, on the grounds that, resulting from, since, thanks to, through

**Own** v., see also Buy, Invest

be a shareholder, be in possession of, be responsible for, be the owner of, become the owner of, belong to, boast, buy out, buy up, control, co-own, dominate, enjoy, gain control of, have, have control of, have in one's ownership, have in one's possession, have to one's name, hold, keep, own a shareholding/stake in, possess, retain ownership, take over, take possession of

**Owner** n., see also Investor

beneficial owner, business owner, buyer, co-owner, founder, holder, joint owner, landlord, landowner, magnate, partner, property owner, proprietor, purchaser, shareholder, stockholder, titleholder, tycoon

**Ownership** n., see also Acquisition, Investment

buy-out, claim, control, controlling interest, co-ownership, dominion, holding, interest, participation, partnership, possession, property, purchase, rights, shareholding, slice, stake, takeover, title

# P

**Part** n., see also Aspect, Feature
area, bit, bite, chunk, component, constituent, contribution, detail, division, element, facet, factor, fraction, fragment, ingredient, interest, involvement, measure, niche, part and parcel, piece, portion, proportion, quota, role, section, sector, segment, share, slice, sliver, splinter, stake, tranche, unit, wedge

**Participate** v., see also Engage, Help
add to, aid, assist, attend, be a participant, be active in, be (a) party to, be a stakeholder in, be included in, be involved, be part of, be present, bring to the party/table, chip in, collaborate, compete, contribute, cooperate, embrace, feature, get involved, have a hand in, join in, lend a hand, partake, play a part/role, share, take an interest in, take part

**Particular** adj., see also Notable, Specific
appropriate, certain, defined, distinct, distinguishing, exact, exceptional, explicit, express, important, individual, intrinsic, marked, noteworthy, painstaking, peculiar, pet, precise, remarkable, respective, separate, signature, significant, singular, special, specialised, specialist, unique, unmistakable, unusual

**Particularly** adv., see also Very
above all, all the more, chiefly, decidedly, distinctly, especially, exceptionally, expressly, extraordinarily, in particular, individually, mainly, markedly, not least, notably, peculiarly, primarily, principally, pronounced, quintessentially, remarkably, singularly, specially, specifically, surprisingly, to say the least, tremendously, undoubtedly, uniquely, unquestionably, unusually

**Partnership** n., see also Business, Collaboration
affiliation, alliance, amalgam, amalgamation, arrangement, association, blend, combination, company, conjunction, cooperation, hook-up, joining, joint effort, marriage, merger, organisation, ownership, pairing, participation, partnering, relationship, sharing, tandem, team, teaming-up, teamwork, tie-up, union, working together

**Passionate** adj., see also Committed, Enthusiastic
ardent, believer in, believing passionately in, burning, champion, crusader, deep, devoted, die-hard, eager, emotional, energised, excited, fanatical, fervent, fierce, fire in the belly, fired up, having a passion for, heartfelt, impassioned, indefatigable, indomitable, intense, invested in, irrepressible, keen, obsessive, proponent of, sincere, single-minded, spirited, staunch, steadfast, stirring, strong, strong believer in, supporter of, tenacious, unflinching, unswerving, unwavering, vehement, wedded to, zealous

**Past** n., see also Experience, History
back in the day, back story, background, bygone era, career to date, days gone by, days of old, days of yore, dim and distant past, (past) form, former glory, former life, good old days, heritage, hindsight, historical events, history books, legacy, life story, living memory, long ago, looking back, old times, olden days, past events, past glories, past life, past performance, past times, previous, record(s), times past, water under the bridge, way back when, years ago, yesterday, yesteryear

**Pay** n., see also Job, Money
commission, compensation, earnings, fee(s), income, pay day, pay packet, payment, payroll, proceeds, recompense, reimbursement, remuneration, reward, salary, settlement, take-home (pay), wage bill, wage packet, wages

**Pay** v., see also Benefit, Buy
advance, bear the cost, chip in, compensate, contribute, cough up, cover (the cost), disburse, foot the bill/cost, fork out, grant, hand over, honour, invest, make payment, meet, offer, open one's chequebook, open one's wallet, pay off, pay out, pay up, pick up the bill/tab, put one's hand in one's pocket, recompense, refund, reimburse, remunerate, repay, reward, settle, shell out, spend, stump up, take care of

**Peak** n., see also Best
all-time high, apex, climax, crest, culmination, height, high point, highest level, highest point, maximum, pinnacle, record, record high, summit, tip, top, zenith

**Penalise** v., see also Criticise, Punish
castigate, chastise, come down hard on, condemn, disadvantage, discipline, dock, fine, hit with a fine/penalty, impose a fine, impose a penalty, levy a fine/penalty, put at a disadvantage, rap on the knuckles, reprove, slap with a fine/penalty, teach a lesson, throw the book at, treat unfairly

**Perfect** adj., see also Accurate, Best
absolute, appropriate, apt, bang on, best choice, beyond reproach, bullseye, can't fault it, classic, complete, consummate, correct, dead on, dream, exact, excellent, exemplary, expert, faithful, faultless, first-rate, flawless, foolproof, holy grail, icing on the cake, ideal, immaculate, impeccable, inimitable, just the job/thing/ticket, last word, matchless, masterpiece, mint condition, not putting a foot wrong, on the button, on the money, optimal, optimum, paragon, peerless, perfect balance, perfect combination, perfect condition, perfect harmony, perfect match, perfection, pinnacle, pitch-perfect, precise, pure, second to none, sheer perfection, spot on, spotless, strict, sublime, suitable, superb, supreme, sweet spot, ten out of ten, textbook, ticking all the boxes, to a T, ultimate, unadulterated, unbeatable, unblemished, uncompromising, unerring, unimpaired, unmarred, unmitigated, unparalleled, unspoilt, untainted, untarnished, utter, very best

**Perform** v., see also Do, Fulfil
accomplish, achieve, acquit oneself, act, action, apply, attain, behave, bring about, bring to fruition, carry out, carry to completion, complete, conduct, deliver, deliver the goods, deploy, discharge, effect, execute, fare, finish, function, generate, implement, impress, operate, post, pull off, realise, record, roll out, satisfy, step up (to the mark/plate), take action, take measures, transact, undertake, work

**Performance** n., see Achievement, Implementation
accomplishment, action, attainment, completion, conduct, earnings performance, effectiveness, efficiency, efforts, endeavours, enforcement, execution, exercise, exploits, feat, form, fortunes, fulfilment, functioning, level (of performance), operation, profit(s), prowess, pursuit, realisation, record, result(s), rich vein of form, run of form, sales performance, showing, track record, triumph, victory, work

**Permanent** adj., see also Continual, Long-term
24/7, abiding, always, ceaseless, come rain or shine, constant, continuous, endless, enduring, entrenched, eternal, ever-present, everlasting, fixed, for keeps, for the long haul, forever, in perpetuity, indefinite, indelible, invariable, lasting, long-lasting, long-lived, never-ending, perennial, permanent fixture, perpetual, persistent, relentless, set in stone, since time immemorial, stable, standing the test of time, steadfast, sustained, unbroken, unchanging, undimmed, undying, unending, uninterrupted, unremitting

**Permission** n., see also Approval, Authorisation
acceptance, acknowledgment, admission, agreement, assent, authority, backing, blessing, carte blanche, concession, consent, dispensation, endorsement, freedom, go-ahead, green light, leave, liberty, licence, mandate, nod, okay, permit, privilege, promise, recognition, rights, sanction, scope, stamp of approval, thumbs up, validation, verification

**Permit** v., see also Enable, Help
accept, acknowledge, admit, agree to, allow, approve, assent to, authorise, concede, condone, consent to, empower, endorse, give/grant one's blessing, give/grant permission, give the go-ahead, give the green light, give the nod, give the okay, give the thumbs up, go along with, grant, grant permission, green-light, indulge, let, license, make possible, okay, open the door, provide the opportunity, provide the scope, recognise, relent, rubber-stamp, sanction, stand by, say yes, sign off on, tolerate, wave through

**Personnel** n., see also Employee, Worker
associates, colleagues, co-workers, crew, employees, headcount, human resources, key employees, manpower, members of staff, men and women, operatives, organisation, peers, people, representatives, staff (members), team, talent, workers, workforce

**Perspective** n., see also Approach, Opinion
angle, attitude, belief, ethos, frame of reference, impression, mentality, mindset, outlook, overview, philosophy, point of view, position, slant, stance, standpoint, style, take, thinking, vantage, vantage point, view, viewpoint, way of looking/thinking

**Persuade** v., see also Advise, Influence
argue, assure, bring round, bring someone to their senses, bulldoze, cajole, coax, convert, convince, demonstrate, encourage, enlist, entice, exhort, impress upon, incentivise, induce, inspire, lead, lure, make a case for, motivate, prevail upon, prompt, reassure, satisfy, seduce, sell, strong-arm, suggest, sway, talk into, talk round, twist someone's arm, urge, use a carrot-and-stick approach, wage a charm offensive, wear down, win the argument, win hearts and minds, win over, woo

**Pessimistic** adj., see also Negative
bearish, bleak, clouds on the horizon, concerned, cynical, dark, defeatist, dejected, depressed, despairing, despondent, discouraged, discouraging,

disenchanted, disheartened, dismal, doom and gloom, doom-laden, doom-monger, down on, downbeat, downcast, downhearted, expecting the worst, fearful, foreboding, glass half empty, gloomy, glum, grim, naysayer, not boding well, not bright, not encouraging, not hopeful, not looking good, not optimistic, not positive, not promising, ominous, resigned, sceptical, worried

**Phase** n., see also Development, Progress
chapter, cycle, juncture, lap, leg, level, milestone, moment, period, point, point in time, point of the process, position, round, quarter, season, spell, stage, stage of development, stage of the process, staging post, state, step, term, time

**Pioneer** n., see also Expert, Inventor
architect, brains behind, champion, creator, crusader, designer, developer, discoverer, early adopter, first, founder, founding father, genius, groundbreaker, innovator, instigator, leader, originator, trailblazer, trendsetter, visionary

**Pioneer** v., see also Innovate, Introduce
be at the forefront, be in the vanguard, be the first, begin, blaze a trail, break new ground, champion, change the face of, change the game, conceive, create, develop, discover, drive, envisage, establish, found, harness, inaugurate, initiate, inspire, instigate, institute, introduce, invent, kick-start, launch, lay the foundations, lay the groundwork, lead the way, originate, oversee, pave the way, preside over, push the envelope, set up, shape, show the way, spawn, spearhead, start, take the lead, think outside the box, usher in

**Place** n., see also Area
bearings, district, environment, geographical position, locale, locality, location, neck of the woods, neighbourhood, point, position, property, region, scene, section, setting, site, situation, spot, territory, venue, vicinity, whereabouts, zone

**Plan** n., see also Approach, Organisation
action plan, agenda, aim, arrangement, blueprint, course of action, deal, design(s), foresight, forethought, formula, framework, game plan, hope, idea, initiative, intent, intention, layout, master plan, method, outline, plan of action, planning, playbook, policy, procedure, programme, project, proposal, road map, scenario, schedule, scheme, stratagem, strategy, structure, suggestion, system, tactics, undertaking, wheeze

**Plan** v., see also Consider, Organise
aim, arrange, brainstorm, calculate, chart (a course), come up with a plan, concoct, contemplate, cook up, design, devise, draft, draw up a plan, engineer, envisage, establish a plan, figure out, foresee, formulate, gear up for, guide, hatch a plan, have a plan, have designs on, have in mind, have in the pipeline, hope, intend, invent, look to, make arrangements, manage, mastermind, orchestrate, outline, oversee, plot, plot a course, prepare, put together, set a timetable, set out, sketch out, supervise, take care of, take charge, think up, wargame, work out

**Pleasant** adj., see also Enjoyable, Good
acceptable, admirable, affable, agreeable, amiable, attractive, brilliant, charming, commendable, considerate, cordial, courteous, decent, delightful, endearing, engaging, entertaining, fab, fabulous, favourable, fine, friendly, genial, good-natured, great, heart-warming, helpful, inviting, kind, likeable, lovely, nice, pleasing, pleasurable, satisfactory, welcome

**Pleased** adj., see also Positive
all smiles, appreciative, chuffed, content, contented, delighted, ecstatic, elated, euphoric, excited, glad, grateful, gratified, happy, heartened, honoured, in high spirits, jubilant, no complaints, over the moon, overjoyed, pleased as punch, proud, psyched, satisfied, smug, thankful, thrilled, tickled pink

**Pledge** n., see also Commitment, Guarantee
agreement, assurance, collateral, confirmation, covenant, firm commitment, oath, pact, promise, security, sincere commitment, surety, undertaking, verification, vow, warranty, word, word of honour

**Plenty** pron., see also Extensive, Large
a lot, abounding, abundance, abundant, acres, all manner, ample, aplenty, array, awash, back to back, bags, boundless, bountiful, brimming, bristling, buckets of, bundles of, bursting, by the truckload, chock-a-block, chock-full, colossal amount, considerable, copious, countless, crammed with, deluge, deluged, depth, dizzying (amounts of), dozens, droves, embarrassment, en masse, endless, excess, exuding, fair few, feast, ***** fest, filled with, flood, flurry, frequent, full of, galore, glut, goldmine, good deal, great amount of, great deal, host, huge quantity, hundreds, in abundance, in force, in numbers, in spades, influx, innumerable, inundated, jam-packed, kaleidoscope, large amount, large numbers, lashings, legion, loaded with, loads, lots, many, many a, masses, millions, mine of, more than enough, mountain, multiple, multitude, myriad, no

end, no shortage, number, numerous, oodles, oozing, packed with, panoply, plentiful, plethora, profuse, profusion, proliferation, quantities, raft, range, reams, rich vein of, rife, scores, series of, slew, spades, spate, spoilt for choice, stacks, stream, string, succession, surfeit, swathes, teeming, thousands, tonnes, torrent, treasure trove, umpteen, untold (amounts of), wall-to-wall, wave, wealth, whole host, wide range, widespread

**Policy** n., see also Approach, Regulation
arrangement, belief, code, core values, course of action, framework, guideline(s), initiative, line, manifesto, method, plan, plan of action, position, practice, principle(s), procedure, programme, proposal(s), protocol, requirement, rule(s), scheme, solution, stance, standpoint, strategy, system, tactics, take, values, view

**Poor** adj., see also Deficient
1. below par, crummy, dire, disappointing, dismal, dubious, dysfunctional, feeble, found wanting, hapless, ill-equipped, impaired, imperfect, inadequate, ineffective, inefficient, inferior, insufficient, lacking, lacklustre, lamentable, low-grade, low-quality, lukewarm, meagre, mediocre, no great shakes, not fit for purpose, not up to scratch, poor-quality, remiss, ropey, scrappy, second-rate, shabby, shambolic, shoddy, slapdash, sorry, subpar, substandard, suspect, unacceptable, underperforming, unfortunate, uninspiring, unproductive, unsatisfactory, wanting, woeful
2. badly off, bankrupt, broke, cash-strapped, deprived, destitute, disadvantaged, empty-handed, fallen on hard times, hard-up, impoverished, in financial difficulties, in need, in straitened circumstances, insolvent, meagre, needy, not well off, on the breadline, penniless, poverty-stricken, skint, strapped for cash, struggling financially, struggling to get by, unable to make ends meet, underprivileged

**Popular** adj., see also Stylish, Successful
à la mode, accepted, accessible, acclaimed, admired, adopted, adored, all the rage, attractive, beloved, best-loved, booming, capturing people's/the popular imagination, catching on, celebrated, cherished, common, contemporary, conventional, crowd-pleasing, darling, desired, endearing oneself, everybody's talking about, familiar, fashionable, favoured, favourite, feted, flavour of the month, gaining currency, gaining traction, general, high-profile, highly regarded, hot, hot property, idolised, in, in demand, in fashion, in favour, in style, in thing, in use, in vogue, latest, leading, liked, mainstream, much-anticipated, much-loved, much-vaunted, must-have, must-see, national

treasure, (very) now, on trend, popularised, preferred, prevailing, prevalent, prominent, renowned, rising star, sought-after, standard, superstar, sweetheart, treasured, trendy, ubiquitous, up-and-coming, well-known, well-liked, well-received, well-regarded, well-thought-of, widespread

**Positive** adj., see also Good, Optimistic
advantageous, affirmative, assured, attractive, beneficial, bullish, can-do, categorical, certain, confident, constructive, convinced, decisive, definitive, effective, emphatic, enthusiastic, favourable, feel-good, forward-looking, healthy, helpful, in a good place, invaluable, optimistic, proactive, productive, progressive, strong, successful, sure, sure-footed, upbeat, uplifting, useful, valuable, welcome, worthwhile

**Possibility** n., see also Ability, Opportunity
chance, circumstance, conceivability, contingency, eventuality, every chance, feasibility, fighting chance, good chance, hope, liability, likelihood, means, odds, off-chance, option, outside chance, permutations, plausibility, potential, practicability, probability, promise, prospect(s), resources, risk, scenario, scope, shot, spectre, stab, viability, workability

**Possible** adj., see also Easy, Probable
accessible, achievable, advisable, anticipated, attainable, available, believable, conceivable, credible, desirable, doable, entirely possible, feasible, future, hopeful, hypothetical, imaginable, liable, likely, not beyond the bounds of possibility, not impossible, obtainable, plausible, potential, practicable, promising, prospective, realisable, sky's the limit, thinkable, up for grabs, viable, within reach, within the realm(s) of possibility, workable, would-be

**Potential** adj., see also Future, Possible
aspiring, budding, conceivable, embryonic, fledgling, having (all) the makings of, having what it takes, hopeful, imminent, impending, in the making, in waiting, latent, likely, looming, nascent, plausible, probable, promising, prospective, rising, threatening, undeveloped, unrealised, untapped, up for grabs, viable, within the realm(s) of possibility, would-be

**Potential** n., see also Possibility
ability, all the makings, bright future, capability, capacity, chance, good chance, makings, opportunity, permutations, promise, prospect(s), what it takes, wherewithal

**Power** n., see also Authority, Strength
ability, authorisation, balance of power, bastion, brawn, capability, capacity, clout, command, competence, connections, control, dominance, domination, drive, driving force, dynamism, effectiveness, energy, firepower, force, force to be reckoned with, forcefulness, grip, heavyweight, influence, intensity, juggernaut, jurisdiction, leadership, licence, mastery, might, muscle, omnipotence, potency, potential, power grab, powerhouse, predominance, prestige, primacy, resilience, robustness, rule, skill, superiority, supremacy, sway, titan, tower of strength, upper hand, vigour, vitality, weight

**Powerful** adj., see also Important, Large
all-powerful, almighty, assertive, authoritarian, authoritative, capable, commanding, compelling, controlling, dominant, dynamic, effective, firm, force to be reckoned with, forceful, formidable, having the upper hand, heavy-duty, high-powered, impactful, impressive, in control, indestructible, influential, mighty, muscular, omnipotent, overwhelming, persuasive, potent, reinforced, resilient, robust, rugged, ruling, significant, solid, steadfast, strong, strong-willed, sturdy, supreme, titanic, vigorous, weighty, with authority

**Praise** n., see also Approval, Success
acclaim, accolade, admiration, adulation, applause, appreciation, approval, brownie points, commendation, compliment(s), congratulations, credit, flattery, endorsement, glory, homage, kudos, ovation, pat on the back, plaudits, positive feedback, recognition, recommendation, shout-out, thanks, tribute

**Praise** v., see also Congratulate, Thank
acclaim, acknowledge, admire, advocate, applaud, appreciate, approve of, be impressed by, celebrate, commend, compliment, endorse, eulogise about, exalt, extol (the virtues of), flatter, give a glowing report of, give credit, hail, heap praise on, honour, hype, laud, lead tributes, make much of, pay homage to, pay tribute to, proclaim, rave about, recognise, recommend, salute, sing the praises of, shout out to, shower with praise, take one's hat off to, talk about in glowing terms, talk up, treasure, value, vaunt, wax lyrical about

**Precise** adj., see Accurate, Specific
bang on, careful, categorical, clear, clear-cut, conscientious, correct, dead on, definite, detailed, distinct, dotting the i's and crossing the t's, exact, explicit, faultless, limited, meticulous, narrow, on the button, on the money, on the nose, painstaking, particular, perfect, picky, proper, right, rigorous, scrupulous, spot on, strict, stringent, to a T, to the letter, true, uncompromising, unequivocal, very, well-defined, with pinpoint accuracy

**Predict** v., see also Estimate, Expect
anticipate, assess, augur, be hopeful, believe, bet, bode, call it, come as no surprise, conjecture, count on, divine, forecast, foresee, foreshadow, foretell, forewarn, gauge, give a foretaste of, guess, have a feeling, have a hunch, hazard a guess, herald, hint, hope for, infer, look ahead to, look forward to, make a forecast/prediction, plan on, pre-empt, prepare for, presage, project, prophesy, read the runes, reason, second-guess, see, see coming, speculate, take a guess, think likely, tip, watch for

**Prediction** n., see also Estimate, Expectation
analysis, anticipation, assumption, best guess, bet, big call, budget, calculation, call, crystal ball, estimation, feeling, forecast, foresight, forewarning, guess, guesstimate, gut feeling, hope, hunch, outlook, planning, prognosis, projection, smart money, speculation, suspicion, tip

**Preparation** n., see also Action, Introduction
alertness, anticipation, arrangement(s), arranging, build-up, contingency planning, countdown, development, dress rehearsal, dry run, foresight, foundation, gearing up, getting ready, groundwork, homework, lead time, making ready, organisation, organising, plan(s), planning, practice, precaution, preparations, preparatory measures, preparedness, preparing, provision(s), readiness, rehearsal, safeguard, setting up, spadework, training

**Prepare** v., see also Organise, Plan
accommodate, adapt, adjust, anticipate, arrange, assemble, batten down the hatches, be prepared, brace for, buckle up, build up, cover the bases, develop, draw up, equip, formulate, fortify, future-proof, gear up, get in order, get into shape, get ready, get set, get up to speed, gird one's loins, hatch a plan, lay the foundations, lay the groundwork, limber up, make preparations, make provision, make ready, muster, outfit, pave the way, position, practise, prep, put in a good position, put in order, put together, ready, rehearse, set up, stand in good stead, stand ready, steel (oneself), strengthen, train

**Prepared** adj., see also Effective, Efficient
able, accessible, adapted, all bases covered, all set, all systems go, anticipating, armed with, arranged, at hand, at one's fingertips, at the ready, available, braced, champing at the bit, completed, eager, enthusiastic, equipped, fit, game, good to go, having a strong basis/platform, ideally placed, in good shape, in order, in place, in position, in readiness, itching to, keen, on call, on guard, on standby, organised, planned, poised, prepped, primed, psyched, raring to go, ***** ready (*e.g. Christmas ready*), ready, ready for anything, ready to go,

rehearsed, set, set fair, set up, stage is set, up and running, up for, waiting, well-drilled, well-equipped, well-positioned, well-prepared, willing

**Present** v., see also Demonstrate, Introduce
announce, award, bestow, cite, confer, display, exhibit, front, give, give a presentation/talk, give an introduction, hand out, hand over, launch, make a pitch, make a presentation, offer, pitch, proffer, proudly present, put before, put forth, put forward, put on, raise the curtain on, release, report, reveal, set forth, set out, show, showcase, show off, spin, stage, submit, take the wraps off, tender, unveil

**Presentation** n., see also Analysis, Report
appearance, big reveal, delivery, demonstration, design, disclosure, display, exhibition, introduction, launch, layout, lecture, offering, performance, pitch, portrayal, production, proposal, proposition, reception, release, reporting, representation, sales pitch, setting, setting out, show, showcase, speech, styling, submission, talk, unveiling

**Pressure** n., see also Challenge, Problem
adversity, albatross (around one's neck), anticipation, attention, burden, clock ticking, coercion, compulsion, constraint, demands, difficulties, duress, expectation, force, hardship, hassle, heat, load, millstone, persuasion, squeeze, squeezing, staring down the barrel, strain, stress, tension, time pressure, trouble, urgency, weight (*e.g. of expectation, of history*), workload

**Pressure** v., see also Force, Persuade
bring pressure to bear on, browbeat, bully, cajole, coerce, compel, convince, drive, exert pressure, exhort, expect (great things), insist, hold someone's feet to the fire, lean on, pile pressure on, press, push around, push, put pressure on, put under pressure, railroad, ramp up pressure on, rush, squeeze, strong-arm, sway, turn the screw, turn up the heat, twist someone's arm, urge, weigh on

**Prevent** v., see also Avoid, Stop
arrest, avert, bar, block, check, clamp down on, combat, crack down on, counter, curb, defend against, derail, deter, disable, foil, forbid, forestall, frustrate, guard against, hamper, head off, hinder, hold back, hold off, impede, inhibit, keep from, knock on the head, nip in the bud, obstruct, preclude, prohibit, put a stop to, put an end to, put paid to, restrain, restrict, rule out, safeguard against, scotch, scupper, shut down, sideline, sidetrack, stamp out, stand in the way of, stave off, step in, stifle, stymie, thwart, torpedo, turn the tide, veto, ward off

**Previous** adj., see also Obsolete, Old
abovementioned, aforementioned, bygone, earlier, erstwhile, ex-*****, former, historical, last, legacy, of old, one-time, out-of-date, outdated, outgoing, past, preceding, predecessor, prior, sometime

**Price** n., see also Cost, Value
amount, asking price, bill, charge, consideration, damage, estimate, expenditure, expense, fee, figure, money, outlay, payment, price band, price point, price tag, pricing, quotation, quote, rate, tariff, toll, valuation, worth

**Principal** adj., see also Important, Key
all-important, basic, biggest, cardinal, central, central plank, chief, core, cornerstone, critical, crucial, defining, definitive, dominant, essential, first (and foremost), flagship, foremost, fundamental, go-to, head, instrumental, integral, keynote, landmark, largest, leading, linchpin, main, mainstay, major, most important, outstanding, overriding, predominant, pre-eminent, premier, prevailing, primary, prime, priority, significant, standout, star, strongest, top, underlying

**Principle** n., see also Approach, Belief
assumption, attitude, axiom, basic principle, basic rule, basis, code, concept, convention, core value, creed, criterion, decency, dictum, doctrine, dogma, ethic(s), formula, foundation, fundamental principle, golden rule, ideal(s), ideology, integrity, law, mantra, maxim, mentality, mindset, morality, morals, position, regulation, rule, rule of thumb, scruples, standard(s), teaching, tenet, theory, value

**Prioritise** v., see also Emphasise, Focus On
accentuate, bring to the fore, concentrate on, consider important, give centre stage, give precedence, give pride of place to, give priority to, give prominence to, highlight, home in on, major on, place importance on, place the emphasis on, prefer, put at the top of the agenda, put first, put front and centre, put the onus on, reiterate, shine a light on, showcase, spotlight, stress, underline, underscore, zero in on

**Priority** n., see also Focus, Importance
centre stage, emphasis, first place, greatest importance, immediate concern, key priority, main concern, most pressing issue, number one priority, onus, paramount importance, precedence, preference, pride of place, primacy, primary concern, prime concern, prime issue, priority issue, prominence, stress, thrust, top of the agenda, urgency

**Private** adj., see also Confidential
behind the scenes, cards close to one's chest, classified, closed-off, concealed, coy, discreet, hushed up, hush-hush, in privacy, in private, inaccessible, independent, individual, inside, intimate, keeping oneself to oneself, non-public, not open, off the record, personal, privately owned, reserved, secret, secretive, separate, under one's hat, undisclosed

**Prize** n., see also Achievement, Win
accolade, award, best, citation, decision, distinction, feather in the cap, first place, first prize, gong, honour, judges' decision, medal, nomination, number one, praise, presentation, ranking, recognition, result, reward, silverware, title, top prize, top ranking, triumph, trophy, verdict, victory

**Probable** adj., see also Future, Potential
anticipated, believable, bound to happen, chances are, conceivable, credible, expected, every chance, feasible, foregone conclusion, hopeful, in all likelihood, in all probability, in the offing, liable, likely, most likely, odds-on, on the cards, plausible, predicted, presumable, reasonable/safe bet, set to, slated

**Problem** n., see also Challenge, Issue
adversity, bind, bump in the road, burden, can of worms, case, catch, complication, concern, conundrum, crisis, crunch, curveball, deep water, difficulty, dilemma, disagreement, doubt, downside, drawback, enigma, episode, fiasco, fix, fly in the ointment, glitch, gremlin, headache, headwind, heart of the problem, hiccup, hitch, hot potato, hot water, hurdle, ill, impasse, incident, inconvenience, issue at hand, matter at hand, mess, millstone, misfortune, nightmare, nub of the problem, nuisance, obstacle, ordeal, Pandora's box, perfect storm, pickle, pitfall, plight, predicament, puzzle, quandary, question, question mark, reality check, riddle, rub, scourge, setback, situation, spanner in the works, speed bump, sticking point, struggle, stumbling block, teething problems, thorn in the side, tight spot, travails, trials and tribulations, tribulation, trouble, turbulence, turmoil, wobble, woes, worry

**Procedure** n., see also Method, System
action, arrangement, approach, course, course of action, creative process, drill, form, formula, framework, game plan, guidelines, measures, mechanism, methodology, operation, plan, plan of action, policy, practice, proceeding, process, programme, route, routine, scheme, setup, step, strategy, style, technique, way

**Proceed** v., see also Continue, Start
advance, carry on, carry out, crack on, develop, follow, forge ahead, full speed/steam ahead, get going, get on with, get underway, go ahead, issue, make a start, make headway, make progress, move forward, press on, progress, pursue, push ahead, put in place, put into action, roll out, set in motion, take action, take the next step, undertake

**Process** n., see also Method, System
action, approach, arrangement, course, course of action, creative process, drill, evolution, form, formula, game plan, guidelines, manner, measures, mechanism, methodology, operation, plan, plan of action, policy, practice, procedure, proceeding, programme, progression, route, routine, scheme, setup, step, strategy, style, technique, way

**Produce** v., see also Create, Manufacture
assemble, bring about, bring out, bring to life, build, cause, churn out, come up with, complete, compose, conceive, concoct, conjure up, construct, craft, cultivate, custom-build, deliver, demonstrate, design, develop, devise, dream up, engender, engineer, establish, generate, give rise to, handcraft, handmake, have in the works, innovate, introduce, invent, launch, lead to, make, make for, mass-produce, offer, present, produce on a large scale, provide, provoke, pump out, put together, reap, result in, roll off the production line, show, spark, spawn, supply, tailor, trigger, turn out, yield

**Product** n., see also Offering, Result
article, by-product, creation, end product, end result, flagship product, goods, handiwork, invention, item, merchandise, offering, output, package, produce, product range, service, stock, unit

**Production** n., see also Activity, Work
assembly, business, construction, crafting, creation, design, development, formulation, generation, making, manufacture, manufacturing, operation(s), output, preparation, production business, production line, production operations, putting together, turning out

**Professional** adj., see also Efficient, Experienced
able, adept, authorised, businesslike, capable, careful, committed, competent, conscientious, dependable, detailed, diligent, effective, expert, expertly done, full-time, good, impressive, knowledgeable, licensed, masterly, methodical, meticulous, polished, practised, proficient, proper, qualified, reliable,

responsible, seamless, serious, sharp, skilful, slick, thorough, trained, trustworthy, well-organised, well-planned, well-qualified, well-run, working as

**Profit** n., see also Achievement, Income
bottom line, cut, earnings, gain, good money, killing, making a killing, margin, markup, money, money-making, money-spinner, money to be made, net income, net profit, nice little earner, percentage, premium, proceeds, profit margin, return(s), surplus, take-home, takings, tidy profit, windfall, yield

**Profitable** adj., see also Successful
advantageous, beneficial, booming, commercial, commercially successful, commercially viable, cost-effective, fruitful, gainful, generating a profit, generating a return, going concern, hit, lucrative, making a profit, money-making, money-spinner, paying, paying for itself, profit-making, quids in, raking it in, rewarding, self-sustaining, sustainable, turning a profit, useful, valuable, viable, well-paying, well-performing, worthwhile

**Progress** n., see also Achievement, Development
advance, advancement, blossoming, boost, breakthrough, enhancement, evolution, forward movement, gain, growth, headway, impetus, improvement, increase, inroads, journey, leap (forward), march, milestone, momentum, movement, optimisation, passage, progression, quantum leap, revolution, rise, shift, step change, step forward, steps, stepping stone, strides, success, traction

**Progress** v., see also Develop, Improve
advance, be on a journey, bear fruit, become better, blossom, boom, come on leaps and bounds, continue, evolve, flourish, forge ahead, gain, gain ground, gain traction, gather momentum, go forward, grow, increase, keep going, leap ahead/forward, make headway, make inroads, make progress, make strides, mature, move forward, move in the right direction, move on, proceed, prosper, see improvement, steal a march, take shape, thrive, turn over a new leaf

**Project** n., see also Assignment, Work
activity, arrangement, campaign, cause, commission, crusade, deal, enterprise, game plan, idea, initiative, job, labour of love, operation, passion project, plan, programme, proposal, scheme, setup, task, undertaking, venture

**Promise** n., see also Agreement, Guarantee
1. affirmation, assurance, bond, certification, commitment, compact, consent, contract, covenant, insurance, oath, obligation, pact, pledge, specification, stipulation, undertaking, vow, warranty, word, word of honour

2. ability, bright future, capability, capacity, chance, encouragement, hope, makings, possibility, potential, prospect(s), talent

**Promise** v., see also Ensure, Guarantee

1. affirm, assert, assure, certify, commit, declare, give a guarantee, give a pledge, give a promise, give one's assurance, give one's word, make a commitment, pledge, provide a guarantee, swear, take an oath, undertake, underwrite, vouch, vow, warrant, with hand on heart

2. appear, augur, be encouraging, bode, have the makings of, hint at, hold out hope of, hold promise, indicate, lead to believe, look like, offer the possibility, show potential, show promise, show signs of, suggest

**Promote** v., see also Advertise, Appoint

1. advance, advocate, aid, assist, back, bang the drum for, boost, build up, champion, contribute, develop, drum up interest, encourage, endorse, espouse, extol (the virtues of), favour, foster, further, get behind, help, hype, improve, increase, market, nurture, peddle, plug, popularise, publicise, push (for), recommend, sell, shout about, sing the praises of, sponsor, strengthen, support, tout, trumpet, urge, vaunt, whip up

2. advance, assign, develop, elevate, give a better position, give a more senior role, give a promotion, put in charge, raise, upgrade

**Proof** n., see also Clear, Real

affirmation, attestation, authentication, borne out by, certification, clincher, clue, confirmation, corroboration, demonstration, documentation, evidence, grounds, hard evidence, hard facts, indication, manifestation, proof positive, sign, smoking gun, speaks for itself, substantiation, testament, testimony, validation, verification

**Property** n., see also Acquisition, Investment

1. ability, aspect, attribute, character, characteristic, DNA, distinguishing feature, element, essence, facet, factor, feature, hallmark, idiosyncrasy, mark, nature, oddity, peculiarity, personality, quality, quirk, trait, uniqueness, virtue

2. assets, belongings, bricks and mortar, building, capital, effects, equity, estate, goods, holdings, intellectual property, land, net worth, ownership, possessions, real estate, resources, riches, wealth, worth

**Proposal** n., see also Idea, Offer

arrangement, bid, concept, game plan, initiative, intention, motion, offer on the table, outline, overture, pitch, plan, presentation, programme, project, proposition, recommendation, sales pitch, submission, suggestion, tender, terms

**Propose** v., see also Offer, Present
advance, advise, advocate, affirm, aim, assert, come up with, contemplate, counsel, drive at, float an idea, have in mind, intend, introduce, invite, lay before, lay out, make a pitch, make a proposal, make an offer, mean, moot, name, nominate, offer a suggestion, pitch, plan, plug, prefer, proffer, promise, propound, put, put forward, put it out there, recommend, refer, remind, set forth, set out, state, submit, suggest, table, tender, urge, volunteer

**Protect** v., see also Defend
assure, care for, cherish, close ranks, come to the defence of, conserve, cushion, ensure, fend off, give refuge, give sanctuary, guard, guard over, harbour, hedge, insulate, keep, keep safe, leap to the defence of, look after, maintain, nurture, preserve, provide a safety net, provide protection, safeguard, save, screen, secure, shelter, shield, stand by, stave off, stick up for, support, take care of, take under one's wing, watch over

**Prove** v., see also Confirm, Demonstrate
attest, authenticate, be found to be, be shown to be, bear out, bear witness, certify, check, clarify, convince, corroborate, determine, document, emerge, end up, establish, explain, find, go to show, have a case, illustrate, justify, make evident, pan out, prove beyond doubt, provide evidence, put to the test, seal, show, show clearly, show proof, show to be true, substantiate, test, testify, transpire, turn out, uphold, validate, verify, vindicate, witness

**Provide** v., see also Offer, Supply
accommodate, add, administer, afford, allocate, allow, arrange, bestow, bring, cater for/to, contribute, create, deliver, dispense, distribute, enable, ensure, equip, establish, feature, furnish, generate, give, grant, hand, hand over, implement, issue, lend, look after, maintain, make, make available, make for, plan, prepare, present, procure, produce, put in place, render, sell, serve (up), stock, submit, support, sustain, take care of, take measures, yield

**Provoke** v., see also Anger, Start
1. arouse, awaken, bring about, call forth, cause, drive, electrify, elicit, encourage, evoke, excite, fan (the flames), fuel, galvanise, generate, give rise to, herald, ignite, incite, induce, inspire, instigate, kick off, kick-start, kindle, lead to, motivate, move, occasion, precipitate, produce, promote, prompt, rally,

result in, rouse, spark, spur, stimulate, stir (up), stoke, summon (up), trigger, usher in
2. affront, aggravate, anger, be a red rag to a bull, enrage, exasperate, gall, get on someone's nerves, get under someone's skin, incense, incite, inflame, infuriate, irk, irritate, make waves, offend, outrage, rile, ruffle feathers, spark/trigger anger, upset

**Public** adj., see also Collective, Famous
accessible, acknowledged, civic, civil, common, communal, community, general, generally known, government, governmental, in the public domain, in the public eye, known, local, municipal, mutual, national, not private, official, open, open to the public, overt, popular, public-sector, published, recognised, shared, social, state, transparent, universal, unrestricted, urban, well-known, widespread

**Publish** v., see also Advertise, Announce
break the news, bring out, broadcast, circulate, communicate, declare, disclose, disseminate, distribute, divulge, issue, issue a statement, let it be known, make available, make public, pen, print, proclaim, produce, promote, publicise, publicly disclose, put out, release, report, reveal, shout about, spread the word

**Punish** v., see also Penalise
blacklist, castigate, chastise, come down hard on, come down like a tonne of bricks on, correct, crack down on, discipline, expel, fine, give a slap on the wrist, issue a sanction, issue punishment, impose punishment on, make an example of, mete out punishment, rap on the knuckles, reprove, slap someone's wrist, scold, sentence, take disciplinary action against, teach a lesson, throw the book at

**Purchase** v., see also Acquire, Pay
agree the purchase of, amass, bag, buy, buy into, buy out, buy up, come by, fork out for, gain, get, get one's hands on, go on a spending spree, go shopping for, grab a bargain, hoover up, invest in, make a purchase, make an acquisition, make an investment, obtain, open one's chequebook, open one's wallet, order, plough/pour money into, procure, put money into, secure, shop (for), snag, snap up, source, treat oneself to

**Purpose** n., see also Aim, Intention
agenda, ambition, aspiration, basis, benefit, big idea, brief, designs, desire, direction, dream, effect, end, expectation, function, gain, goal, grounds, hope, idea, intent, justification, meaning, mission, motivation, motive, object, objective, plan, point, principle, proposal, raison d'être, rationale, reason, remit, scope, target, use, usefulness, utility, value, view, wish

# Q

**Quality** n., see also High-quality, Property

1. calibre, class, condition, craftsmanship, distinction, excellence, gold standard, grade, high quality, measure of excellence, merit, perfection, pre-eminence, rank, standard, standing, state, stature, status, superiority, value, worth
2. advantage, aspect, attribute, benefit, capacity, character, characteristic, distinction, DNA, element, essence, facet, factor, feature, hallmark, individuality, mark, merit, nature, nature of the beast, peculiarity, strength, trait, value, virtue

**Quantity** n., see also Extent, Level

abundance, amount, bulk, capacity, chunk, dose, entirety, extent, helping, load, magnitude, mass, measure, no less than, number, percentage, portion, proportion, quota, scale, scope, score, size, slice, sum, tidy sum, total, value, volume, weight, whole

**Question** n., see also Issue, Problem

1. argument, bone of contention, can of worms, challenge, contention, controversy, conundrum, debate, difficulty, discussion, dispute, food for thought, heart of the matter, issue at hand, matter, misgiving, nub of the matter, objection, point, point at issue, proposal, proposition, question at hand, subject, theme, topic, uncertainty
2. confusion, conundrum, contention, dispute, doubt, enigma, enquiry, examination, inquest, inquiry, inquisition, investigation, misgiving, mystery, poll, puzzle, Q and A, quandary, query, question at hand, question mark, questioning, riddle, survey, third degree, uncertainty

**Quick/Quickly** adj./adv., see also Agile, Brief

abrupt, accelerated, all of a sudden, animated, apace, at a blistering pace, at a fair lick, at full tilt, at pace, at speed, before you know it, blistering, breakneck, brisk, bustling, double-quick (time), energetic, ephemeral, express, fast, fast-changing, fast-growing, fast-growth, fast-moving, fast-paced, flat out, fleet, fleet of foot, fleeting, full speed ahead, full throttle, furious, hasty, headlong, hell for leather, high-speed, hurried, immediate, in a flash, in a jiffy, in an instant, in no time, in the blink of an eye, instant(ly), instantaneous, keen, lightning-quick, like a bat out of hell, like a rocket, like a shot, like lightning, lively, meteoric, momentary, nimble, nippy, no slouch, overnight, post haste, promptly, quick as a flash, quick-and-dirty, quick-witted, rapid, short-lived, short-term, snappy, speedy, sprightly, sudden, supersonic, swift, unhesitating, urgent, whirlwind

# R

**Raise** v., see also Expand, Increase

1. accelerate, add to, advance, aid, amplify, augment, beef up, bolster, boost, broaden, build up, bump up, buoy, crank up, deepen, develop, dial up, elevate, enhance, enlarge, escalate, extend, facilitate, fortify, foster, further, heighten, hike, improve, inflate, inspire, intensify, lift, magnify, make bigger, make more, promote, raise, ramp up, ratchet up, reinforce, scale up, send through the roof, spur, step up, stoke, strengthen, supercharge, supersize, support, take higher, take to new levels, take to the next level, turbocharge, up, upgrade
2. advance, arouse, awaken, bring up, broach, cause, encourage, evoke, excite, express, highlight, introduce, kindle, mention, moot, note, pose, provoke, put forward, start, stimulate, suggest

**Range** n., see also Area, Assortment

1. armoury, array, arsenal, battery, breadth, broad spectrum, cannon, cocktail, collection, cross section, diversity, everything from…to…, family, field, gamut, group, line, line-up, mixed bag, mixture, number, offering, palette, portfolio, product range, raft, repertoire, roster, scope, selection, sort, span, spectrum, spoilt for choice, suite, …to name but a few, variation, variety, wide range
2. breadth, confines, distance, domain, extent, magnitude, orbit, parameters, radius, reach, realm, scope, space, span, spectrum, sphere (of influence), spread, sweep, territory

**Rare** adj., see also Few, Unusual

abnormal, almost never, almost unprecedented, atypical, elusive, exceptional, few and far between, hardly ever, infrequent, like gold dust, limited, little, not common, not often, not your everyday, occasional, once in a blue moon, out of the ordinary, outlier, precious (little), preserve of, refreshingly different, scant, scarce, seldom, singular, sparing, sparse, special, sporadic, strange, surprising, thin on the ground, uncommon, unexpected, unfamiliar, unique, unlikely

**Reach** v., see also Achieve, Fulfil

accomplish, amount to, approach, arrive at, attain, be as much as, bottom out, carry, catch up, come to, complete, extend to, gain, get as far/high as, get to, grasp, land, make, make contact with, manage, peak at, rack up, reach a high/low of, realise, reel in, satisfy, score, seize, show up, total, turn up, win

**React** v., see also Comment, Respond
acknowledge, act, answer, behave, bounce back, come back, conduct oneself, counter, counteract, do as a reaction/in response, feel, give a reaction/response, hit back, proceed, reciprocate, recoil, recover, reply, retaliate, retort, rise to the bait, take action, take the bait

**Reaction** n., see also Result
acknowledgement, aftermath, answer, backlash, blowback, comeback, consequence, counter, counterattack, countermove, effect, fallout, feedback, feeling, gut reaction, knee-jerk reaction, reception, reciprocation, rejoinder, repercussion, reply, reprisal, response, retaliation, retort, revenge, reverberation, riposte, tit-for-tat, upshot, verdict, witty response

**Ready** adj., see also Effective, Efficient
able, accessible, adapted, all bases covered, all set, all systems go, anticipating, armed with, arranged, at hand, at one's fingertips, at the ready, available, braced, champing at the bit, close at hand, completed, convenient, eager, enthusiastic, equipped, fit, game, good to go, handy, in good shape, in order, in place, in position, in readiness, itching to, keen, on call, on guard, on standby, organised, poised, planned, poised, prepared, prepped, primed, processed, psyched, raring to go, ***** ready (*e.g. Christmas ready*), ready for anything, ready to go, rehearsed, ripe, set, set fair, set up, stage is set, up and running, up for, waiting, well-drilled, well-equipped, well-positioned, well-prepared, willing

**Real** adj., see also Authentic, Genuine
absolute, actual, authenticated, bona fide, certain, concrete, convincing, de facto, earnest, evident, existing, factual, genuine article, heartfelt, honest, irrefutable, legitimate, material, original, palpable, perceptible, physical, proper, real deal, real-life, real McCoy, rightful, sincere, specific, substantive, tangible, true, true colours, undeniable, unfeigned, unquestionable, veritable

**Realise** v., see also Achieve, Understand
1. accept, appreciate, become aware of, become conscious of, come to the realisation, comprehend, cotton on, cross one's mind, dawn on, get it, grasp, have a reality check, hit, hit home, notice, occur, penny drops, see sense, see the light, sense, sink in, take on board, tumble, twig, wake up to

2. accomplish, attain, bring about, bring to fruition, carry out, carry through, complete, deliver, do, execute, fulfil, get something done, implement, make happen, perfect, put into action, see through (to completion)

**Realistic** adj., see also Logical, Sensible
accepting reality, businesslike, clear-eyed, clear-sighted, common-sense, down-to-earth, facing facts, hard-headed, hard-nosed, honest (with oneself), in the cold light of day, level-headed, matter-of-fact, no-nonsense, not sugar-coating, phlegmatic, practical, pragmatic, prudent, rational, reasonable, sanguine, sober, stoic, stoical, tough, truthful, unemotional, unromantic, unsentimental, viable, with eyes open, workable

**Reason** n., see also Argument, Cause
1. agenda, aim, basis, case, catalyst, defence, driver, driving force, excuse, explanation, goal, grounds, idea, impetus, incentive, inspiration, intent, intention, justification, key driver, logic, mission, motivation, motive, object, objective, origin, point, pretext, principle, purpose, raison d'être, rationale, root, root cause, sense, spark, stimulus, target, trigger, underlying reason, why and wherefore, whole idea
2. analysis, common sense, deduction, judgement, logic, reasoning, sense, understanding, wisdom

**Reasonable** adj., see also Inexpensive, Sensible
acceptable, advisable, average, common-sense, credible, equitable, fair, feasible, grown-up, honest, intelligent, judicious, justifiable, legitimate, level-headed, logical, mature, moderate, modest, normal, okay, plausible, practical, proper, prudent, rational, restrained, sane, satisfactory, sensible, sound, stands to reason, suitable, tenable, thoughtful, tolerable, understandable, valid, viable, wise, within reason

**Recall** v., see also Consider
arouse, awaken, be nostalgic about, bring to mind, call to mind, cast one's mind back, cite, commemorate, elicit, evoke, hark back to, have a memory of, have fond memories of, have the benefit of hindsight, look back on, recollect, refer to, remember, remind, reminisce, revisit, revive, ring a bell, stir, strike a chord/note, take a trip down memory lane, think back on, think of

**Receive** v., see also Acquire, Gain
accept, accept delivery, access, accommodate, assume, bag, be awarded, be given, be issued with, be paid, be sent, be the recipient of, bear, benefit from, collect, come by, earn, endure, experience, garner, generate, get, get hold of,

get one's hands on, grab, gross, make, meet with, net, obtain, pick up, pocket, reap, secure, snag, suffer, sustain, take, take home, take in, take possession/receipt of, undergo, welcome, win

**Recession** n., see also Downturn, Economy
collapse, contraction, crash, crisis, decline, depression, deterioration, economic collapse, economic crisis, economic downturn, economic slowdown, hard times, meltdown, reversal, slide, slowdown, slowing, slump, stagnation, weakening

**Recommend** v., see also Praise, Suggest
a lot to be said for, advise, advocate, approve, back, cannot speak highly enough of, counsel, encourage, endorse, extol (the virtues of), favour, give a glowing report of, heartily recommend, hype, justify, make a recommendation, plug, promote, propose, put forward, put in a good word for, rave about, sing the praises of, speak highly of, strongly/warmly recommend, swear by, talk up, tip, urge, vouch for, wax lyrical about

**Reconsider** v., see also Change
back down, back-pedal, backtrack, change one's mind, change one's tune, change tack, climb down, come around, go back on, go back to the drawing board, have a change of heart, have a rethink, have second thoughts, make a U-turn, overturn, reappraise, reassess, re-evaluate, re-examine, rehash, relent, renege, rethink, retract, review, review one's position, revise, revisit, rework, row back on, see in a new light, sleep on, take a step back, take another look at, take back, think again, think better of, think over, think twice

**Recover** v., see also Improve, Resume
be back in the game, be back on track, be on the mend, be on the road to recovery, be out of the woods, be reinvigorated, bounce back, breathe new life into, bring back, claw back, come back (from the brink/dead), come back stronger, dust oneself down/off, fight back, gain a new lease of life, get back on one's feet, get back on track, get better, get over, lick one's wounds, make a comeback, make a recovery, make up for (lost time), overcome, perk up, pick oneself up, pick up, play catch-up, pull through, put it behind you, rally, reassert oneself, rebuild, recapture, recharge one's batteries, reclaim, recoup, recuperate, rediscover, re-emerge, regain, regain strength, regroup, rekindle, repair, rescue, restore, resurrect, retrieve, return to form, reverse, revitalise, revive, right the ship, salvage, save face, steady the ship, survive, take a turn for the better, turn the corner, turn the tide, turn things around, win back

**Recovery** n., see also Change, Improvement
comeback, fightback, improvement in fortunes, pickup, progress, rally, reawakening, rebirth, reboot, rebound, rebuilding, reclaim, reconstruction, recuperation, regeneration, rehabilitation, reinstatement, rejuvenation, relaunch, renaissance, renewal, rescue, restoration, resumption, resurgence, resurrection, resuscitation, return, return to form, revival, road to recovery, turn for the better, turnaround, upswing

**Recruit** v., see also Appoint, Employ
assemble, assign, bring in, bring on board, call up, draft (in), engage, enlist, enrol, find, find a role for, give responsibility, give someone a job/role, hand someone a job/role, headhunt, hire, invite, parachute in, poach, procure, put in charge, put in place, select, sign up, take on, welcome

**Reduce** v., see also Decrease, Inhibit
alleviate, bring down, check, cool, cull, curb, curtail, cut, cut back (on), cut down, dampen, de-escalate, depress, devalue, dial down, dilute, diminish, dip, discount, downgrade, downsize, drag down, drive down, drop, ease, eat into, erode, fall, have a negative impact on, hit, impair, lessen, lower, make less, make lower, make smaller, make worse, mark down, minimise, moderate, narrow, pare, prune, push down, rationalise, rein in, relegate, sap, scale back, scale down, shave, shorten, shrink, slash, slim down, slow (down), subdue, take down, taper, tighten, tone down, trim, turn down, undermine, weaken, weigh on, whittle down

**Reduction** n., see also Collapse, Deterioration
abatement, blip, contraction, crash, crumbling, cull, curtailment, cut, cutback, decline, decrease, demise, dent, depreciation, depression, descent, devaluation, dip, discount, dive, downfall, downgrade, downsizing, downturn, downward spiral, downward trend, drop, drop-off, dwindling, easing, ebb, erosion, fall, falling off, fall-off, flagging, freefall, lessening, limiting, loss, lowering, lull, meltdown, minimisation, narrowing, nosedive, plunge, retreat, rout, shortening, shrinkage, slide, slip, slippery slope, slowdown, slowing, slump, softening, tumble, wane, waning, weakening, withering, worsening

**Refer** v., see also Concern, Say
1. acknowledge, address, allude to, be relevant, bring up, broach, cite, comment on, connect, detail, disclose, draw attention to, give a nod to, give an example, have a bearing on, have to do with, hint at, indicate, introduce, involve, link, make mention of, make reference to, mention, name, observe, pertain, point out, recount, relate, remark, report, reveal, speak about, specify, touch on/upon

2. address, apply to, consult, direct, hand over, recommend, resort to, seek information from, submit, turn to

**Reflect** v., see also Demonstrate, Represent
allude to, be a reflection of, be characterised by, be indicative of, be representative of, bear witness to, correspond to, denote, display, echo, embody, epitomise, exemplify, exhibit, express, hint at, illustrate, indicate, manifest, mirror, point to, portray, present, resonate, reveal, show, speak volumes, suggest, symbolise, typify

**Reform** n., see also Change, Improvement
adjustment, amendment, correction, innovation, major change, makeover, modernisation, modification, overhaul, reboot, rectification, regeneration, rehabilitation, renewal, renovation, reorganisation, restructuring, rethink, review, revision, revolution, reworking, shake-up, shift, step change, transformation, transition, turnaround, turning point, wholesale change, update, ushering in of a new era

**Reform** v., see also Change, Update
adjust, amend, convert, correct, disrupt, improve, introduce change/reforms, make over, modernise, modify, overhaul, put right, rearrange, reboot, rebuild, reconstruct, rectify, regenerate, rehabilitate, rejig, remake, remedy, remodel, renew, renovate, reorganise, repair, restore, restructure, rethink, revise, revolutionise, rework, ring the changes, shake up, transform, turn around, turn over a new leaf, upend, upgrade, usher in a new era

**Refuse** v., see also Reject
balk at, be stubborn, brook no, decline, deny, dig one's heels in, dismiss, dodge, draw the line, evade, give the cold shoulder, give the thumbs down, have no truck with, ignore, not agree to, not budge, pass up, rebuff, refute, resist, say no, shun, spurn, turn away, turn down, turn one's back on, veto, will not, withdraw, withhold

**Regret** v., see also Apologise, Reconsider
admit, ask forgiveness, be chastened, be contrite, be mortified, be regretful, be sad, be sorry, bemoan, deplore, express regret/remorse, feel remorse, feel uneasy, have misgivings, have qualms, in hindsight, in retrospect, kick oneself, lament, offer excuses, recant, reproach oneself, rue, show contrition, wish one had not, with a heavy heart, with hindsight, with regret

**Regular** adj., see also Frequent, Normal
1. average, bog-standard, classic, common, common-or-garden, commonplace, conventional, day-to-day, established, everyday, general, go-to, habitual, ordinary, orthodox, plain-vanilla, regulation, routine, run-of-the-mill, standard, standard-issue, standardised, staple, traditional, typical, unexceptional, usual
2. coherent, common, consistent, constant, cyclical, day-to-day, even, every (day/week, etc.), homogenous, invariable, organised, periodic, recurring, regular as clockwork, regulated, religious, routine, standardised, steady, systematic, uniform

**Regulate** v., see also Control, Govern
adjust, administer, balance, check, command, coordinate, determine, dictate, direct, guide, have oversight, legislate, manage, marshal, moderate, monitor, orchestrate, order, organise, oversee, police, preside over, require, rule, run, set the requirements/rules, standardise, stipulate, supervise, watch over

**Regulation** n., see also Requirement, Rule
administration, arrangement, bible, checks and balances, code, control, coordination, direction, directive, framework, governance, governing, government, guidelines, law, legislation, management, monitoring, order, oversight, precedent, principle, procedures, provisions, restriction, rule book, rules and regulations, standard(s), statute, supervision, systematisation

**Reject** v., see also Dislike, Oppose
abandon, block, break with, brook no, brush aside, cast aside, decline, deny, discard, disdain, dismiss, disown, dispel, distance oneself from, ditch, drop, eschew, exclude, give short shrift, give the cold shoulder, give the thumbs down, have no truck with, ignore, jettison, junk, pass on, pour cold water on, push back on, rebuff, refuse, refute, reject out of hand, renounce, repudiate, resist, rubbish, say no to, scorn, scrap, shoot down, shun, snub, spurn, stand in the way of, take with a pinch of salt, throw out, turn down, turn one's back on, turn one's nose up at, veto, walk away from, wash one's hands of, write off

**Rejection** n., see also Criticism, Opposition
aversion, backlash, brush-off, cold shoulder, denial, disapproval, dislike, dismissal, elimination, eschewal, frosty reception, heave-ho, kick in the teeth, knockback, misgivings, no, outcry, rebuff, rebuttal, refusal, renunciation, repudiation, short shrift, slap in the face, snub, thumbs down, veto

**Relate** v., see also Concern, Link
apply to, associate, be about, be connected, be related, be relevant, be synonymous, chime with, compare, concur, connect, correlate, correspond, couple, echo, encompass, equate, feed into, fit with, have a bearing on, have to do with, impact, interconnect, interlink, interrelate, involve, orient, orientate, owe a debt to, pertain, refer, reflect, regard, resonate with, speak to, tally with, tie in with, touch (on)

**Related** adj., see also Relevant, Similar
accompanying, affiliated, akin, allied, ancillary, associated, bedfellow, bound up with, connected, correlated, corresponding, coupled, cousin, dependent, fused, having a bearing on, having implications for, in keeping with, in line with, in the vein of, in tune with, integrated, inextricably linked, interconnected, interrelated, intertwined, interwoven, linked, matching, mutual, parallel, pertinent, reciprocal, reminiscent, sibling, sister, spin-off, synonymous

**Relationship** n., see also Agreement, Link
affiliation, alliance, association, attachment, axis, bond, camaraderie, collaboration, communication, connection, connotation, cooperation, correlation, cross-over, dependence, dynamic, exchange, friendship, interdependence, interrelationship, liaison, link, network, pairing, partnership, rapport, ratio, relation, relevance, similarity, solidarity, symbiosis, synergy, teamwork, tie-in, tie-up, working together

**Relax** v., see also Enjoy, Lessen
1. bask, be laid back, be relaxed, breathe easy, calm, chill, compose oneself, cool off, escape, feel at ease, feel at home, find relaxation, forget cares/worries, get away (from it all), get some peace and quiet, get some R & R, kick back, lay back, let go, let one's hair down, make oneself at home, put one's feet up, recharge (one's batteries), rest, rest on one's laurels, settle back, sit back, slow down, switch off, take a break, take a breather, take it easy, take one's time, take time out, unwind
2. curb, dilute, ease, ease back on, ease off, let up, loosen, lower, lower one's guard, moderate, reduce, relieve, temper, tone down, weaken

**Relevant** adj., see also Appropriate, Significant
applicable, apt, compatible, concerning, connected, correlated, corresponding, fitting, germane, good fit, having a bearing on, having to do with, ideal, important, in keeping, linked, material, of importance, of interest, of relevance, of significance, of value, perfect, pertaining to, pertinent, poignant, referring to, related, relative, resonant, suitable, suited, to the point, useful

**Reliability** n., see also Stability, Strength
accuracy, assurance, authenticity, availability, certainty, consistency, credibility, dependability, durability, efficiency, fidelity, honesty, loyalty, peace of mind, predictability, professionalism, quality, reliable reputation, resilience, robustness, safety, security, soundness, stability, steadfastness, sturdiness, trustworthiness, uptime

**Reliable** adj., see also Stable, Strong
assured, bulletproof, certain, comforting, conscientious, consistent, constant, decent, dependable, devoted, fail-safe, faithful, foolproof, good old, honest, ironclad, loyal, never missing a beat, peace of mind, predictable, proven, reassuring, reputable, robust, rock-solid, rock-steady, safe pair of hands, solid, solid as a rock, sound, stable, stalwart, steadfast, steady, sturdy, sure, sure-fire, tried-and-tested, trusted, trustworthy, trusty, unfailing, unflinching, workhorse

**Rely** v., see also Relate, Require
bank on, be at the mercy of, be based on, be conditional on, be contingent on, be dependent on, be founded on, be grounded on, be influenced by, be reliant on, be subject to, be underpinned by, bet on, build on, count on, depend on, fall back on, hang on, hinge on, need, pend, pivot on, rest on, rest with, revolve around, trust in, turn on

**Remain** v., see also Continue, Maintain
abide, be left, become established, become part of the furniture, bide one's time, carry on, endure, go on, hang in there, keep at/on, keep going, last, linger, live on, outlast, outlive, persist, persevere, press on, prevail, put down roots, remain standing, settle, sit out, stay, stay put, stay/remain standing, stick around, stick at/to/with, still be, stop, survive, tough it out, wait

**Remember** v., see also Celebrate
arouse, awaken, be nostalgic about, bring to mind, call to mind, cast one's mind back, cite, commemorate, elicit, evoke, hark back to, have a memory of, have fond memories of, have the benefit of hindsight, in retrospect, look back on, mark an occasion, recall, recollect, refer to, remind, reminisce, revisit, revive, ring a bell, stir, take a trip down memory lane, think back, think of

**Remove** v., see also Cancel, Replace
abolish, axe, banish, bin, call time on, can, chuck out, clear out, cull, cut (off/out), delete, deprive of, discard, dismiss, dispose of, ditch, do away with, drive out, drop, eject, eliminate, eradicate, erase, exclude, expel, get rid of, good riddance to, jettison, junk, kick out, kill (off), oust, purge, rid, root out,

scrap, scratch, shelve, stop, strip of, sweep away, take an axe to, take away, take out, terminate, throw out, unseat, wipe out, withdraw

**Repair** v., see also Improve, Resolve
adjust, amend, correct, counter, debug, find a solution, fix, get to grips with, make good, mend, overhaul, patch up, put back together, put in order, put right, rebuild, recalibrate, recover, rectify, refurbish, remedy, renovate, restore, revamp, revise, revisit, revive, service, solve, sort, sort out, stabilise, stop the rot, tackle, tinker with, turn around, tweak, work around, work out

**Repeat** v., see also Continue, Copy
be déjà vu, be in a vicious circle, carry on, do again, do all over again, do the same again, double up, drum into, duplicate, echo, keep doing/going, labour the point, occur again, persevere, persist, reaffirm, reappear, reassert, recur, redo, regurgitate, rehash, rehearse, reiterate, renew, repeat the feat/trick, replay, reprise, reproduce, rerun, restate, resume, revert, stick at

**Replace** v., see also Change, Dismiss
be a replacement for, be a stand-in for, be a successor to, deputise for, displace, exchange, fill in for, follow, give a new look to, give way to, make way for, oust, pick up the baton from, put in someone's stead, reconfigure, re-establish, regain, reinstate, remove, renew, restore, retrieve, shake up, stand in for, stand in lieu of, step into the shoes of, substitute, succeed, supersede, supplant, swap (out), swap places, switch (up), take over, take the place of, trade in, usurp

**Report** n., see also Analysis, Information
account, article, blow-by-blow account, briefing, buzz, chronicle, communication, communiqué, critique, description, findings, grapevine, hearsay, intelligence, latest, memo, message, narrative, news, opinion, outline, picture, presentation, record, reports, revelation(s), review, rumours(s), statement, story, submission, summary, version, write-up

**Report** v., see also Announce, Communicate
advise, articulate, brief, declare, depict, describe, detail, disclose, divulge, document, elaborate, give an account of, inform, issue a report, list, make known, make public, mention, note, notify, outline, post, present, provide an account, provide details, publish, put out, record, recount, relate, reveal, set forth, set out, submit a report, summarise, tell

**Represent** v., see also Demonstrate, Illustrate
1. act as, be a model of, be representative of, characterise, correspond to, denote, depict, describe, embody, epitomise, equate, evoke, exemplify, exhibit, express, hint, immortalise, mean, mirror, personify, portray, present, reflect, serve as, show, stand for, suggest, symbolise, typify
2. act for, assume the role of, be a representative for, be a spokesperson for, be the face of, front, hold office, serve as, speak for/on behalf of, work for

**Representative** adj., see also Typical
archetypal, average, characteristic, classic, classic case of, emblematic, embodiment, epitome, evocative, exemplary, ideal, illustrative, model, normal, personification, quintessential, reflective, standard, stereotypical, symbolic

**Representative** n., see also Employee, Leader
agent, affiliate, ambassador, associate, delegate, deputy, embodiment, emissary, envoy, epitome, face of, incarnation, official, on behalf of, personification, personnel, proxy, rep, salesperson, spokesperson, stand-in, stereotype, substitute, symbol, typical

**Reputation** n., see also Brand, Popular
acclaim, air, approval, aura, authority, bad press, bad rap, cachet, character, credentials, credibility, distinction, fame, image, impression, influence, name, notoriety, position, prestige, prominence, rank, regard, reliability, renown, repute, respect, respectability, standing, stature, status, synonymous, trustworthiness, word of mouth

**Request** n., see also Inquiry
appeal, application, behest, call, claim, convening, demand, desire, enquiry/inquiry, entreaty, invitation, offer, order, petition, plea, polite request, query, question, solicitation, urging

**Request** v., see also Consult, Inquire
appeal, apply, ask, beg, beseech, call for, charge, claim, demand, desire, enquire/inquire, entreat, implore, invite, make an enquiry/inquiry, make a request, offer, order, petition, plead, politely request, require, solicit, urge

**Require** v., see also Must, Need
ask, be crying out for, be in need of, be incumbent on, be obliged, be short of, behove, call for, call upon, claim, command, compel, could do with, could use, crave, demand, depend on, expect, force, had better, have call for, have need of, have requirement of, have to, impose requirements, insist on, involve, lack,

look for, necessitate, oblige, occasion, order, push for, put pressure on, rely on, request, resort to, set requirements, specify, stipulate, take

**Requirement** n., see also Necessity, Obligation
call for, claim, commitment, compulsion, condition, core requirement, deficiency, demand, desire, dire need, dos and don'ts, duty, essential, expectation, fundamental, fundamental requirement, imperative, inadequacy, key component, lack, must, must-have, necessary evil, need, obligation, precondition, prerequisite, proviso, rule, shortage, specification, stipulation

**Rescue** v., see also Defend, Recover
bail out, be a lifeline/lifesaver, come to the rescue, deliver from, extricate, free, help (out), liberate, preserve, protect, pull out of the fire, redeem, retrieve, safeguard, salvage, save, save someone's bacon, save someone's life, save someone's skin, save the day, set free, spare, spare someone's blushes, throw a lifeline

**Resign** v., see also End, Leave
abandon, abdicate, bail out, bow out, call it a day, cease working, cede, end one's service/time at, escape, fall on one's sword, give notice, give up, hand in notice, hand in one's resignation, hand over (the reins) to, jump ship, move on (to pastures new), part company with, part ways, quit, relinquish, renounce, retire, sign off, stand aside, stand down, step down, tender one's resignation, throw in the towel, vacate, walk, walk away, walk out, wash one's hands of

**Resilient** adj., see also Durable, Flexible
adaptable, bouncing back, buoyant, capable, determined, firm, formidable, fortitude, hardy, indefatigable, indomitable, invincible, irrepressible, never-say-die, putting up with, quick to recover, resolute, robust, rolling with the punches, sanguine, steadfast, stoic, stoical, strong, strong-willed, stubborn, sustainable, tenacious, thick-skinned, tough, tough as old boots, unfazed, unflinching, unperturbed, unstinting, unswerving, unstoppable

**Resolve** v., see also Address, Decide
1. answer, clear up, confront, crack, deal with, decipher, fathom, figure out, find a (re)solution, fix, get on top of, get to grips with, iron out, meet head on, navigate, nip in the bud, overcome, put in order, put right, rectify, remedy, respond to, settle, solve, sort (out), stop the rot, tackle, take care of, undertake, unlock, untangle, work around, work out, work out/through
2. agree, approve, choose, conclude, determine, intend, make a decision, make up one's mind, rule, settle, undertake, vote

**Resources** n., see also Ability, Personnel
assets, backing, budget, capabilities, capability, capacity, capital, clout, collateral, deep pockets, expertise, facilities, financial resources, funds, human resources, know-how, materials, means, money, muscle, natural resources, power, reserves, resourcefulness, strength, supplies, tools, wealth, what is required, what it takes, wherewithal

**Respond** v., see also Address, React
acknowledge, act in response, answer, behave, come back, comment, confront, counter, counteract, deal with, feed back, fight back, get back to, get in touch, give a reaction, give a response, handle, hit back, meet, meet a challenge, move, provide feedback, reciprocate, reply, resolve, retaliate, retort, rise to the bait, rise to the challenge, silence one's critics, step up (to the mark/plate), take a stance, take action/measures/steps, take the bait

**Response** n., see also Result, Solution
acknowledgement, action, aftermath, answer, backlash, blowback, comeback, comment, consequence, counter, counterattack, countermove, fallout, feedback, gut reaction, knee-jerk reaction, measure, move, reaction, reception, reciprocation, rejoinder, repercussion, reply, reprisal, retaliation, retort, revenge, riposte, stance, step, tit-for-tat, verdict, witty response

**Responsibility** n., see also Authority, Power
1. accountability, blame, buck (stops here), burden, commitment, control, culpability, duty, fault, guilt, liability, obligation, onus
2. authorisation, capacity, care, charge, competency, concern, control, decision-making, dependability, duties, function, importance, job, job description, jurisdiction, leadership, level-headedness, management, mantle, maturity, oversight, ownership, position, powers, professionalism, reliability, role, task, trustworthiness, work

**Responsible** adj., see also Important, Reliable
1. accountable, answerable, at fault, blamed, buck stops here, carrying the can, culpable, culprit, duty-bound, guilty, liable, obliged, obligated, on the hook, taking responsibility, to blame, under obligation, with responsibility for
2. capable, committed, competent, conscientious, dependable, diligent, effective, ethical, level-headed, loyal, mature, professional, rational, safe pair of hands, sensible, steady, trustworthy
3. at the helm, concerned with, duty-bound, have the job of, in authority, in charge, in control, mandated with, overseeing, with responsibility for

**Restrict** v., see also Prevent, Reduce
block, cap, check, circumscribe, clamp down on, confine, constrain, constrict, contain, control, crack down on, curb, curtail, define, delimit, demarcate, diminish, draw a line in the sand, draw the line, earmark, fence in, fix, freeze, hamper, hamstring, hem in, hinder, hold back, hold in check, impede, inhibit, keep a lid on, keep within limits, lessen, limit, lock down, minimise, moderate, narrow, pin down, place restrictions on, prescribe, put a brake on, put a limit on, ration, regulate, rein in, repress, restrain, ring-fence, set a limit, specify, stifle, temper, thwart, tie, tighten

**Restriction** n., see also Extent
ban, cap, ceiling, check, confines, constraint, control, crackdown, curb, curtailment, cut-off point, deadline, demarcation, earmarking, limitation, limit(s), lockdown, maximum, most, proviso, regulation, reservation, restraint, ring-fencing, rule, stipulation, threshold, tops, upper limit, veto

**Result** n., see also Performance, Profit
achievement, after-effect, aftermath, bottom line, by-product, chain reaction, conclusion, consequence, development, earnings, effect, end, end product, end result, fallout, financial results, finding, fruits (of one's labour), fruition, impact, implication(s), influence, issue, knock-on effect, outcome, payback, pay-off, product, ramifications, reaction, reckoning, repercussion, return, reverberations, side effect, significance, thrust, upshot, verdict, wake

**Result In** v., see also Cause, Start
breed, bring, bring about, come to a head, conclude in, contribute to, create, culminate in, end in, engender, ensure, evoke, fan (the flames), form the basis of, fuel, generate, give rise to, incite, influence, kick-start, kindle, lay the ground for, lead to, make for, occasion, pave the way for, precipitate, produce, prompt, provoke, see, sow the seeds, spark, spawn, stoke, trigger, unleash

**Resume** v., see also Recover, Start
begin again, bring back, carry on, come back to, continue, finish, go back to the drawing board, go back to basics, go on, keep on, keep up, pick up (from where one started), proceed, reassume, reboot, recommence, regain, reignite, reinstate, reopen, reset, restart, retake, return, revert, revisit, start again, start from square one, start over, take up

**Retailer** n., see also Business, Company
agent, chain, dealer, dealership, distributor, merchant, outlet, peddler, proprietor, purveyor, reseller, retail outlet, salesperson, sales representative, seller, shop, shopkeeper, store, store owner, storekeeper, trader, vendor

**Retain** v., see also Continue, Sustain
accumulate, amass, be in charge of, be responsible for, care for, cherish, conserve, contain, control, defend, encourage to stay, hang on to, have, have charge of, hoard, hold, hold back, hold onto, keep, keep control of, keep hold of, keep possession of, keep up, look after, maintain, manage, nurture, oversee, own, preserve, protect, reserve, retain ownership, safeguard, save, store, support, withhold

**Reveal** v., see also Announce, Discover
acknowledge, admit, bare, be honest, break news, bring out into the open, bring to light, communicate, concede, confess, confide, declare, disclose, display, divulge, expose, get off one's chest, give away, inform, introduce, launch, lay bare, lay cards on the table, let slip, let the cat out of the bag, level with someone, make known, make public, notify, open, present, publish, report, shine a light on, showcase, spill the beans, take the wraps off, tell, uncover, unearth, unmask, unveil

**Revenue** n., see also Performance, Sales
cash flow, commission, compensation, earnings, income, income generated, livelihood, money, pay, proceeds, receipts, remuneration, revenue generated, revenue stream, salary, sales figures, sales revenue, sales turnover, takings, top line, trade, turnover, wage

**Review** n., see also Analysis, Report
another look, appraisal, appreciation, assessment, audit, check, comment, consideration, criticism, critique, discussion, enquiry/inquiry, evaluation, examination, exploration, fresh look, inspection, investigation, judgement, look at, reappraisal, reassessment, reconsideration, re-evaluation, re-examination, rethink, revision, scrutiny, study, survey, verification, write-up

**Review** v., see also Analyse, Assess
appraise, check, comment on, consider, critique, discuss, evaluate, examine, gauge, give an opinion, go over, grade, inspect, investigate, judge, look at/into/over, look at again, monitor, probe, rank, rate, reassess, reconsider, re-evaluate, re-examine, reflect on, rethink, revise, revisit, run over, screen, scrutinise, study, summarise, take another look at, take stock of, verify

**Revise** v., see also Adjust, Improve
adapt, alter, amend, change, correct, develop, edit, enhance, facelift, fix, go over, hone, look over, make over, modify, optimise, overhaul, perfect, polish, reboot, recalibrate, reconsider, rectify, redesign, redraft, re-examine, refine, relaunch, remodel, reorganise, restyle, revamp, review, revisit, rework, take another look at, tinker with, tweak, update, upgrade

**Ridiculous** adj., see also Unlikely, Unusual
absurd, amusing, beggars belief, bizarre, beyond belief, beyond a joke, comical, crazy, curious, daft, fanciful, fantastic, fantastical, farce, farcical, folly, foolish, funny, goofy, hare-brained, illogical, impossible, incredible, insane, irrational, laughable, losing/lost the plot, ludicrous, mad, mockery, nonsense, nonsensical, not making sense, nuts, odd, outrageous, pie in the sky, pipedream, preposterous, risible, rubbish, senseless, silly, strange, stupid, unbelievable, unconventional, wacky, weird, wrongheaded, zany

**Right** adj., see also Accurate, Appropriate
acceptable, advantageous, all right, apt, authentic, befitting, convenient, correct, decent, deserved, desirable, due, ethical, exact, factual, fair, favourable, fine, fitting, good, honest, honourable, ideal, just, lawful, legal, legitimate, merited, normal, on the money, on the nose, only right, opportune, perfect, precise, preferable, proper, rational, reasonable, right approach, right thing to do, satisfactory, sound, spot on, suitable, sure, true, unerring, valid, watertight, wise

**Right** n., see also Ability, Authority
authorisation, birth right, claim, due, entitlement, facility, fairness, freedom, human rights, independence, legality, liberty, licence, mandate, permission, position, power, prerogative, privilege, rights, scope, user rights

**Rise** n., see also Boost, Expansion
acceleration, accretion, accumulation, addition, advance, amplification, appearance, augmentation, blossoming, bolstering, boom, bounce, broadening, build-up, burgeoning, climb, development, elevation, emergence, enlargement, escalation, explosion, extension, gain, groundswell, growing, growth, growth spurt, heightening, hike, improvement, increase, increment, inflation, intensification, jump, leap, meteoric rise, multiplication, mushrooming, pick-up, progress, proliferation, rally, rebound, rising tide, spike, spurt, step-up, strengthening, surge, swell, upsurge, upswing, uptick, upturn

**Rise** v., see also Expand, Increase
abound, accelerate, accumulate, advance, appreciate, ascend, balloon, be on the increase, be on the rise, be on the up, be up, become larger, boom, build, build up, burgeon, climb, creep up, develop, edge higher, emerge, enlarge, escalate, explode, flourish, gain, gain ground, gather pace, get bigger, go through the roof, go up, grow, heighten, hot up, improve, jump, leap, mount, move up, multiply, mushroom, notch up, pick up, progress, proliferate, prosper, rocket, shoot up, skyrocket, snowball, soar, spike, spread, sprout, strengthen, surge, swell, take off, thrive, zoom

**Risk** n., see also Possibility, Threat
chance, contingency, danger, exposure, gamble, hazard, jeopardy, leap in the dark, liability, likelihood, opportunity, peril, pitfall, potential, prospect, scope, spectre, speculation, stake, susceptibility, uncertainty, unpredictability, vulnerability

**Risky** adj., see also Bold, Dangerous
asking for trouble, bringing risks, delicate, delicate balance, dicey, dodgy, flirting with danger, fraught with danger/risk, hairy, hazardous, higher-risk, high-risk, living dangerously, long shot, not without risk, on dangerous ground, on thin ice, perilous, playing with fire, precarious, rocky, sailing close to the wind, sensitive, speculative, touch and go, tricky, uncertain, under threat, unpredictable, unsafe, unsound, vulnerable

**Robust** adj., see also Reliable, Strong
alive and kicking, booming, built on strong foundations, deep-rooted, dependable, durable, dynamic, fighting fit, firm, fit, flourishing, forceful, formidable, hale and hearty, hardy, hard-wearing, healthy, hearty, hefty, holding its own, in fine fettle, in good health, in good shape, in rude health, in the pink, ironclad, muscular, potent, powerful, powerhouse, resilient, rock-solid, rugged, safe, secure, solid, solid as a rock, sound, stable, steadfast, steady, sturdy, thriving, tough, vigorous, well-built, well-founded, well-made

**Role** n., see also Job, Work
aspect, assignment, brief, business, capacity, contribution, duties, duty, function, guise, involvement, line of work, occupation, office, operation, part, participation, position, post, purpose, remit, responsibility, status, task, trade

**Rough/Roughly** adj./adv., see also Almost, General(ly)
about, approaching, approximate(ly), around, at a guess, ballpark figure, bordering on, close to, crude, estimated, generally, imprecise, in the ballpark

of, in the region of, in the vicinity of, just over/under, more or less, near, nearly, nigh on, not far off, odd, or so, relatively, roughly speaking, some (*e.g. some £1 million*), somewhere around, (there or) thereabouts, verging on

**Rule** n., see also Regulation, Requirement
basic rule, basis, belief, bible, checks and balances, code, command, convention, cornerstone, criterion, custom, decree, directive, dos and don'ts, edict, ethos, formula, general rule, golden rule, guideline(s), instruction, keystone, law, letter of the law, mantra, maxim, method, order, philosophy, policy, practice, precedent, principle, procedure, protocol, restriction, rule book, rule of thumb, ruling, standard, statute, tenet

**Rumour** n., see also News, Reputation
anecdotal evidence, buzz, chat, chatter, comment, gossip, grapevine, hearsay, hint, indication(s), inside story/track, intelligence, low-down, mood music, report(s), rumour has it, rumour mill, story, suggestion, swirling rumours, tale, talk, tittle-tattle, tongues wagging, whisper, word, word has it, word on the street

# S

**Sack** v., see also Dismiss, Reject
axe, call for someone's head, can, cast out, dispense with, ditch, drop, eject, eliminate, exclude, expel, fire, force out, get rid of, give marching orders, give notice, give the boot, give the elbow, give the heave-ho, give the push, kick out, lay off, let go, make redundant, oust, part company with, part ways, reduce headcount/personnel/workforce, release, remove, replace, send packing, show the door, strip of, terminate employment

**Safe** adj., see also Cautious, Certain
1. alive and kicking, defended, dependable, free from harm, harmless, healthy, home and dry, in safe hands, intact, not dangerous, okay, out of danger, out of harm's way, out of the woods, protected, reliable, risk-free, safe and sound, safe as houses, safe haven, safeguarded, secure, sheltered, shielded, sitting pretty, stable, sure, unassailable, undamaged, unharmed, unscathed
2. belt-and-braces, careful, circumspect, conservative, dependable, guarded, hedging one's bets, on the safe side, playing it safe, prudent, reliable, risk-averse, safe pair of hands, safety first, sure, tame, tried-and-tested, trustworthy, unadventurous, vigilant, wary, watchful

**Sales** n., see also Income, Performance
business, demand, proceeds, receipts, revenue(s), revenue generated, revenue stream, sales activity, sales figures, sales performance, sales revenue, sales turnover, selling, takings, top line, trade, trading, turnover

**Same** adj., see also Similar, Unchanged
alike, carbon copy, clone, comparable, consistent, constant, copy, corresponding, dead ringer, ditto, dual, duplicate, equal, equivalent, exactly alike, fellow, identical, imitation, indistinguishable, interchangeable, invariable, look-alike, no difference, nothing between them, one and the same, photocopy, replica, rip-off, self-same, spitting image, spot the difference, twin, two peas in a pod, unaltered, unchanging, uniform, unvarying, very same, virtually identical

**Sanction** v., see also Approve, Punish
agree (to), allow, authorise, back, certify, confirm, consent to, empower, encourage, endorse, give backing, give blessing, give permission, give the go-ahead, give the green light, give the nod, grant, green-light, license, mandate, okay, permit, ratify, support, validate

**Satisfactory** adj., see also Enough, Reasonable
acceptable, adequate, all right, average, competent, decent, does the job, fair, fine, fit, fit for purpose, good, good enough, okay, passable, respectable, solid, sound, sufficient, suitable, tolerable, unexceptional, up to scratch, up to standard, up to the job, valid, will do

**Satisfy** v., see also Achieve, Fulfil
accomplish, address, answer, appease, assuage, assure, be adequate, be enough, be sufficient, be up to scratch, comfort, comply with, conform to, convince, correspond, deliver, do the trick, fit the bill, fit with, gladden, gratify, hit the mark/spot, humour, indulge, keep a promise, make good, make the grade, match, meet, meet expectations, meet requirements, mollify, pacify, pass muster, perform, persuade, placate, please, provide, put at ease, qualify, quench, reassure, sate, satisfy requirements, serve its purpose, suffice, suit

**Save** v., see also Defend, Invest
1. bail out, be a lifeline/lifesaver, come to the rescue, deliver, extricate, free, help (out), liberate, preserve, protect, pull out of the fire, recover, redeem, rescue, retrieve, safeguard, salvage, save, save someone's bacon, save someone's life, save someone's skin, save the day, set free, spare, spare someone's blushes, throw a lifeline
2. amass, be frugal, be thrifty, build a nest egg, cache, conserve, economise, eke out, hoard, keep, penny-pinch, put aside, put by, reserve, save for a rainy day, save money, save up, scrape together, scrimp and scrape, set aside, skimp, squirrel away, stash, stockpile, store, tighten one's belt

**Say** v., see also Announce, Comment
add, affirm, answer, assert, break silence, claim, clarify, communicate, conclude, continue, convey, declare, detail, disclose, divulge, elaborate, explain, express, hint, imply, infer, interject, joke, maintain, make a comment, make a/the point, make a statement, mention, note, outline, point out, put forth, put into words, question, quip, relay, remark, repeat, reply, report, respond, retort, reveal, set out, share, speak, speak out, state, stress, suggest, summarise, tell, underscore, urge, voice

**Schedule** n., see also Plan, Time
agenda, appointments, arrangements, calendar, chronology, countdown, diary, engagements, itinerary, line-up, movements, order of business, order of the day, planning, programme, progress, record, sequencing, time management, timeline, timetable, timing, (on) track

**Scope** n., see also Amount, Extent
ability, area, area of expertise, authority, bounds, breadth, brief, capacity, competence, comprehensiveness, confines, degree, dimensions, elbow room, field, field of reference, flexibility, freedom, headroom, influence, latitude, leeway, magnitude, mandate, margin, measure, opportunity, outlet, possibility, radius, range, reach, realm, remit, room, scale, size, span, sphere, spread, volume, wriggle room

**Search** v., see also Explore
cast about, chase after, check, comb, delve into, dig, enquire, examine, go in quest of, go in search of, go over with a fine-tooth comb, go through, hunt, inquire, inspect, investigate, leave no stone unturned, look everywhere, look for, look high and low, pore over, probe, prospect, pursue, research, scan, scour, scout, scrutinise, search high and low, seek, sift, study, track down, trawl

**Secret** adj., see also Private
behind closed doors, behind the scenes, cards close to one's chest, clandestine, classified, cloak-and-dagger, cloaked, closed, closely guarded, concealed, confidential, covert, coy, cryptic, dirty little secret, discreet, elusive, enigmatic, furtive, hidden, hush-hush, incognito, inside, intimate, little-known, mysterious, need-to-know basis, off the record, personal, restricted, secretive, sensitive, shadowy, shrouded in secrecy/mystery, surreptitious, tight-lipped, top-secret, under lock and key, under one's hat, under wraps, undercover, underground, undisclosed, well-kept secret

**Sector** n., see also Area, Market
activity, area of activity, arena, bracket, branch of industry, business, category, commerce, discipline, domain, enterprise, field, game, industry, landscape, line, line of business, line of work, niche (market), practice, profession, scene, segment, space, sphere, trade, world of

**Secure** adj., see also Certain, Safe
assured, confident, defended, established, firm, guarded, immune, impregnable, in safe hands, in the bag, locked in, nailed on, out of harm's way, protected, reliable, robust, rock-solid, safe and sound, safe as houses, safe pair of hands,

sheltered, shielded, shoo-in, solid, solid as a rock, sound, stable, steady, strong, sure, unassailable, under lock and key, unharmed

**Secure** v., see also Ensure, Guarantee
access, achieve, acquire, assure, build, buy, capture, cement, clinch, close, defend, establish, fix, gain, guard (against), get, get hold of, have, implement, land, make sure, obtain, pick up, procure, protect, put in place, receive, safeguard, score, seal, settle, shield, source, strengthen, take, win

**Security** n., see also Reliability, Strength
assurance, care, certainty, confidence, defence, dependability, force, freedom, guarantee, insurance, muscle, peace of mind, precaution, protection, reassurance, refuge, robustness, safeguard, safekeeping, safety, safety measure, safety net, sanctuary, security measure, sense of security, shelter, shield, soundness, surveillance

**Seem** v., see also Indicate, Suggest
allude to, appear, augur, be apparently, be on the face of it, be ostensibly, be seemingly, be set to, be suggestive of, bode, come across as, create the impression, evoke, give/create the impression, have the air of, have the appearance, hint, imply, insinuate, intimate, look as though, look like, make for, promise, reflect, resemble, set to be, shape up, show every sign of, smack of, sound, strike one as

**Select** v., see also Decide, Specify
adopt, agonise over, appoint, assign, bite the bullet, cherry-pick, choose, conclude, consider, curate, decide on, designate, determine, elect, embrace, favour, go for, handpick, hem and haw/hum and haw, judge, make a call, make a choice, make a decision, make a selection, make up one's mind, opt for, pick, pick and choose, pick one's battles, plump for, ponder, prefer, settle on, shortlist, single out, take a decision, um and ah, weed out, weigh, whittle down

**Selection** n., see also Assortment, Decision
1. assessment, call, choice, choosing, determination, election, evaluation, judgement, nomination, outcome, pick, preference, result, verdict, vote
2. alternatives, array, broad spectrum, choice, collection, cross section, diversity, everything from…to…, gamut, group, line-up, medley, menu, mix, mixture, number, offering, option, palette, portfolio, raft, range, scope, smorgasbord, spectrum, spoilt for choice, suite, variation, variety, wide range

**Sell** v., see also, Promote, Supply
advertise, auction, be an outlet for, close a deal, complete a sale, deal in, dispose of, distribute, divest, fetch (a price), flog, fly off the shelves, give the hard sell, hawk, make a deal, make a sale, make available, market, offer, offload, peddle, persuade, pitch, plug, purvey, push, put up for sale, retail, sell by the truckload, sell like hotcakes, sell off, shift, ship, stock, tap into, trade

**Seller** n., see also Business, Company
agent, broker, chain, dealer, dealership, distributor, merchant, operator, outlet, peddler, purveyor, representative, reseller, retail outlet, retailer, salesperson, sales representative, shop, shopkeeper, store, store owner, storekeeper, trader, vendor, wholesaler

**Sensible** adj., see also Logical, Reasonable
acceptable, appropriate, astute, calm, canny, clear-eyed, common-sense, discerning, down-to-earth, far-sighted, feet on the ground, grown-up, informed, intelligent, judicious, justifiable, legitimate, level-headed, mature, perfect sense, practical, proper, prudent, rational, realistic, reasoned, right, right-minded, sage, sane, shrewd, smart, sound, straightforward, suitable, thoughtful, well-advised, well-reasoned, well-thought-out, wise

**Sensitive** adj., see also Controversial
1. conscious, delicate, easily affected, easily offended, elephant in the room, emotional, emotive, fragile, hot potato, hypersensitive, nervous, on thin ice, oversensitive, precarious, raw nerve, sensitive subject, susceptible, temperamental, tender, tense, thin-skinned, thorny, touchy, touchy subject, treading on eggshells, tricky, volatile
2. attentive, aware, conscious, considerate, kind, patient, receptive, responsive, sympathetic, tactful, tender, thoughtful, understanding

**Separate** adj., see also Different, Unusual
alone, apart, autonomous, cut off, detached, disconnected, discrete, disjointed, distinct, distinctive, divided, divorced, earmarked, fenced off, free, free-standing, independent, individual, isolated, particular, removed, ring-fenced, segregated, separated, sole, solitary, specific, stand-alone, unconnected, unique, unrelated

**Serious** adj., see also Important, Worrying
acute, alarming, austere, businesslike, careful, challenging, committed, concerning, critical, crucial, dangerous, deep, deliberate, detailed, determined, difficult, down to brass tacks, earnest, far-reaching, fateful, genuine, grave,

grim, humourless, in earnest, life-and-death, major, make-or-break, make-your-mind-up time, meaningful, means business, moment of truth, momentous, no laughing matter, no-nonsense, of consequence, passionate, pivotal moment, pressing, professional, profound, reflective, resolute, severe, significant, sincere, sober, sobering, solemn, sombre, sophisticated, stern, strict, stringent, thoughtful, tough, troubling, unsmiling, urgent, watershed moment, weighty

**Service** n., see also Product, Support
advantage, advice, aid, assistance, benefit, business, client/customer service, client/customer support, consulting, contribution, duty, experience, expertise, guidance, help, know-how, maintenance, offer, package, provision, services, servicing, solution, supply, support, use, utility, value, work

**Setback** n., see also Disappointment, Problem
bitter pill to swallow, blow, body blow, bump in the road, challenge, complication, concern, damage, defeat, difficulty, disadvantage, disaster, disastrous, double whammy, embarrassment, hammer blow, hiccup, hindrance, hitch, humiliation, impediment, inconvenience, knock-back, let-down, loss, misfortune, obstacle, reality check, reversal, reversal of fortune, scourge, snag, spanner in the works, stumbling block, test, trouble, upset, worry

**Share** v., see also Combine, Include
allocate, allot, apportion, assign, be (a) party to, be involved, collaborate, contribute, cooperate, dispense, distribute, divide, divvy (up), do jointly, do together, empathise, experience, give and take, go fifty-fifty, go halves, have a hand in, have in common, inform, join, partake, participate, pool, provide information, ration, split, swap, sympathise, take part in, use jointly

**Shared** adj., see also Common, Public
collaborative, collective, combined, communal, community, concerted, consolidated, cooperative, cumulative, global, group-wide, joint, mass, mutual, national, organisation-wide, pooled, social, unified, united, *****-wide

**Shift** n., see also Change
about-face, adjustment, change of tack, changeover, changing face of, changing of the guard, conversion, departure, development, deviation, lurch, move, new approach, new era, paradigm shift, pivot, pivotal moment, rearrangement, rethink, revolution, sea change, seismic shift, shifting, step change, switch, tipping point, transformation, transition, turnaround, turning point, U-turn, veering, volte-face, watershed moment

**Shock** v., see also Surprise
amaze, anger, appal, astonish, astound, awe, beggar belief, bowl over, come out of nowhere, daze, dismay, disturb, drop a bombshell, electrify, flabbergast, give a shock, horrify, jar, jolt, leave aghast, leave open-mouthed, leave speechless, offend, outrage, overwhelm, raise eyebrows, rock, scandalise, shake (up), shell-shock, stagger, startle, stir up, stun, stupefy, throw, unnerve, unsettle, wow

**Shop** n., see also Business, Retailer
boutique, chain, chain store, dealer, dealership, emporium, establishment, outlet, purveyor(s), retail business, seller, showroom, store, supplier, trader

**Show** v., see also Demonstrate, Indicate
bare, be visible, bear out, brandish, capture, clarify, depict, direct, disclose, display, elucidate, emerge, emphasise, epitomise, establish, exemplify, exhibit, explain, expose, feature, flag up, flaunt, guide, herald, highlight, illustrate, introduce, lay bare, lead the way, make clear, make known, make visible, manifest, mark, materialise, offer, outline, parade, point out, point to, portray, present, proclaim, profile, prove, represent, reveal, set out, show off, showcase, signify, sport, spotlight, symbolise, testify to, typify, uncover, unveil, vaunt

**Shrink** v., see also Decrease, Deteriorate
abate, be eroded, be in decline, be in retreat, be on the wane, become smaller, contract, crumble, cut, decline, decrease in size, deflate, die away, diminish, dip, drop off, dry up, dwindle, ebb, fade, fall away, fall off, get smaller, grow smaller, lessen, narrow, peter out, plummet, plunge, recede, reduce, retreat, shorten, shrivel, slash, slide, spiral down, wane, weaken, wilt, wither

**Sign** n., see also Forecast, Warning
barometer, bellwether, benchmark, bright spot, canary in the coal mine, caution, clue, cue, encouraging signs, evidence, flag, foreboding, foretaste, forewarning, gauge, glimmer, guide, harbinger, hint, indication, indicator, mark, marker, measure, milestone, omen, pointer, precursor, prediction, proof, red flag, reminder, signal, signpost, suggestion, symbol, symptom, taster, tip of the iceberg, trace, wake-up call, writing on the wall

**Significance** n., see Emphasis, Focus
bearing, bottom line, concern, connotation, consequence, crux, distinction, essence, factor, force, gravity, heart of the matter, implication, import, importance, influence, key element, magnitude, meaning, poignancy, principle,

priority, prominence, relevance, ramifications, sense, seriousness, stress, substance, tenor, usefulness, value, weight, worth

**Significant** adj., see also Main, Vital
all-important, be all and end all, bedrock, big, big deal, cardinal, central, chief, considerable, core, cornerstone, critical, crucial, crunch, decisive, defining, distinctive, dominant, dramatic, drastic, emphatic, epic, essential, extensive, far-reaching, foremost, fundamental, game-changer, game-changing, going to the heart of, grave, great, heavy, historic, impactful, imperative, important, indispensable, influential, integral, it matters, key, landmark, large, leading, lifeblood, linchpin, looming large, mainstay, major, material, meaningful, mission-critical, momentous, necessary, notable, noteworthy, of (great) importance, of note, of significance, paramount, pertinent, pivotal, poignant, pressing, primary, prime, prominent, real, red-letter day, relevant, resonant, salient, seismic, seminal, serious, sharp, speaks volumes, special, strategic, strong, substantial, substantive, telling, topping the agenda, urgent, valuable, valued, vital, watershed moment

**Similar** adj., see also Related
à la, akin, alike, along the same lines, analogous, chiming with, close to, commensurate with, comparable to, copy, corresponding to, cut from the same cloth, déjà vu, echoing, equivalent to, *****esque, following in the footsteps of, having an affinity with, having echoes of, having parallels with, having shades of, identical to, in keeping with, in line with, in step with, in the mould of, in the same vein, in the vein of, in tune with, indistinguishable from, kindred (spirit), like, like-minded, matching, much of a muchness, much the same, not a million miles away from, not dissimilar to, on a par with, owing a debt to, parallel, rehash, reminiscent of, resembling, rip-off, similar picture, taking inspiration from, tantamount to

**Simple** adj., see also Basic, Easy
1. breeze, child's play, cinch, clear, comprehensible, direct, doddle, easy as pie, effortless, elementary, foolproof, fundamental, hassle-free, honest, meat and drink, no-fuss, no-nonsense, no problem, no sweat, not rocket science, piece of cake, plain, pure and simple, pushover, self-explanatory, simplicity itself, smooth, straightforward, transparent, trouble-free, uncomplicated, undemanding, understandable, walk in the park, walkover, with ease
2. bare-bones, classic, clean, direct, honest, minimalist, modest, no-frills, no-nonsense, pared-back, plain, practical, pure and simple, sincere, spartan, stark,

unadulterated, unaffected, uncluttered, uncomplicated, unfussy, unpretentious, unsophisticated

**Situation** n., see also Circumstances, Issue
case, climate, conditions, context, dilemma, episode, event, how things are, incident, juncture, lie of the land, location, matter, narrative, picture, plight, position, predicament, quandary, reality, result, scenario, scene, setting, stage, standpoint, state, state of affairs, state of play, status, status quo, the way it is/things are

**Size** n., see also Amount, Level
area, breadth, bulk, capacity, content, diameter, dimension(s), extent, footprint, format, height, immensity, length, magnitude, mass, measurements, proportion(s), range, room, scale, scope, space, spread, stature, vastness, volume, width

**Skill** n., see also Ability, Experience
accomplishment, acumen, adeptness, aptitude, artistry, capabilities, capability, command, competence, craft, craftsmanship, credentials, deftness, dexterity, expertise, facility, faculty, finesse, flair, flourish, forte, genius, gift, grasp, ingenuity, intelligence, knack, know-how, knowledge, magic touch, masterclass, masterpiece, masterstroke, mastery, Midas touch, professionalism, proficiency, prowess, skilfulness, skillset, speciality, strength, stroke of genius, strong suit, talent, technique, top of one's game, trump card, versatility, what it takes, wherewithal, wisdom

**Skilled** adj., see also Experienced, Talented
able, accomplished, adept, aficionado, blessed, capable, competent, connoisseur, consummate professional, dab hand, deft, distinguished, exceptional, expert, gifted, good at, handy, highly regarded, hotshot, intelligent, knowledgeable, leading, masterful, masterly, practised, professional, proficient, qualified, respected, seasoned, skilful, top-rated, trained, versatile, veteran, virtuoso, virtuosic, well-versed, widely respected, whizz, wizard

**Slightly** adv., see also Little, Moderate
barely, bit, ever so slightly, hardly, hint of, imperceptibly, insignificantly, *****ish, just a little, lightly, marginally, moderately, modestly, modicum of, on the ***** side, only just, partially, scarcely, shade, somewhat, suggestion of, tad, tinged, to some degree, to some extent, touch

**Slogan** n., see also Advertising, Brand
banner, brand name, branding, byword, catchphrase, emblem, expression, label, logo, mantra, marque, motto, phrase, rallying cry, saying, strapline, tagline, trademark, watchword

**Slow** adj., see also Gradual, Unsuccessful
at a leisurely pace, at a slow pace, at a snail's pace, at one's leisure, behind, belated, careful, cautious, crawling, creeping, delayed, drawn-out, hesitant, hindered, idling, impeded, inactive, in no hurry, lackadaisical, lagging, late, lazy, leisurely, lethargic, lingering, listless, low-speed, measured, moderate, not fast, plodding, ponderous, postponed, procrastinating, prolonged, protracted, relaxed, reluctant, sleepy, slow burner, slow-footed, slow-moving, slow out of the blocks, sluggish, snail-like, stagnant, steady, tame, tardy, tedious, time-consuming, trailing, uneventful, unhurried, unproductive, unpunctual

**Slow (Down)** v., see also Decline, Delay
abate, act as a brake on, bog down, brake, check, choke, curb, curtail, dampen, decelerate, decrease, depress, detain, deteriorate, diminish, ease off, ease up, get bogged down, go slower, grind to a halt, hinder, hobble, hold back, impede, inhibit, keep waiting, lag (behind), lessen, lose speed, lose steam, mire, moderate, postpone, put the brakes on, reduce, reduce speed, rein in, relax, restrict, run out of steam, set back, slacken, slow to a halt, stall, stunt, subdue, take one's time, temper, weigh on, wind down

**Small** adj., see also Few, Lack
almost no, baby, barely, bite-size(d), brief, compact, concise, deficiency, diminutive, dinky, few and far between, fleeting, fun-size(d), hardly any, humble, immaterial, imperceptible, in short supply, inadequate, inappreciable, inconsequential, inconsiderable, insignificant, insufficient, junior, lesser, light, limited, little, meagre, measly, mere, microscopic, mini, miniature, minnow, minor, minuscule, minute, miserly, modest, muted, narrow, negligible, next to nothing, not large, not many, not much, paltry, paucity of, petite, piffling, pint-size(d), pocket-size(d), portable, potted, precious little, reduced, scaled-down, scant, scarcely, scarcity, short of/on, short-lived, slender, slight, slightly, slim, small but perfectly formed, small fry, smallish, small-scale, small-time, smattering, smidgeon, sparse, succinct, tad, teeny, thin on the ground, tiny, trifling, trivial, undersize(d), ungenerous, unimportant, unsatisfactory, vanishingly small, virtually no, wanting, wee

**Smart** adj., see also Intelligent, Stylish
1. able, agile, astute, brains, bright, brilliant, canny, capable, clever, discerning, effective, far-sighted, genius, gifted, incisive, ingenious, insightful, intellectual, keen, knowledgeable, logical, nimble, on the ball, perceptive, quick-witted, resourceful, savvy, sharp, shrewd, skilful, switched on, thoughtful, whizz, wise
2. attractive, chic, classy, dapper, dashing, debonair, elegant, fashionable, fetching, fine, graceful, handsome, high-end, in fashion, natty, neat, polished, posh, snazzy, swanky, trendy, upmarket, well-dressed, well-turned-out

**Solution** n., see also Action, Idea
antidote, answer, approach, big idea, breakthrough, conclusion, explanation, fix, hack, key, knack, panacea, plan, proposal, quick fix, remedy, repair, resolution, secret, silver bullet, strategy, trick, way to solve something, way forward, way out, workaround

**Solve** v., see also Fix, Resolve
answer, clear up, crack, deal with, debug, decipher, decode, determine, explain, fathom, figure out, find out, find the answer/solution to, get, get to grips with, get to the bottom, identify, iron out, make something a thing of the past, navigate, nip in the bud, overcome, patch up, pinpoint, put right, put two and two together, reason, rectify, settle, sort out, stop the rot, turn around, unlock, unravel, untangle, work around, work out

**Somewhat** adv., see also Little, Moderate
barely, ever so slightly, hardly, hint of, imperceptibly, insignificantly, *****ish, just a little, lightly, marginally, moderately, modestly, on the ***** side, only just, partially, scarcely, shade, slightly, suggestion of, tad, tinged, to some degree, to some extent, touch

**Soon** adv., see also Future, Quick
any moment now, around the corner, before long, before you know it, imminently, in a while, in a minute, in a moment, in due course, in no time, in short order, in the near future, in time, it won't be long, presently, promptly, quickly, rapidly, shortly, suddenly, very soon, within a short space of time

**Source** n., see also Inventor, Start
beginning, birthplace, centre, cradle, crucible, dawn, derivation, epicentre, foundation, fount, heart, home, homeland, hot spot, hotbed, hub, inspiration, nerve centre, nucleus, origin, point of supply, provenance, root, spark, spring, springboard, starting point, where it all began

**Special** adj., see also Impressive, Notable
celebrated, characteristic, definitive, designated, different, distinctive, distinguished, earmarked, eminent, exceptional, exclusive, extra-special, extraordinary, handpicked, important, individual, landmark, life-changing, limited-edition, magical, memorable, momentous, no ordinary, not just any, not your average, notable, noteworthy, one in a million, out of the ordinary, particular, peculiar, pre-eminent, primary, purpose-built/designed/made, rare, remarkable, reserved, select, significant, singular, specialised, specialist, speciality, specific, standout, striking, tailored, tailor-made, trademark, uncommon, unconventional, unique, unorthodox, unusual

**Specialise** v., see also Focus On, Specify
be a leader/leading light in, be a master of one's craft, be a specialist in, be an authority on, be an expert in, be into, be in one's element, be known for, come into one's own, concentrate on, develop skill in, devote oneself to, do one's own thing, excel in, go in for, have a reputation for, major in, practise, pursue, train in, work in, zero in on

**Specific** adj., see also Precise, Special
categorical, characteristic, clear, clear-cut, concrete, dedicated, definite, definitive, detailed, distinct, distinguishing, exact, explicit, individual, itemised, limited, niche, particular, peculiar, personal, purpose-built/designed/made, specialised, specialist, tailored, targeted, unambiguous, unequivocal, unique

**Specify** v., see also Clarify, Focus On
be particular, be specific, cite, decide, define, designate, detail, determine, establish, get down to brass tacks, get to the point, go into detail, hit the nail on the head, identify, indicate, itemise, lay out, limit, list, make clear, name, pin down, point out, put one's finger on, set out, spell out, stipulate

**Spoil** v., see also Affect, Damage
be the fly in the ointment, blemish, blight, blot, botch, bungle, cast a shadow over, corrode, deface, demolish, dent, derail, desolate, destroy, detract from, devastate, diminish, disfigure, erode, harm, hurt, impair, let down, mar, mess up, overshadow, put a dampener on, put a downer on, rain on (someone's parade), ruin, sabotage, sully, taint, take away from, take the shine off, tarnish, throw a spanner in the works, trash, undermine, undo, upset, waste, wreck

**Spread** v., see also Distribute, Expand
advertise, balloon, become (better) known, become larger, become popular, become wider, branch off, branch out, broadcast, burgeon, cast, catch on,

circulate, cover, develop, diffuse, disperse, disseminate, diverge, encompass, engulf, enlarge, escalate, extend, flow, get bigger, grow, grow in popularity, grow in size, increase, make known, make public, multiply, mushroom, pass on, pervade, proliferate, promote, propagate, publish, radiate, reach, roll out, scatter, snowball, sow, span, sprawl, spread like wildfire, spread the word, stretch, sweep across, swell, tell about, transmit, unfold, widen

**Stabilise** v., see also Calm, Stagnate
balance out, become stable, bring under control, calm down, cool, dampen, ease, equalise, gain stability, hold up, keep stable, keep steady, level out, maintain, make stable, make steady, normalise, plateau, provide stability, remain level, remain unchanged, right the ship, settle, settle down, steady, steady the ship, sustain

**Stability** n., see also Reliability, Strength
assurance, balance, calm, certainty, certitude, cohesion, confidence, dependability, durability, endurance, equilibrium, even keel, firm foundations, foundations, maturity, peace of mind, reassurance, resilience, resistance, robustness, security, solid basis, solidity, solidness, soundness, steadfastness, steadiness, strong foundations, sturdiness, support, toughness

**Stable** adj., see also Reliable, Unchanged
balanced, calm, consistent, constant, continuing, deep-rooted, dependable, durable, enduring, established, firm, fixed, invariable, lasting, on an even keel, persistent, predictable, resilient, resistant, resolute, robust, rock-solid, rock-steady, safe, secure, solid, solid as a rock, sound, stable, stalwart, steadfast, steady, strong, strong foundations, sturdy, sure, sustainable, ticking along, trustworthy, unchanging, unvarying, unwavering, well-founded

**Staff** n., see also Employee, Worker
colleagues, co-workers, crew, employees, human resources, manpower, members of staff, men and women, office, officers, operatives, organisation, peers, people, personnel, representative, talent, team, workers, workforce

**Stage** n., see also Development, Progress
chapter, cycle, juncture, lap, leg, level, milestone, moment, period, phase, point, point in time, point of the process, position, quarter, round, season, spell, stage of development, stage of the process, staging post, state, state of play, step, stepping stone, term, time

**Stagnate** v., see also Deteriorate, Underperform
be flat, be in a rut, be in a slump, be in retreat, be in the doldrums, be stagnant, cool, decay, decline, fester, flatline, founder, go nowhere, idle, languish, level out, lie dormant, lie fallow, not budge, not move, not progress, plateau, remain unchanged, settle, slump, stall, stand still, stumble, stutter, suffer stagnation, tail off, tread water

**Standard** adj., see also Average, Normal
accepted, approved, basic, bog-standard, business as usual, classic, common, common-or-garden, conventional, customary, default, definitive, established, everyday, familiar, general, go-to, intermediate, mainstay, off-the-peg, official, orthodox, popular, prevailing, recognised, regular, regulation, requisite, run-of-the-mill, standardised, standard-issue, staple, stock, traditional, typical, uniform, usual, plain-vanilla, widespread, your everyday

**Standard** n., see also Level, Quality
average, benchmark, best practice, calibre, code, criterion, ethics, gauge, gold standard, grade, guideline, ideal, level of achievement, level of performance, litmus test, norm, normal, par (for the course), principle, requirement, rule (of thumb), specification, standing, status, touchstone, yardstick

**Start** n., see also Innovation, Introduction
advent, baptism (of fire), beginning, birth, breakthrough, catalyst, commencement, creation, curtain-raiser, dawn, dawning, day one, debut, early days, embryonic, emergence, establishment, first steps, flying start, foundation(s), genesis, germ of an idea, get-go, green shoots, groundwork, inauguration, inception, infancy, initiation, inroads, inspiration, just the beginning/start, kick-off, launch, launch pad, nascent, off, onset, opening, origin, outset, preface, prelude, premiere, rise, roots, source, spark, springboard, square one, start of something (big/great), starting point, start-up, stirring(s), thin end of the wedge, tip of the iceberg, top, unveiling

**Start** v., see also Innovate, Launch
activate, appear, arise, be a catalyst for, be born, be first, be in its infancy, begin, blaze a trail, blow up, break new ground, bring about, cause, come into existence, commence, conceive, creep in, cut one's teeth, dawn, debut, embark on, emerge, enter upon, establish, fire the starting gun, fire up, found, get cracking, get going, get the ball rolling, get the show on the road, get underway, give birth to, give rise to, herald, inaugurate, induce, initiate, inspire, instigate, institute, introduce, jump-start, kick off, kick-start, kindle, lay the foundations, lay the groundwork, light the fuse, make a start, mark the

beginning/start of, mount, open, originate, pioneer, precipitate, premier, proceed, provoke, raise the curtain, scratch the surface, set about, set in motion, set to, sow the seed(s), spark, spawn, start from scratch, start life, start off, start out, start up, stem from, stimulate, take off, take root, take the initiative, trigger, undertake, unleash, unveil, usher in

**Status** n., see also Capacity, Circumstances
category, class, condition, footing, grade, importance, level, mode, notoriety, office, position, prestige, prominence, quality, rank, rating, reputation, setting, situation, stage, standing, state, state of affairs, state of play, stature, status quo, title

**Stay** v., see also Continue, Maintain
abide, be left, become established, become part of the furniture, bide one's time, carry on, endure, go on, hang in there, keep going, keep at/on, last, linger, live on, outlast, outlive, persevere, persist, press on, prevail, put down roots, remain, remain standing, settle, sit out, stay, stay put, stay/remain standing, stick around, stick at/to/with, still be, stop, survive, tough it out, wait

**Stop** v., see also Cancel, Prevent
arrest, axe, bar, be over, bin, block, break off, bring the curtain down on, bring to a conclusion, bring to an end, bring to a standstill, call a halt to, call it a day, call it quits, call off, call time on, can, cease, close, combat, come to an end, come to a standstill, come to the end of the line/road, crack down on, curb, curtail, cut off, cut short, desist, deter, discontinue, disrupt, ditch, down tools, draw a line in the sand, draw a line under, draw to a close, drop, dry up, end, eradicate, finish, fizzle out, freeze, frustrate, halt, hinder, hit the brakes, hold, hold fire, interrupt, kick into the long grass, kill off, knock on the head, nip in the bud, pack in, peter out, pull, pull the plug on, put an end to, put a stop to, put paid to, quit, refrain, run its course, scotch, scrap, scupper, shelve, shut down, sign off, snuff out, stamp out, stand in the way of, staunch, stem, stop in tracks, stop the rot, stymie, suspend, terminate, throw in the towel, thwart, torpedo, turn off, turn out, veto, wave goodbye to, wind up, withdraw, wrap up

**Store** n., see also Business, Retailer
boutique, chain, chain store, dealer, dealership, emporium, establishment, outlet, purveyor(s), retail business, seller, shop, showroom, supplier, trader

**Strange** adj., see also Surprising, Unusual
against the grain, alien, anomaly, at odds, atypical, bewildering, bizarre, curious, different, distinctive, eccentric, eerie, enigmatic, esoteric, exceptional,

extraordinary, far-out, funny, idiosyncratic, left-field, little-known, mysterious, new, not your everyday, obscure, odd, odd one out, oddball, oddity, offbeat, off-piste, original, out of place, out of the ordinary, outlier, peculiar, perplexing, puzzling, quirky, random, rare, remarkable, sticking out like a sore thumb, strange bedfellows, surreal, uncommon, unconventional, unexpected, unfamiliar, unheard-of, unique, unorthodox, unprecedented, wacky, weird, weird and wonderful

**Strategy** n., see also Approach, Method
action, angle, attitude, big idea, blueprint, game plan, grand design, manoeuvre, manoeuvring, mentality, mindset, perspective, philosophy, plan, plan of action, planning, playbook, policy, procedure, programme, project, proposition, road map, scheme, slant, system, tactic(s), tack, take, thinking, vision, way of thinking

**Strength** n., see also Advantage, Power
1. backbone, bastion, brawn, brute force, capacity, character, clout, courage, depth, determination, dominance, durability, effectiveness, energy, firepower, firmness, force, force to be reckoned with, fortitude, grit, gusto, health, intensity, mettle, might, muscle, oomph, potency, powerhouse, resolve, robustness, security, severity, stability, stamina, steadfastness, strength in depth, strength of character, stronghold, sturdiness, tenacity, toughness, tower of strength, utility, vehemence, vigour, vitality, willpower
2. ability, aptitude, asset, beauty, benefit, blessing, boon, capacity, edge, effectiveness, feature, forte, merit, plus, plus point, selling point, skill, speciality, strong point, strong suit, superiority, talent, trump card, upper hand, value, virtue, weight

**Strengthen** v., see also Improve, Increase
add (to), add fuel to the fire, add strength, amplify, augment, back up, become stronger, beef up, bolster, boost, brace, build up, buttress, complement, consolidate, deepen, drive, embolden, empower, encourage, enhance, enlarge, extend, flourish, fortify, fuel, further, gain (in) strength, galvanise, give a boost, give support, give weight to, grow in strength, grow stronger, harden, hearten, heighten, intensify, invigorate, make more robust, make stronger, nourish, nurture, power, prop up, prosper, provide support, raise, ramp up, ratchet up, ready, reinforce, restore, scale up, shore up, steel, step up, strengthen someone's hand, supercharge, supersize, support, toughen, turbocharge, underpin, up, uphold, upgrade

**Strict** adj., see also Accurate, Serious

absolute, austere, authoritarian, autocratic, demanding, disciplined, draconian, exact, exacting, faithful, firm, hard-and-fast, harsh, inflexible, meticulous, no-nonsense, particular, pedantic, perfect, picky, precise, rigid, rigorous, scrupulous, severe, stern, stickler, stringent, to the letter, tight, total, tough, uncompromising, unyielding

**Strong** adj., see also Effective, Powerful

acute, ardent, assertive, authoritative, avowed, big, bold, capable, clear, compelling, considerable, convincing, core, decisive, dedicated, deep, deep-rooted, deep-seated, determined, die-hard, distinct, dominant, dramatic, drastic, durable, dyed-in-the-wool, dynamic, emphatic, entrenched, extreme, fervent, fierce, fighting fit, firm, focused, forceful, formidable, full, full-blown, full-bodied, good, great, gutsy, hard-line, healthy, heartfelt, heavy-duty, Herculean, high, impactful, impassioned, impressive, in-depth, integral, intense, ironclad, keen, large, marked, might, mighty, muscular, numerous, one hundred percent, overpowering, overwhelming, passionate, potent, profound, pronounced, real, redoubtable, reinforced, reliable, resilient, resolute, resourceful, rich, rich vein of, robust, rock-solid, rock-steady, running deep, severe, sharp, significant, solid, solid as a rock, sound, stable, stalwart, stark, staunch, steadfast, steady, steep, strong-willed, sturdy, substantial, tenacious, tough, trenchant, unbridled, uncompromising, undiluted, unflinching, unmistakable, unmitigated, vehement, vigorous, well-equipped, well-established, well-founded

**Strongly** adv., see also Completely, Especially

absolutely, achingly, acutely, adamantly, all-out, ardently, avidly, awfully, big time, brazenly, certainly, comprehensively, concertedly, conclusively, considerably, decidedly, deeply, demonstrably, downright, dramatically, drastically, eminently, emphatically, every inch, exceedingly, excessively, extensively, extraordinarily, extremely, firmly, full-on, genuinely, glaringly, greatly, heavily, highly, hugely, immeasurably, impossibly, in earnest, incredibly, insanely, intensely, irretrievably, model of, monumentally, most, nothing short of, noticeably, obscenely, off the charts, off the scale, overwhelmingly, particularly, patently, profoundly, quintessentially, quite, radically, really, remarkably, resolutely, resoundingly, richly, rigorously, screaming, severely, sharply, shouting, smacks of, staunchly, steadfastly, steeped in, substantially, super-*****, supremely, sure-fire, surprisingly, terribly, to put it mildly, tremendously, truly, ultra*****, unanimously, unashamedly, uncompromisingly, undisputedly, undoubtedly, unequivocally, unquestionably, unusually, unwavering, utmost, utterly, vastly, vehemently, veritably, very, very much, well and truly, wholeheartedly, wonderfully

**Structure** n., see also Method, Organisation
architecture, arrangement, basis, composition, configuration, construction, design, fabric, form, format, formation, framework, hierarchy, layout, make-up, network, order, organisational structure, plan, platform, process, shape, structural arrangement, structural organisation, system

**Struggle** v., see also Endeavour, Underperform
1. attempt, battle, bend over backwards, combat, compete, contend, contest, cope, do one's best, exert oneself, fight, fight tooth and nail, get stuck in, go all out, grapple, grind out, have one's nose to the grindstone, make every effort, move heaven and earth, plug away, put up a fight, roll one's sleeves up, scramble, seek to, slave, slog, strain, strain every sinew, strive, tackle, toil, tough it out, try, try one's hardest, tussle, undertake, work flat out, work tirelessly, wrestle with
2. be beset by (*e.g. problems*), be embroiled/engulfed in (*e.g. a crisis*), be hard pressed, be haunted by, be mired in (*e.g. a crisis*), be on one's knees, be plagued by, be under pressure, bite off more than one can chew, bomb, come unstuck, face difficulties, face headwinds, fail to cope, fall on hard times, fall short, fight a losing battle, flounder, founder, go backwards, go down like a lead balloon, go off the boil, have a hard time, have trouble, labour, make heavy weather of, miss the mark, suffer (difficulties), run aground, stagnate, stall, stutter, tread water

**Study** v., see also Analyse, Train
assess, bone up on, brainstorm, brush up on, check out, consider, contemplate, deliberate, delve into, do one's homework, enquire, evaluate, examine, explore, go over, inquire, inspect, investigate, learn, learn the ropes, look closely at, look into, mug up on, mull (over), ponder, pore over, probe, read (up on), reflect on, research, scour, scrutinise, shine a light on, survey, swot up on, take a course in, think, think over, undergo training

**Stylish** adj., see also Attractive, Good
à la mode, attention-grabbing, beautiful, bold, charming, chic, classic, classy, contemporary, cool, coordinated, dapper, dazzling, debonair, designer, discerning, dressed to kill, elegant, exuding class/style, eye-catching, fashionable, fetching, flawless, funky, glamorous, good-looking, graceful, handsome, head-turning, hot, iconic, in, in fashion, in style, in vogue, latest, looks the part, must-have, natty, (very) now, on-trend, polished, posh, refined,

resplendent, sartorial, sharp, showy, sleek, slick, smart, snazzy, sophisticated, statement, striking, stunning, sumptuous, swish, tasteful, to die for, trendy, up-to-date, up-to-the-minute, well-turned-out

**Subject** n., see also Idea, Issue
affair, business, case, core, debate, discipline, discussion, field, field of reference, focus, food for thought, front, heart of the matter, issue at hand, item, material, matter, matter at hand, object, point, point in question, problem, proposal, question, speciality, subject matter, substance, talking point, theme, thought, topic

**Subtle** adj., see also Little, Slightly
balanced, complex, delicate, delicate balance, faint, fine, fine line, gentle, hair-splitting, hint of, implied, insinuated, marginal, mild, moderate, muted, narrow, not black and white, nuanced, slight, soft, sophisticated, subdued, suggestion of, suggestive, tacit, tenuous, tinged, toned down, understated, undertone of

**Succeed** v., see also Achieve, Replace
1. accomplish, ace, advance, arrive, bask in the glory, be a hit, be a success, be effective, be flying high, be going places, be on fire, be on a high, be on the front foot, be successful, bear fruit, benefit, boss it, carry the day, click, come off, come up trumps, conquer, deliver the goods, do successfully, do well, earn, fall into place, fare well, find one's feet, fire on all cylinders, flourish, forge ahead, gain, gain victory, gel, get to the top, go down a storm, go down well with, go gangbusters, go great guns, go well, have the wind in one's sails, hit one's stride, hit the big time, hit the ground running, hit the heights, hit the jackpot, hit the mark, land, make a killing, make it, make it big, nail it, not disappoint, not put a foot wrong, obtain, overcome, pass with flying colours, perform well, prevail, profit, prosper, pull something off, realise, revel in, ride high, rise to the occasion, shine, star, strike gold, surmount, take by storm, take off, take to new heights, thrive, triumph, turn the tide, win, wow
2. accede, be successor to, come after, come next, fill someone's boots/shoes, follow on from, inherit from, take over from, take up the baton

**Success** n., see also Achievement, Performance
accomplishment, advance, ascendancy, big league, big time, boom, coup, fame, fame and fortune, favourable outcome, flying colours, fortune, fruits of labour, gain, golden era, good times, happy days, heyday, hit, making of, march of, master stroke, masterpiece, meteoric rise, Midas touch, pièce de résistance, positive result, progress, prosperity, prowess, purple patch, realisation, resounding/roaring success, reward, rise, runaway success, sensation, smash

hit, stroke of genius, successful outcome, success story, top spot, triumph, victory, win, winning formula, win-win

**Successful** adj., see also Effective, Popular
acclaimed, accomplished, acknowledged, at the top (of one's game), at the top of the tree, award-winning, bestselling, booming, bumper, celebrated, champion, constructive, commendable, famed, favourable, feted, flourishing, fortunate, fruitful, going places, high-flying, high-performance, high-performing, hit, in a good place, in the ascendancy, legendary, lucrative, momentous, notable, noteworthy, on a roll, on everyone's lips, on fire, on the front foot, out in front, outstanding, pre-eminent, prize-winning, productive, profitable, prosperous, resounding success, respected, rewarding, roaring success, rosy, second to none, sitting pretty, standout, stellar, storming, strong, talk of the town, thriving, to be commended, top, triumphant, tour de force, victorious, well-known, winning, win-win, with aplomb

**Sudden/Suddenly** adj./adv., see also Quick, Unexpected
abrupt(ly), all at once, all of a sudden, at a stroke, bolt from the blue, fleeting(ly), from nowhere, hastily, hasty, hurried(ly), immediate(ly), impetuous(ly), impromptu, impulsive(ly), in one fell swoop, in the blink of an eye, on the spur of the moment, out of a clear blue sky, out of nowhere, out of the blue, overnight, rapid(ly), rashly, surprising(ly), swift(ly), unannounced, unawares, unforeseen, unplanned, urgent, with immediate effect, within seconds/minutes etc., without warning

**Suffer** v., see also Endure, Negatively Affected
be affected by, be afflicted by, be embroiled in, be engulfed by, be hit by, be impacted by, be in the grip of, be negatively affected/impacted, be rocked by, be stricken with, be subjected to, be under fire, be victim to, bear, bear the brunt of, bear the scars, encounter, experience, face, fall foul of, fall victim to, feel, feel the effects of, go through, hurt, live with, meet with, pay the price, receive, resign oneself to, survive, sustain, sustain damage, take, take a battering, undergo, weather

**Sufficient** adj., see also Adequate, Satisfactory
acceptable, agreeable, all right, ample, aplenty, appropriate, as necessary, as required, comfortable, competent, decent, does the job, enough, good enough, more than enough, plentiful, plenty, proportionate, reasonable, requisite, sufficing, suitable, that will do, tolerable, unexceptional

**Suggest** v., see also Advise, Indicate
1. advance, advocate, affirm, aim, assert, come up with, contemplate, counsel, drive at, float an idea, have in mind, get at, give a tip, hint, intend, introduce, invite, lay before, lay out, make a pitch, make a proposal/suggestion, mean, moot, name, nominate, nudge, offer, offer a suggestion, pitch, plan, plug, prefer, proffer, propose, propound, put, put forward, put it out there, recommend, set forth, set out, submit, table, tender, urge, volunteer
2. allude to, be a sign of, be reminiscent of, evoke, hint (at), imply, insinuate, intimate, point to, promise, put in mind of, refer to, remind, signal

**Suggestion** n., see also Advice, Idea
1. approach, bid, big idea, brainchild, encouragement, game plan, hint, motion, notion, nudge, opinion, outline, pitch, plan, presentation, proposal, proposition, recommendation, scheme, thought, tip, urging
2. allusion, clue, connotation, echoes, hint, implication, indication, inkling, insinuation, intimation, notion, sense, sign, suspicion, tinge, trace, undercurrent, undertone, whiff

**Suit** v., see also Correspond, Match
accommodate, accord, adapt, adjust, agree, be a good fit, be a good match, be a match made in heaven, be acceptable, be appropriate, be cut out for, be ideal, be just the ticket, be suitable, become, befit, conform to, enhance, fit, fit in, fit the bill, follow suit, fulfil, gel, go together, go with, harmonise with, make the grade, meet a need, mesh, please, satisfy, serve, sit well with, suit down to the ground, tailor, tally with, tick all the boxes

**Suitable** adj., see also Correct, Right
acceptable, applicable, appropriate, apt, at home, befitting, compatible, conducive, consistent, convenient, corresponding, cut out for, deserved, done thing, fit for purpose, fitting, geared towards, good, good fit, go-to, horses for courses, ideal, in keeping, in one's comfort zone, just the thing/ticket, legitimate, made for, meeting with approval, one's cup of tea, only right, opportune, optimal, optimum, perfect, pertinent, proper, purpose-built/designed/made, quite right, relevant, right, right and proper, satisfactory, stacks up, successful, suited, suit down to the ground, tailored, tailor-made, ticking all the boxes, to taste, up one's street, useful, well-judged, well-suited

**Summarise** v., see also Conclude, Find
abridge, boil down, brief, compile, condense, cut down, cut to the chase, distil, encapsulate, epitomise, get to the point, give a rundown, give the gist, in a

nutshell, keep it brief, list the main points, look back on, outline, recap, rehash, review, round up, run through, shorten, simplify, skim, sum up

**Summary** n., see also Brief, Conclusion
abstract, analysis, at a glance, big picture, bottom line, brief statement, briefing, bullet points, compilation, digest, essence, in a nutshell, long story short, look back, main points, outline, overview, potted history, precis, recap, report, review, round-up, rundown, run-through, salient points, sense, substance, summing-up, synopsis, takeaway

**Supply** v., see also Provide, Sell
be a contractor/provider/supplier, cater for/to, contribute, deliver, dispense, distribute, equip, feed, fulfil, furnish, give, make, make available, meet, offer, produce, purvey, satisfy, serve, ship, stock, source, transfer, transport

**Support** n., see also Help, Strength
advocacy, aid, approval, assistance, backing, backup, basis, bedrock, benefit, blessing, buy-in, championing, cornerstone, empowerment, encouragement, endorsement, fallback, foundation, funding, guidance, helping hand, interest, linchpin, loyalty, mentoring, moral support, pillar, platform, protection, reassurance, reinforcement, tailwind, underpinning, vote of confidence

**Support** v., see also Enable, Encourage
advocate (for), aid, approve of, assist, back (up), bankroll, be a lifeline/lifesaver, be a source of strength, be a supporter of, be all for, be by someone's side, be pro something, be there for someone, bear out, believe in, bolster, buttress, buy into, care for, carry, champion, cheer on, contribute, defend, empower, endorse, facilitate, finance, foster, fund, get behind, give help, give a leg up, give approval, give endorsement, give space, give support, have someone covered, have someone's back, help, keep an eye on, lend support, look after, maintain, make possible, nourish, nurture, promote, prop up, prove, provide support, rally behind/round, reassure, reinforce, root for, safeguard, shore up, shoulder (the burden), side with, stand by someone, stick up for, stick with, strengthen, subsidise, supplement, sustain, take under one's wing, throw one's weight behind, underpin, uphold, vouch for

**Supporter** n., see also Customer, Investor
adherent, admirer, advocate, ally, backer, believer, champion, cheerleader, collaborator, defender, devotee, enthusiast, fan, fan base, financier, follower, following, friend, funder, helper, patron, proponent, stalwart, strong believer in, superfan, volunteer, well-wisher

**Sure** adj., see also Confident, Likely
absolute, adamant, assured, banking on, beyond a shadow of (a) doubt, bound to, cast-iron, categorical, certain, certified, clear, clear-cut, conclusive, convinced, counting on, cut and dried, dead cert, decisive, definite, dependable, determined, emphatic, established, fail-safe, fait accompli, firm, foregone conclusion, genuine, gimme, given, guaranteed, incontrovertible, inevitable, ironclad, irrefutable, nailed-on, never/not in doubt, positive, predictable, resolved, satisfied, secure, settled, shoo-in, solid, sure thing, sure-fire, tried-and-tested, true, trusty, unambiguous, undeniable, undisputed, undoubted, unmistakable, unquestionable, unshakable, untroubled, unwavering, watertight, with certainty, without a shadow of a doubt, without doubt

**Surplus** adj./n., see also Large, Lots
balance, excess, extra, extravagance, flood, glut, in excess, left over, more than enough, over, overabundance, overflow, overkill, overload, overrun, oversupply, plethora, remainder, remaining, spare, superfluous, surfeit, too much, unused, waste

**Surprise** v., see also Shock
amaze, ambush, astonish, astound, beggar belief, blindside, blow away, bowl over, buck a trend, catch off guard, catch unawares, cause amazement/surprise, confound, creep up on, dazzle, defy (the odds, predictions, etc.), disconcert, dismay, drop a bombshell, dumbfound, electrify, flabbergast, leave open-mouthed, leave speechless, overwhelm, raise eyebrows, rattle, rock, shake up, shell-shock, spring something on, stagger, startle, stun, take aback, take by surprise, take one's breath away, throw, throw a curveball, unsettle, wow, wrong-foot

**Surprised** adj., see also Unexpected, Unusual
alarmed, amazed, astonished, astounded, at a loss, blindsided, caught off guard/unawares, dazed, disconcerted, dismayed, dumbfounded, flabbergasted, gobsmacked, hit for six, incredulous, lost for words, not believing one's ears/eyes, reeling, shocked, speechless, staggered, startled, stunned, taken aback, taken by surprise, thrown, unable to believe (one's eyes/ears)

**Surprising** adj., see also New, Unexpected
against (all) the odds, alarming, amazing, astonishing, astounding, beggars belief, bombshell, counterintuitive, curveball, dark horse, deceptive, disbelief, extraordinary, eye-opener, eye-opening, out of left field, full of surprises, gobsmacking, going under the radar, inconceivable, jaw-dropping, lo and behold, mind-blowing, miraculous, out of nowhere, out of the blue, remarkable,

revelation, rude awakening, shock, shocking, sobering, source of amazement, staggering, startling, stunning, sudden, surprise, trick up one's sleeve, turn-up for the books, twist, unanticipated, unbelievable, uncharted, unforeseen, unknown quantity, unlikely, unplanned, unpredicted, unusual, without warning

**Sustain** v., see also Continue, Suffer
1. aid, assist, back, bolster, buoy, buttress, defend, develop, endorse, foster, keep, keep alive, keep going, keep up, maintain, nourish, nurture, preserve, prolong, prop up, save, shore up, stand by, stand up for, stick up for, subsidise, support, underpin, uphold, validate
2. bear, encounter, endure, experience, face, feel, live with, put up with, stand, stomach, take, tolerate, undergo, withstand

**Sustainability** n., see also Environment, Ethics
carbon footprint, care for the environment/nature/natural world/planet, ecological footprint, ecological impact, environmental awareness, environmental consideration, environmental footprint, environmental impact, environmental responsibility, environmental sustainability, environmentally sustainable approach, ESG (environmental, social and corporate governance), green approach, low-carbon approach, low emissions, sustainable approach, sustainable development

**Sustainable** adj., see also Ethical, Long-term
1. carbon-negative, carbon-neutral, clean, climate-friendly, eco-conscious, eco-friendly, eco-labelled, ecologically sustainable, environmentally friendly, environmentally sustainable, ESG (environmental, social and corporate governance), green, low-carbon, low-emissions, low-impact, renewable, respecting the environment/nature/natural world/planet, responsible, with consideration for the environment, zero-emissions
2. continual, continuous, durable, feasible, lasting, permanent, resilient, stable, steady, supportable, tenable, viable, workable, worthwhile

**System** n., see also Method, Process
application, approach, architecture, arrangement, basis, classification, coordination, design, ecosystem, framework, mentality, methodology, mindset, order, organisation, philosophy, plan, platform, policy, practice, procedure, routine, rules, scheme, setup, software, strategy, structure, systematic approach/process, tactics, technique, thinking

# T

**Tackle** v., see also Address, Resolve
attend to, challenge, clear up, combat, confront, cope with, deal with, engage in/with, ensure, face up to, find a solution, get on top of, get stuck into, get to grips with, grapple with, grasp, handle, iron out, manage, meet, meet the challenge, navigate, nip in the bud, respond to, rise to the challenge, see to, seize, set about, settle, solve, sort (out), take in hand, take measures, take on, take steps, take the bull by the horns, take up, undertake, work on, wrestle with

**Take Advantage** v., see also Exploit, Utilise
apply, avail oneself of, benefit from, bring into play, capitalise on, cash in on, convert into, deploy, draw on, drive home an advantage, employ, establish, exercise, extract, fleece, get mileage out of, grasp an opportunity, harness, impose, inflict, leverage, make the most of, make (good) use of, maximise, milk, profit by, profit from, put to use, seize the opportunity, tap into, translate into, turn into, turn to one's advantage, use, use to one's advantage, work with

**Talented** adj., see also Experienced, Skilled
able, accomplished, adept, admired, adroit, aficionado, blessed, brilliant, capable, clever, connoisseur, consummate, cut out for, dab hand, distinguished, exceptional, expert, gifted, handy, highly respected, hotshot, intelligent, knowledgeable, many strings to one's bow, master, master of one's craft, masterful, multitalented, prodigiously talented, professional, proficient, qualified, respected, skilful, smart, top, top-rated, trained, versatile, virtuoso, well-regarded, well-versed, whizz

**Target** n., see also Aim, Objective
ambition, aspiration, desire, destination, determination, end, end goal, expectation, express aim, focus, goal, holy grail, hope, idea, intent, intention, mission, object, plan, point, purpose, sights, stated aim, ultimate objective, vision

**Target** v., see also Aim, Forecast
aspire to, direct at, endeavour, eye, focus on, go after, have an ambition, have an intention, have in one's sights, have one's eye on, hope for, intend, look

ahead/forward to, look to, plan, propose, pursue, seek to, set a target, set one's sights on, shoot for, strive towards, want, work towards, zero in on

**Task** n., see also Job, Responsibility
activity, assignment, brief, business, challenge, duties/duty, exercise, expectation, function, job at hand, job description, mammoth task, mission, occupation, position, project, remit, requirement, role, undertaking, work, workload

**Teach** v., see also Explain, Prepare
advise, brief, coach, communicate, counsel, demonstrate, develop, drill, educate, encourage, enlighten, expound, familiarise, give lessons, ground, guide, hone skills, illustrate, impart knowledge, indoctrinate, initiate, instil, instruct, lecture, mentor, nurture, open someone's eyes, prepare, provide guidance, provide lessons, provide training, put through paces, share knowledge, school, show, show the ropes, supervise, take under one's wing, train, tutor

**Team** n., see also Cooperation, Personnel
alliance, band, bunch, contingent, crew, crop, dream team, employees, family, gang, group, inner circle, line-up, management team, members, organisation, pairing, participants, squad, taskforce, team effort, teamwork, troop, unit, workers

**Technique** n., see also Approach, Strategy
arrangement, art, capability, craft, craftsmanship, delivery, execution, facility, fashion, form, format, formula, know-how, manner, means, mechanism, method, methodology, modus operandi, plan, practice, procedure, process, routine, scheme, skill, style, system, tack, tactic(s), take, technical skill, touch, way, workmanship

**Technology** n., see also Device, High-tech
advancement, advances (in technology), AI, apparatus, appliance, application(s), artificial intelligence, automation, big data, communications technology, computing, digital economy, digital revolution, digital transformation, digitalisation, electronics, gadget, gadgetry, hardware, information technology, innovation, IT, latest developments, next big thing, online, progress, robotics, scientific knowledge, software, tech, technical advances, technical knowledge, technological progress, (technical) wizardry

**Temporary** adj., see also Brief
acting, ad hoc, backup, brief, ephemeral, fleeting, for a (short) while, for the time being, for a limited period, interim, make-do, makeshift, momentary, not for long, not permanent, passing, provisional, shifting, short, short-lived, short-term, stand-in, stopgap, substitute, transient, transitional, transitory

**Terms** n., see also Circumstances, Condition(s)
agreement, basis, clause, conditions, details, fine print, minutiae, nitty-gritty, points, premise, provisions, regulations, relationship, requirements, restrictions, rules, rules and regulations, small print, specifications, stipulations, terms and conditions, t's and c's

**Test** n., see also Attempt, Evaluation
acid test, analysis, appraisal, approval, assessment, benchmark, challenge, check, criteria/criterion, examination, experiment, inquiry, inspection, investigation, litmus test, probe, probing, quiz, scrutiny, search, test bed, test run, testing, touchstone, trial, trial run, trial and error, verification, yardstick

**Test** v., see also Evaluate, Try
analyse, appraise, assess, carry out testing, challenge, check, check out/over, confirm, demonstrate, dip one's toe in the water, examine, experiment, explore, gauge, give a trial run, give a whirl, investigate, judge, look into, monitor, pilot, probe, prove, put to the test, question, road-test, screen, scrutinise, study, subject to testing, substantiate, suck it and see, survey, test out, test the waters, trial, try out, use trial and error, validate, verify

**Thank** v., see also Appreciate, Praise
acknowledge, admire, applaud, be grateful, be indebted, be obliged, be thankful, celebrate, compliment, credit, express/extend gratitude, express one's (warmest) thanks, offer one's thanks, owe a debt of gratitude to, pay tribute, recognise, say (a big) thank you, show appreciation, show gratitude, value, welcome

**Theme** n., see also Idea, Trend
argument, central plank, central theme, claim, concept, crux, emphasis, essence, focus, gist, heart, issue, keynote, leitmotif, line, matter, motif, point, question, recurring theme, running joke, running theme, statement, strand, subject, subject matter, thesis, thought, topic, unifying idea

**Therefore** adv., see also Consequence, Impact
accordingly, as a consequence, as a result, because of this, consequently, for that reason, hence, in that event, on account of, owing to, since, so, that is why, thus, to that end

**Think** v., see also Believe, Consider
analyse, anticipate, appreciate, assume, be convinced, be of the opinion, be under the impression, bear in mind, brainstorm, chew over, comprehend, conceive, conclude, contemplate, cross one's mind, deduce, deem, deliberate, determine, envisage, espouse, estimate, evaluate, examine, expect, feel, figure out, foresee, get one thinking, give pause for thought, give (serious) thought to, guess, imagine, judge, make of, mull (over), muse, occur, ponder, presume, put one's thinking cap on, rack one's brains, realise, reason, reckon, reflect, resolve, scratch one's head, see, speculate, spring to mind, stop and think, strike, suppose, surmise, suspect, take stock, take the view, think carefully, think long and hard, think outside the box, understand, view, weigh (up)

**Thorough** adj., see also Comprehensive, Detailed
absolute, accurate, all-encompassing, assiduous, attentive, careful, complete, conscientious, consummate, deep, die-hard, diligent, dyed-in-the-wool, efficient, end-to-end, exhaustive, expansive, extreme, far-reaching, full, full-blown, full-on, inclusive, in detail, in-depth, intensive, lock stock and barrel, methodical, meticulous, out-and-out, painstaking, perfect, probing, professional, profound, proper, root-and-branch, scrupulous, staunch, strong, sweeping, systematic, total, unmitigated, utter, veritable, wholehearted, works

**Threat** n., see also Problem, Risk
challenge, clear and present danger, concern, danger, foreboding, hazard, indication, intimidation, jeopardy, menace, omen, peril, pitfall, possibility, potential threat, prospect, sign, spectre, vulnerability, warning, worry, writing on the wall

**Threaten** v., see also Jeopardise, Pressure
approach, be brewing, be in the air, be in the offing, be on the horizon, bully, caution, challenge, come for, endanger, flex one's muscles, forewarn, gather, hang over, impend, imperil, intimidate, lean on, loom (over), make a threat, menace, pose a danger/risk/threat, pressure, pressurise, push around, put at risk, put in danger/jeopardy, put under pressure, raise the stakes, risk, scare, spell danger, spook, warn

**Time** n., see also Future, Timetable
aeon, age, chronology, clock, countdown, date, day, duration, epoch, era, eternity, generation, hands of time, heyday, hour, interval, juncture, length of time, life, life cycle, lifespan, lifetime, minutes, moment, occasion, opportunity, pace, past, period, period of time, phase, point, point in time, present, prime, quarter, sands of time, season, seconds, space of time, span, spell, stage, stint, term, tide, time and tide, time frame, time immemorial, time period, times, timeline, timescale, timespan, timing, while, year

**Timetable** n., see also Plan, Time
agenda, appointments, arrangements, calendar, chronology, countdown, diary, engagements, itinerary, line-up, movements, order of business, order of the day, planning, programme, progress, record, schedule, sequencing, status, time management, timeframe, timeline, timescale, timing

**Together** adv., see also Collaboration, Combination
alongside, as a group, as a team, as one, close-knit, closely, collaboratively, collectively, combined, concerted(ly), concurrently, cooperatively, en masse, hand in glove, hand in hand, in cahoots, in chorus, in close collaboration, in company, in concert, in conjunction, in cooperation, in harmony, in parallel, in partnership, in solidarity, in synch, in tandem, in the company of, in unison, jointly, mutually, pulling together, sharing, shoulder to shoulder, side by side, simultaneously, unanimously, united, with each other, with one voice

**Tool** n., see also Device, Method
aid, apparatus, appliance, approach, contraption, gadget, gizmo, implement, instrument, invention, lever, machine, means, mechanism, platform, range of tools, resource, system, technique, toolbox, toolkit, utensil, way, weapon

**Top** adj., see also Best, First
award-winning, best-selling, biggest, chief, class-leading, commanding, dominant, elite, eminent, excellent, finest, first-class, first-rate, five-star, flagship, foremost, greatest, highest, high-quality, high-ranking, important, incomparable, key, lead, leading, main, most, most important, most successful, number one, outstanding, pre-eminent, premier, premium, primary, prime, principal, renowned, respected, second to none, standout, state-of-the-art, superior, supreme, top-flight, topmost, top-notch, top-quality, top-ranked, top-rated, ultimate, unequalled, unrivalled, uppermost, well-regarded, well-respected, world-class

**Total** adj./n., see also All, Entire
absolute, across the board, aggregate, all told, altogether, amassed, amount, complete, comprehensive, cumulative, entirety, exhaustive, full, full amount, full-blown, full-on, in total, out-and-out, outright, overall, quantity, result, sum, sum total, sweeping, tally, thorough, totality, unmitigated, utter, whole

**Totally** adv., see also Strongly
absolutely, completely, comprehensively, conclusively, deeply, downright, effectively, entirely, exhaustively, firmly, from start to finish, full-on, fully, heart and soul, in earnest, in full, lock stock and barrel, on all counts, one hundred percent, overwhelmingly, perfectly, quite, root and branch, roundly, soundly, steadfastly, thoroughly, truly, unanimously, undisputedly, unquestionably, utterly, veritably, very, well and truly, wholeheartedly, wholly

**Tough** adj., see also Challenging, Durable
1. arduous, backbreaking, baffling, beset by problems, bruising, brutal, complex, demanding, difficult, exhausting, formidable, gruelling, hard, hard work, harsh, heavy, heavy lifting, laborious, no picnic, not easy, onerous, out of one's comfort zone, painful, perplexing, puzzling, severe, strenuous, taxing, testing, thorny, torrid, tough going, tricky, troublesome, trying, uncomfortable, unenviable, uphill (battle/task)
2. determined, dogged, doughty, fit, hard, hard as nails, hard-nosed, hardwearing, hardy, indomitable, indestructible, mighty, resilient, resolute, robust, rugged, ruthless, seasoned, solid, steely, stern, stout, strict, strong, sturdy, tenacious, tough as old boots, unyielding

**Train** v., see also Explain, Prepare
advise, brief, coach, communicate, counsel, demonstrate, develop, develop professionally, drill, educate, enlighten, equip, exercise, expound, familiarise, give lessons, ground, guide, hone, illustrate, impart knowledge, improve, initiate, instil, instruct, lecture, mentor, nurture, open someone's eyes, practise, provide guidance, provide lessons, provide training, put through paces, qualify, receive training, rehearse, school, sharpen, show, show the ropes, study, supervise, take lessons, take under one's wing, teach, tutor, undergo training, upskill, work out

**Training** n., see also Education, Prepare
apprenticeship, background, basics, coaching, course, crash course, credentials, development, discipline, drill, education, exercise, foundation, grounding, groundwork, guidance, honing, improvement, instruction, learning curve, lessons, mentoring, practice, preparation, professional development, rehearsal,

schooling, strengthening, supervision, support, teaching, training course, tuition, upskilling, workout

**Transaction** n., see also Acquisition, Agreement
business, business deal, contract, deal, dealings, disposal, divestment, investment, matter, move, purchase, sale, selling, settlement, trade, undertaking, venture

**Transform** v., see also Disrupt, Improve
be transformative, become, bring about a sea change/transformation/etc., change completely, change the complexion of, change the face of, convert, dramatically change, have a major impact on, make over, mark a revolution/shift, metamorphose, morph, overhaul, pivot, reboot, rebuild, recast, reconstruct, redraw the map, reimagine, renew, reorganise, reset, restructure, revamp, revolutionise, rewrite the rule book, ring the changes, rip up (the rule book), rock, shake to the foundations/core, shake up, tear up, transfigure, transition, turn around, turn into, turn on its head, upend, usher in a new era

**Transport** v., see also Deliver, Supply
bring, carry, convey, courier, deliver to your door, dispatch, drop off, ferry, fetch, haul, lug, move, run, send, shift, ship, take, transfer, truck, wing its way

**Treat** v., see also Manage, Tackle
act towards, address, administer, approach, attend to, behave towards, cater for, conduct (oneself), consider, cope with, deal with, engage with, get to grips with, govern, handle, look after, maintain, play, process, rate, react towards, regard, resolve, respect, respond to, serve, supervise, take care of, undertake, use, value, work with

**Trend** n., see also Development
change, course, craze, current, direction, direction of travel, fad, fashion, flow, general direction, inclination, latest thing, leaning, mania, mood, move away from/towards, movement, narrative, orientation, progression, rage, shift, swing, tendency, theme, trajectory, uptake, vogue, wave, what's in, zeitgeist

**Trouble** n., see also Challenge, Difficulty
adversity, anxiety, bother, catastrophe, challenging times, complication, concern, conflict, crisis, danger, deep water, dilemma, dire straits, disarray, discontent, discord, disquiet, dissatisfaction, distress, disturbance, effort, fiasco, grief, hard times, hardship, hassle, headache, heartache, hiccup, hitch, hot potato, hot water, incident, inconvenience, mess, misfortune, nightmare,

nuisance, pain, perfect storm, pickle, plight, predicament, problem, quandary, scourge, setback, stress, strife, struggle, teething problems, testing times, thorn in the side, travails, trials and tribulations, troubling picture, trying times, tumult, turmoil, unhappiness, unpleasantness, unrest, upheaval, uproar, woes, worry

**Trouble** v., see also Hamper, Worry
afflict, annoy, arise, assail, bedevil, beset, bother, bug, burden, cause trouble, concern, disconcert, distress, disturb, dog, embroil, engulf, faze, fester, get to, harass, haunt, hound, inconvenience, interfere, irk, irritate, mire, nag, niggle, pain, perturb, plague, rattle, spell trouble, strain, stress, torment, upset, vex

**True** adj., see also Accurate, Correct
actual, appropriate, authentic, authoritative, bona fide, confirmed, dependable, exact, factual, faithful, genuine, gospel truth, honest, kosher, legitimate, loyal, precise, proper, pure, real, right, rightful, ring of truth, ring true, sincere, spot on, staunch, steadfast, straight, striking a chord, trustworthy, truthful, typical, undeniable, unerring, unquestionable, valid, verified

**Trust** v., see also Believe, Confidence
anticipate, bank on, be confident, be convinced, be sure of, bet on, bet one's bottom dollar, commit, confide in, count on, credit, depend on, entrust, expect, have belief, have confidence in, have (complete) faith in, hope, imagine, lean on, look to, place confidence in, place trust in, presume, put faith in, reckon on, rely on, show faith, show loyalty, suppose, swear by, take as gospel, think likely

**Try** v., see also Endeavour, Test
1. aim, aspire, attempt, bid, buckle down, chip away, dig deep, do one's best, do one's damnedest, exert oneself, experiment, get stuck in, give it one's all, give it one's best shot, go after, go for, go for broke, have a crack, have a go, have a shot, have a stab, hope, leave no stone unturned, make a bid, make a fist of, make an attempt/effort, make a foray into, move heaven and earth, plan, pull out all the stops, push for, push the boat out, put one's best foot forward, put one's heart (and soul) into, put one's mind to, roll up one's sleeves, seek, set one's sights on, shoot for, step up (to the mark/plate), strain every sinew, strive, struggle, target, try one's hand, try one's hardest, undertake, venture, work, work flat out, work tirelessly
2. appraise, check, check out, dip one's toe in (the water), evaluate, examine, give it a whirl, inspect, investigate, judge, put to the test, sample, scrutinise,

suck it and see, take the plunge, taste, test the waters, trial, try one's hand, try out

**Turbulent** adj., see also Uncertain, Volatile
agitated, anxious, blowing hot and cold, bumpy, changeable, chaotic, choppy, confused, confusing, disorderly, erratic, febrile, fierce, fitful, furious, haywire, hectic, raging, raucous, restless, riotous, rollercoaster (ride), rough, rowdy, seething, shifting, stormy, tempestuous, topsy-turvy, tumultuous, unpredictable, unruly, unsettled, unstable, up and down, ups and downs, violent, wild

**Turmoil** n., see also Chaos, Volatility
agitation, anxiety, bedlam, changeability, commotion, confusion, crisis, disorder, disquiet, distress, disturbance, flurry, free-for-all, hubbub, instability, maelstrom, pandemonium, restlessness, riot, rollercoaster (ride), ruckus, storm, strife, trouble, tumult, turbulence, uncertainty, unpredictability, unrest, upheaval, uproar, ups and downs

**Turnover** n., see also Income, Performance
business, business activity, demand, proceeds, receipts, revenue(s), revenue generated, revenue stream, sales, sales activity, sales figures, sales performance, sales revenue, sales turnover, takings, top line, trade, trading

**Type** n., see also Category, Group
character, class, classification, description, designation, family, form, genre, ilk, like, kind, model, nature, persuasion, sort, standard, style, variant, variety, version

**Typical** adj., see Average, Common
archetypal, bog-standard, byword, characteristic, classic, clichéd, common-or-garden, commonplace, conventional, emblematic, epitome, epitomised by, epitomising, everyday, exemplary, from central casting, general, incarnation, model, normal, ordinary, orthodox, prime example, proverbial, quintessential regular, representative, routine, run-of-the-mill, standard, standardised, standard-issue, stereotypical, stock, symbolic, textbook, trademark, true to form, usual, very model, vintage, wont to do

# U

**Ultimately** adv., see also End, Finally
after all, at heart, at its most basic, at long last, at the end of the day, basically, conclusively, deep down, essentially, eventually, fundamentally, in conclusion, in due time, in the end, in the final analysis, to conclude, when all is said and done, when it comes down to it, when it comes to the crunch, when push comes to shove

**Unable** adj., see also Unsuccessful, Weak
cannot, daren't, doomed, helpless, ill afford, ill-equipped, ill-prepared, impotent, inadequate, incapable, incompetent, ineffective, ineffectual, inept, in no position, not able, not capable, not cut out for, not cutting it, not equal to, not fit for purpose, not in a position to, not making the grade, not ready, not up to, not up to scratch, powerless, struggling, unfit, unprepared, unqualified

**Unacceptable** adj., see also Disappointing, Inappropriate
bad, below par, below the belt, beyond the pale, detrimental, disagreeable, disconcerting, distasteful, dubious, forbidden, ill-advised, ill-conceived, ill-judged, improper, inadequate, inadmissible, indefensible, inexcusable, insupportable, intolerable, not fit for purpose, not on, not suitable, not up to scratch, objectionable, offensive, out of order, poor, reflecting poor judgement, regrettable, reprehensible, repugnant, serious, taboo, undesirable, unforgivable, unpleasant, unsatisfactory, unsavoury, unsuitable, unwanted, unwelcome, won't do, won't stand for, wrong

**Uncertain** adj., see also Unclear, Volatile
all bets are off, all to play for, ambiguous, ambivalent, anyone's guess, caught in two minds, changeable, conflicted, confused, doubtful, dubious, grey area, hanging in the balance, hazy, hesitant, hit and miss, in the balance, in two minds, inconclusive, inconsistent, indefinite, insecure, jury is out, no telling, not black and white, not certain, not clear, on a knife edge, on the fence, precarious, questionable, risky, rudderless, sketchy, torn, touch and go, unconfirmed, unconvinced, undecided, unpredictable, unreliable, unresolved, unsettled, unsettling, unstable, unsure, up for grabs, up in the air, vague, wavering, woolly

**Uncertainty** n., see also Doubt, Instability
ambiguity, ambivalence, anxiety, concern, confusion, conjecture, disquiet, distrust, guesswork, hesitancy, hesitation, inconclusiveness, indecision, lack of certainty, lack of confidence, misgivings, mistrust, quandary, question mark, scepticism, speculation, suspicion, uneasiness, unknown, unpredictability, unreliability, vagueness, volatility, wavering, worry

**Unchanged** adj., see also Reliable, Same
at the same level, consistent, constant, continual, continuous, equal, fixed, level, no difference, on a level, on a par, permanent, perpetual, remaining the same, remaining unchanged, resilient, stable, stagnant, steady, still the same, unaffected, unaltered, unmodified, unmoved, untouched, unvaried, unvarying, unwavering, virtually unchanged

**Unclear** adj., see also Uncertain
ambiguous, baffling, blurred, clear as mud, cloudy, complex, complicated, confused, confusing, disjointed, elusive, evasive, fudged, fuzzy, grey area, hazy, imprecise, intangible, lacking certainty, lacking clarity, muddying the waters, nebulous, no telling, not certain, not clear, not obvious, obscure, opaque, perplexing, question marks, rudderless, unsettled, vague, woolly

**Undecided** adj., see also Almost, Unclear
all bets are off, all to play for, ambiguous, ambivalent, anyone's guess, at a crossroads, borderline, caught in two minds, close, conflicted, debatable, dithering, doubtful, down to the wire, hanging by a thread, hesitant, hit and miss, in play, in the balance, in two minds, inconclusive, jury is out, make or break, make-your-mind-up time, moot, neck and neck, neither nor, nip and tuck, noncommittal, not set in stone, not sure, on a knife edge, on the fence, open, tentative, too close to call, torn, touch and go, uncertain, uncommitted, undetermined, unsettled, unsure, up for grabs, up in the air, vague, wavering

**Underestimate** v., see also Dismiss, Wrong
be complacent, belittle, bite off more than one can chew, doubt, fail to achieve, fall short, get wrong, give a conservative estimate, make light of, manage expectations, minimise, miscalculate, misconstrue, misinterpret, misjudge, mislead, misread, not do justice, not fully appreciate, not go far enough, place too little emphasis on, play down, sell short, set too little store by, trivialise, underrate, undersell, undervalue

**Underperform** v., see also Fail, Inefficient
be ailing, be at a low ebb, be beset by (*e.g. problems*), be flat, be found lacking, be found wanting, be in a rut, be in the doldrums, be out of sorts, be subdued, be under pressure, be unsuccessful, blunder, bomb, buckle, bungle, come a cropper, come unstuck, come up short, crash, crash and burn, disappoint, drop the ball, dwindle, fade, fall by the wayside, fall flat, fall from grace, fall short, falter, feel the pinch, fizzle out, flag, flatline, flop, flounder, founder, go astray, go down like a lead balloon, go into a tailspin, go nowhere, go off the boil, go wrong, implode, labour, lag (behind), languish, limp, make heavy weather of something, misfire, miss the mark, not firing on all cylinders, not make the grade, pale in comparison, perform below expectations, peter out, reel, run aground, show lacklustre performance, stagnate, stall, stand still, struggle, stumble, stutter, succumb, suffer, tank, tread water, underachieve, unravel, wane, wheels come off

**Understand** v., see also Analyse, Identify
accept, appreciate, apprehend, ascertain, assume, be alive to, be aware, be conscious of, be conversant with, be familiar with, be in tune with, be under no illusion(s), be under the impression, be up on, calculate, cast light on, catch on, click, come to terms with, comprehend, conceive, conclude, cotton on, dawn on, decipher, deduce, digest, discern, discover, distinguish, face facts, face up to reality, fathom, figure out, find out, follow, forgive, gather, get, get a handle on, get one's head round, get the hang of, get the idea, get to grips with, get to the bottom of, glean, grasp, have a grasp of, have an insight, have one's finger on the pulse, have sympathy, hear what someone says, heed, interpret, know, know inside out, know like the back of one's hand, learn, make out, make sense of, master, navigate, penny drops, perceive, presume, put things into perspective, read between the lines, realise, reckon, recognise, register, resonate with, see, see sense, see the light, sense, shed light on, shine a light on, sink in, suppose, surmise, suspect, sympathise, take away, take in, take on board, take the point, think, tolerate, tumble, tune in, twig, wake up to

**Undertake** v., see also Agree, Do
address, attempt, attend to, begin, carry out, commence, commit, conduct, deal with, devote, embark, endeavour, engage in, enter upon, execute, get involved, go about, grapple with, handle, implement, initiate, launch, manage, pledge, promise, resort to, respond to, set about, set out, shoulder, step up (to the mark/plate), tackle, take on, take ownership of, take responsibility for, take up, try, venture, work on

**Underway** adj., see also Continue, Start
afoot, begun, being developed, being prepared, being worked on, brewing, evolving, happening, in full swing, in motion, in preparation, in process, in progress, in the making/works, in the process of, initiated, launched, ongoing, progressing, started, taking place, undertaken, unfolding

**Unethical** adj., see also Corrupt, Unfair
breach of ethics, cheating, crooked, deceitful, dishonest, dishonourable, disreputable, dodgy, fake, fishy, fly-by-night, illegal, immoral, improper, inappropriate, murky, nefarious, not acceptable, not ethical, scam, shady, unacceptable, unauthorised, underhand, unlawful, unprincipled, unprofessional, unscrupulous, wrong

**Unexpected** adj., see also Surprising, Unusual
abrupt, accidental, against the odds, amazing, arbitrary, astonishing, chance, coming as a surprise, eye-opening, impromptu, impulsive, new, not bargained for, not expected, not on the cards, out of left field, out of nowhere, out of the blue, pleasant surprise, random, remarkable, rude awakening, shock, staggering, startling, stunning, sudden, surprise, unannounced, unanticipated, unchartered, unforeseen, unheralded, unplanned, unpredictable, unpredicted, without warning

**Unfair** adj., see also Unethical, Wrong
arbitrary, biased, cruel, discriminatory, dishonest, disproportionate, hard done by, harsh, improper, inequitable, low, not a level playing field, not fair, one-sided, partisan, prejudiced, punitive, stacked against, travesty of justice, unacceptable, undue, unjust, unjustifiable, unjustified, unmerited, unprincipled, unreasonable, unscrupulous, unsporting, unwarranted

**Unfortunate** adj., see also Bad, Unsuccessful
accidental, adverse, afflicted, bad luck, calamitous, cruel, cursed, damaging, disappointing, disastrous, doomed, down on one's luck, hapless, ill-advised, ill-fated, inappropriate, inauspicious, inopportune, jinxed, lamentable, luckless, misfortune, ominous, out of luck, regrettable, shambolic, tough luck, tragic, unfair, unfavourable, unhappy, unlucky, unsuitable, untimely, unwelcome

**Unhappiness** n., see also Anger, Disappointment
annoyance, bitterness, blues, chagrin, dejection, depression, despondency, disaffection, discontent, displeasure, dissatisfaction, distress, exasperation, frustration, gloom, grief, heartache, irritation, low spirits, malaise, misery, misfortune, sadness, sorrow, vexation

**Unhappy** adj., see also Angry, Disappointed
aggrieved, bitter, bleak, blue, blues, cheerless, crestfallen, dejected, depressed, despondent, disaffected, disconsolate, disenchanted, disgruntled, disillusioned, dispirited, displeased, dissatisfied, distraught, down, down in the dumps, down in the mouth, downbeat, downcast, fed up, forlorn, frustrated, gloomy, glum, grim, heavy-hearted, incensed, irked, let down, livid, low, miffed, miserable, not impressed, sad, saddened, sorry, sour grapes, troubled, unfortunate, unimpressed, unsatisfied, upset, with a heavy heart

**Unique** adj., see also Different, Unusual
alone, bespoke, custom-built/made, customised, distinctive, exceptional, exclusive, extraordinary, groundbreaking, in a class of its own, incomparable, individual, individualised, inimitable, landmark, matchless, never-before-seen, never-to-be-repeated, once-in-a-lifetime, one and only, one-in-a-million, one-of-a-kind, one-off, particular, peerless, personalised, pioneering, radical, rare, revolutionary, signature, singular, special, *****-specific (*e.g. customer-specific*), standout, strange, tailored, tailor-made, trademark, trailblazing, uncommon, unequalled, unmatched, unmistakeable, unparalleled, unprecedented, unrivalled, unsurpassed, without compare, without equal, without parallel, without precedent

**Unknown** adj., see also Surprising, Unusual
alien, anonymous, dark horse, enigma, foreign, hidden, hidden gem, incognito, languishing in obscurity, little-known, minor, mystery, mysterious, nameless, niche, obscure, plucked from obscurity, secret, strange, uncelebrated, uncharted, under the radar, undiscovered, undiscovered gem, undistinguished, unexplained, unexplored, unfamiliar, unheard-of, unheralded, unidentified, unknown quantity, unknown territory, unrecognised, unspecified, unsung (hero), untold, virgin territory, wild card

**Unlikely** adj., see also Impossible, Surprising
against the odds, distant chance, doubtful, dubious, fanciful, far-fetched, implausible, improbable, inconceivable, little chance, long shot, million to one, nonstarter, not a hope, not happening, not likely, not a prayer, not realistic, outside chance, pie in the sky, pipedream, questionable, remote possibility, suspect, unbelievable, unconvincing, unimaginable, unrealistic, unthinkable

**Unlucky** adj., see also Bad, Unsuccessful
accidental, adverse, afflicted, bad luck, calamitous, cruel, cursed, damaging, disappointing, disastrous, doomed, down on one's luck, hapless, harsh, ill-advised, ill-fated, inappropriate, inauspicious, inopportune, jinxed, lamentable,

luckless, misfortune, ominous, out of luck, regrettable, shambolic, tough luck, tragic, unfair, unfavourable, unfortunate, unhappy, unsuitable, untimely, unwelcome

**Unpleasant** adj., see also Negative, Unacceptable
antisocial, appalling, atrocious, awful, awkward, bad, despicable, diabolical, disagreeable, displeasing, distasteful, foul, harsh, improper, inappropriate, malicious, nasty, not nice, not on, objectionable, obnoxious, offensive, off-putting, reprehensible, rude, troublesome, ugly, unattractive, unbecoming, undesirable, unedifying, unfortunate, unfriendly, unkind, unlikeable, unpalatable, unsavoury, unwelcome, upsetting

**Unpopular** adj., see also Dislike, Unknown
avoided, cast aside, despised, detested, disliked, hate figure, hated, ignored, loathed, much-maligned, not a favourite, not liked, not one's cup of tea, not popular, not sought after, out in the cold, out of fashion, out of favour, pariah, rejected, scorned, shunned, turn-off, unappealing, unattractive, undervalued, unfashionable, unloved, unvalued, unwanted, unwelcome

**Unprecedented** adj., see also Unique, Unusual
abnormal, all-time high/low, as never before, best/worst/highest/lowest ever, bizarre, black-swan event, exceptional, extraordinary, first, first of its kind, freak event, groundbreaking, highly unusual, incomparable, miraculous, never seen the like before, new, noteworthy, novel, one-off, original, previously unknown/unseen, rare, record, record-breaking, remarkable, singular, strange, uncharted territory/waters, uncommon, unexpected, unheard-of, unimaginable, unparalleled, unrivalled, unseen, without parallel, without precedent

**Unprofessional** adj., see also Deficient, Unethical
amateurish, cavalier, cutting corners, improper, inappropriate, incompetent, inefficient, inexperienced, irresponsible, lacking professionalism, lax, negligent, not professional, not up to scratch, not up to standard, poor, poor-quality, remiss, shoddy, slapdash, sloppy, unacceptable, unbefitting, unbusinesslike, unimpressive, unfitting, unprincipled, unreliable, unsuitable

**Unprofitable** adj., see also Unsuccessful
ailing, cash-strapped, failing, failure, feeling the pinch, haemorrhaging money, leaking money, losing money (hand over fist), loss-making, making no money, not a commercial success, not a going concern, not breaking even, not economically/financially viable, not lucrative, not making/turning a profit, not

making ends meet, not profitable, out of pocket, struggling, uneconomic, unrewarding

**Unrestricted** adj., see also Large, Many
boundless, broad, countless, endless, extensive, free, generous, great, immeasurable, immense, incalculable, independent, knowing no bounds, liberal, liberated, limitless, no limits, no restrictions, sweeping, unbounded, unconditional, unconstrained, unfettered, unhampered, unhindered, unimpeded, unlimited, unobstructed, unregulated, vast, without limits, without restrictions

**Unstable** adj., see also Volatile, Weak
changeable, chaotic, doubtful, dubious, erratic, fitful, flimsy, fluctuating, fragile, inconsistent, insecure, jittery, lacking stability, lacking strong foundations, not robust, not stable, precarious, rickety, risky, rocky, rollercoaster (ride), sensitive, shaky, shifting, temperamental, turbulent, uncertain, unpredictable, unreliable, unsettled, unsound, unsteady, up and down, variable, wavering, wobbly

**Unsuccessful** adj., see also Disappointing, Negatively Affected
abortive, ailing, also-ran, beaten, beleaguered, beset by problems, counterproductive, crisis-hit, dead and buried, defeated, defunct, disastrous, disgraced, doomed, embattled, embroiled in (*e.g. a crisis*), engulfed in (*e.g. a crisis*), failed, failing, feeling the pinch, floundering, foiled, foundering, fruitless, futile, gone pear-shaped, hapless, hard-pressed, has-been, hopeless, ill-fated, in a bad place, in vain, ineffective, ineffectual, irretrievable, lacklustre, languishing, losing, loss-making, off the boil, on the ropes, out of kilter, out of one's depth, out of sorts, shambolic, stricken, struggling, stumbling, stuttering, subdued, tainted, thwarted, under pressure, underachieving, underperforming, unfavourable, unlucky, unprofitable, wanting, washed-up, weak, wide of the mark, wheels coming off, worthless

**Unsuitable** adj., see also Inadequate, Unacceptable
bad, ill-judged, ill-suited, ill-timed, inapplicable, inappropriate, inauspicious, incompatible, incongruous, incorrect, inopportune, irrelevant, not appropriate, not fit for purpose, not fitting, not ideal, not (quite) right, not suitable, not up to scratch, out of place, poor, shoddy, sloppy, unbecoming, unbefitting, undue, unfit, unsatisfactory, unsuited, untimely, wrong

**Unsure** adj., see also Unclear, Volatile
all bets are off, all to play for, ambiguous, ambivalent, anyone's guess, caught in two minds, changeable, confused, doubts, doubtful, dubious, grey area,

hanging in the balance, hazy, hesitant, hit and miss, in the balance, in two minds, inconclusive, inconsistent, indecisive, indefinite, insecure, jury is out, no telling, not certain, not clear, not confident, not sure, on a knife edge, on the fence, precarious, questionable, risky, sketchy, torn, touch and go, uncertain, unconfirmed, unconvinced, undecided, unpredictable, unreliable, unresolved, unsettled, up for grabs, up in the air, vague, wavering, woolly

**Untrue** adj., see also Error, Wrong
baseless, bogus, cooked-up, counterfeit, covering up, deceitful, deceptive, dishonest, dissembling, distorted, erroneous, fabricated, fake, fallacious, fallacy, false, falsehood, fanciful, feigned, fictitious, fishy, flawed, forged, fraudulent, hollow, imprecise, inaccurate, inconsistent, incorrect, invalid, lie, lying, made-up, misleading, mistaken, myth, not correct, not true, nothing could be further from the truth, phoney, ringing hollow, sham, spurious, two-faced, unfair, unfaithful, unfounded, unreliable, unsound, untrue, untrustworthy, untruthful, way off, wide of the mark

**Unusual** adj., see also Different, Surprising
anomaly, astonishing, at odds with, atypical, breaking the mould, breaking the rules, breath of fresh air, bizarre, contrasting, contradiction (in terms), counterintuitive, curious, distinctive, esoteric, exceptional, extraordinary, going against the grain, idiosyncratic, in (sharp) contrast to, incredible, ironic, irregular, left-field, maverick, memorable, mysterious, not your everyday, noteworthy, novel, odd, oddity, odd one out, oddball, offbeat, off-piste, original, out of left field, out of the ordinary, outlier, oxymoron, paradox, peculiar, phenomenal, quirky, random, rare, refreshing, remarkable, singular, special, standing out from the crowd, standing apart, sticking out like a sore thumb, strange, strange bedfellows, uncharted territory/waters, uncommon, unconventional, unexpected, unfamiliar, unheard-of, unique, unorthodox, unparalleled, unpredicted, unprecedented, weird, with a difference, with a twist

**Unwilling** adj., see also Disagree, Opposition
against, averse, begrudging, disapproving, disinclined, grudging, half-hearted, hesitating, hostile, ill-disposed, in opposition, loath, not happy about, not in the mood, not keen, not ready, not willing, not wanting/wishing, objecting, opposed, reluctant, resistant, slow, unaccommodating, uncooperative, unenthusiastic, unhelpful

**Update** v., see also Adjust, Change
add, alter, amend, breathe new life into, bring up to date/speed, develop, enhance, facelift, improve, keep current, keep fresh, keep relevant, make better,

make current, make over, modernise, modify, overhaul, reboot, reconfigure, reform, refresh, refurbish, rejuvenate, remodel, renew, renovate, replace, restore, revamp, review, revise, revisit, shake up, spruce up, tweak, upgrade

**Upset** v., see also Anger, Trouble
alarm, alienate, annoy, bewilder, bother, cause consternation, cause dismay, cause trouble, cause upset, confound, destabilise, disconcert, dismay, disrupt, distress, disturb, fluster, make waves, mess up, offend, overturn, perturb, rattle, rock the boat, rub up the wrong way, ruffle feathers, send shock waves through, spoil, spook, turn upside down, unnerve, unsettle, worry

**Upturn** n., see also Boom, Improvement
acceleration, bonanza, boom in business, boost, bounce, economic boom, expansion, explosion, growth, higher economic activity, increase, jump, leap, momentum, pickup, prosperity, purple patch, rally, rebound, recovery, recuperation, revival, rise, spike, spurt, strengthening, swell, turnaround, upsurge, upswing, uptick

**Urgent** adj., see also Essential, Important
acute, burning, compelling, critical, crucial, crying out for, desperate, emergency, every second counts, exigent, grave, high-priority, high time, immediate, imperative, indispensable, instant, life-and-death, necessary, now or never, of vital importance, paramount, pressing, priority, requiring immediate attention, sudden, time is of the essence, top priority, vital

**Use** v., see also Exploit, Take Advantage Of
administer, adopt, apply, avail oneself of, bring into play, bring to bear, call upon, consume, control, deploy, draw on, employ, engage with, exercise, exert, find a use for, get the most from/out of, handle, harness, leverage, manage, make the most of, make use of, manage, mobilise, operate, put into action, put to (good) use, put to work, repurpose, resort to, set in motion, take up, tap into, use to one's advantage, utilise, wield, work (with)

**Useful** adj., see also Effective, Valuable
advantageous, all-purpose, appropriate, beneficial, boon, can't do without, capable, clever, coming into its own, convenient, efficient, essential, favourable, *****-friendly (*e.g. family-friendly*), fruitful, functional, general-purpose, godsend, good, handy, helpful, ideal, important, indispensable, informative, ingenious, instrumental, integral, invaluable, must, of benefit, of help, of use, of value, practical, pragmatic, sensible, serve well, suitable, suited, versatile, worth its weight in gold, worthwhile

**Usual** adj., see also Normal, Regular
accepted, average, bog-standard, bread and butter, business as usual, classic, common, commonplace, constant, conventional, customary, everyday, expected, familiar, frequent, general, habitual, mainstream, matter of course, meat and drink, natural, ordinary, orthodox, prevailing, routine, run-of-the-mill, standard, standard-issue, stock, traditional, true to form, typical, unexceptional, unremarkable, unsurprising, usual suspects, widespread, workaday

**Utilise** v., see also Exploit, Take Advantage Of
administer, adopt, apply, avail oneself of, bring into play, bring to bear, call upon, consume, convert, deploy, draw on, employ, engage with, exercise, exert, find a use for, get the most from/out of, handle, harness, leverage, make the most of, make use of, manage, maximise, mobilise, operate, put into action, put to (good) use, put to work, repurpose, resort to, seize the opportunity, set in motion, take up, tap into, transfer, translate into, turn into/to, turn to one's advantage, use, use to one's advantage, wield, work with

# V

**Vague** adj., see also Uncertain, Undecided
ambiguous, ambivalent, blurred, cannot pin down, cloudy, coy, dithering, doubtful, dubious, enigmatic, equivocal, evasive, fudged, fuzzy, general, hazy, hesitant, ill-defined, imprecise, inconclusive, indistinct, muddy, nebulous, noncommittal, nonspecific, not clear, obscure, on the fence, sketchy, unclear, uncommitted, unresolved, unsettled, unspecific, unspecified, unsure, wavering, wishy-washy, woolly

**Valuable** adj., see also Effective, Useful
1. advantageous, appreciated, beneficial, boon, can't do without, cherished, constructive, essential, godsend, handy, helpful, important, indispensable, inestimable, integral, invaluable, irreplaceable, key, lifesaver, much-needed, must, of benefit, of use, of value, positive, precious, priceless, prized, profitable, relevant, respected, top-notch, treasured, valued, vital, worth its weight in gold, worth every penny, worthwhile, worthy
2. costly, dear, expensive, high-end, high-priced, precious, priceless, pricey, profitable, treasured, worth a lot (of money)

**Value** n., see also Advantage, Benefit
1. amount, bang for buck, calibre, capitalisation, cost, desirability, distinction, expense, fair value, good value, help, import, importance, market price/value, meaning, merit, practicality, price, price tag, profit, quality, rate, relevance, significance, stature, support, use, usefulness, utility, valuation, virtue, worth
2. approach, attitude, behaviour, belief, code of conduct, core values, corporate culture, culture, ethical standards, ethics, ethos, mentality, mindset, morals, mores, philosophy, principles, set of values, standards, value set, watchword

**Value** v., see also Evaluate, Like
acknowledge, admire, applaud, appraise, appreciate, approve of, assess, assign a value to, be appreciative of, be grateful for, be indebted to, celebrate, cherish, consider important, count one's blessings, endorse, estimate the cost/value, favour, have admiration for, hold dear, hold in high esteem, measure (the value of), praise, prize, put a price/value on, rate highly, recognise, regard highly, respect, set a price, treasure, welcome

**Variation** n., see also Difference, Variety
alternative, array, assortment, change, departure, deviation, discrepancy, disparity, distinction, divergence, diversity, exception, fluctuation, flux, medley, mixed bag, mixture, nonconformity, patchwork, permutation, range, selection, shift, spectrum, ups and downs, variant, version

**Varied** adj., see also Different, Unusual
all kinds/manner of, array of, assorted, broad church of, broad spectrum of, changeable, cocktail of, contrasting, disparate, diverse, eclectic, fluctuating, fragmented, heady mix of, kaleidoscopic, manifold, miscellaneous, mix-and-match, mixed, mixed bag of, multifaceted, multifarious, potpourri of, rich and varied, scattergun, smorgasbord, spectrum of, spoilt for choice, sundry, sweeping, variety of, various, varying, versatile, wide-ranging

**Variety** n., see also Assortment, Choice
1. array, all kinds/manner, all sorts, armoury, arsenal, battery, breadth, broad spectrum, cocktail, collection, cornucopia, cross section, divergence, diversification, diversity, everything from…to…, fragmentation, gamut, heady mix, hodgepodge, kaleidoscope, line-up, medley, mix, mixture, melting pot, miscellany, mishmash, mixed bag, mixture, offering, pick 'n' mix, portfolio, potpourri, range, repertoire, scope, smorgasbord, soup, spectrum, spoilt for choice, stew, suite, variation, wide range
2. brand, category, class, classification, grade, kind, make, model, nature, quality, sort, strain, type, variant, version

**Vary** v., see also Change, Differ
add variety, alter, alternate, be different, be dissimilar, be unlike, blow hot and cold, change (things) up, chop and change, come and go, depart, deviate, digress, disagree, diverge, diversify, fluctuate, go up and down, mix and match, mix (it) up, modify, offer variety, pick and mix, range, see-saw, separate, shift, span, swing

**Verify** v., see also Check, Confirm
acknowledge, affirm, ascertain, assure, attest, authenticate, back up, be certain/sure, bear out, certify, check out/up, corroborate, debunk, demonstrate, determine, document, double-check, ensure, establish, examine, find out, inspect, justify, make certain/sure, monitor, prove, scrutinise, study, substantiate, test, validate, vouch for, warrant

**Very** adv., see also Completely, Especially
absolutely, achingly, acutely, adamantly, all-out, ardently, avidly, awfully, brazenly, certainly, comprehensively, concertedly, conclusively, considerably, decidedly, deeply, demonstrably, devilishly, downright, dramatically, drastically, eminently, emphatically, every inch, exceedingly, exceptionally, excessively, extensively, extraordinarily, extremely, firmly, full-on, genuinely, glaringly, greatly, highly, hugely, immeasurably, immensely, impossibly, in earnest, incredibly, insanely, intensely, irretrievably, model of, monumentally, most, nothing short of, noticeably, obscenely, off the charts, off the scale, overwhelmingly, particularly, patently, profoundly, quintessentially, quite, radically, really, remarkably, resolutely, resoundingly, richly, rigorously, seriously, severely, sharply, sheer, smacks of, staunchly, steadfastly, steeped in, strongly, substantially, super-*****, supremely, surprisingly, terribly, totally, to put it mildly, tremendously, truly, ultra*****, unanimously, unashamedly, uncompromisingly, undisputedly, undoubtedly, unequivocally, unquestionably, unusually, unwavering, utmost, utterly, vastly, vehemently, veritably, very much, well and truly, wholeheartedly, wonderfully

**View** n., see also Approach, Belief
analysis, angle, appraisal, argument, assessment, attitude, comment, conclusion, consensus, considered opinion, consideration, conviction, estimation, evaluation, feeling, idea, impression, in one's book, judgement, matter of opinion, mindset, notion, opinion, outlook, perception, perspective, philosophy, point of view, position, reaction, school of thought, sense, sentiment, slant, stance, standpoint, supposition, take, theory, thinking, thought, vantage point, verdict, viewpoint, way of thinking

**View** v., see also Believe, Think
assess, adjudge, be minded, be of the opinion, be of the view, conclude, consider, deem, espouse, evaluate, feel, judge, maintain, make of, perceive, reckon, reflect on, regard, take the view, treat, weigh (up)

**Vital** adj., see also Important, Key
all-important, basic, bedrock, can't do without, cardinal, chief, core, cornerstone, critical, crucial, de rigueur, decisive, essential, fundamental, imperative, indispensable, inherent, innate, integral, intrinsic, life-or-death/life-and-death, lifeblood, linchpin, lost without, main, mainstay, mandatory, mission-critical, must-have/read/see, necessary, needed, obligatory, of utmost importance, paramount, pivotal, prerequisite, primary, principal, required, required reading/viewing, sorely needed, unmissable, urgent

**Volatile** adj., see also Turbulent, Uncertain
anyone's guess, blowing hot and cold, capricious, changeable, chaotic, choppy, confused, confusing, erratic, explosive, fast-changing, febrile, fickle, fitful, fluctuating, fraught, haywire, inconsistent, jittery, lively, lottery, mercurial, messy, no telling, precarious, raucous, restless, rocky, rollercoaster (ride), sensitive, shaky, shifting, stormy, temperamental, tempestuous, topsy-turvy, torrid, unpredictable, unreliable, unsettled, unsettling, unstable, unsteady, up and down, variable

**Volatility** n., see also Instability, Turmoil
bumpy ride, changeability, chaos, combustibility, confusion, crisis, disorder, disquiet, erratic nature, excitability, explosiveness, fluctuation, inconsistency, instability, jitters, rollercoaster ride, turbulence, uncertainty, unpredictability, unpredictable nature, unsteadiness, upheaval, ups and downs, variability

**Vulnerable** adj., see also Unsuccessful, Weak
at risk, at the mercy of, defenceless, exposed, helpless, in danger, in jeopardy, open, open to attack, out on a limb, powerless, precarious, prone, sensitive, sitting duck, susceptible, under pressure, under threat, unguarded, unprotected, unsafe, weak point, wide open

# W

**Wages** n., see also Job, Money
commission, compensation, earnings, fee, income, pay, pay day, pay packet, payment, payroll, proceeds, recompense, reimbursement, remuneration, reward, salary, take-home (pay), wage bill, wage packet

**Wait** v., see also Delay
await, be in a holding pattern, be kept waiting, be on tenterhooks, be patient, bear with, bide one's time, expect, hang around, hang in there, hang on, have patience, have the patience of a saint, hesitate, hold fire, hold off, hold out, kick one's heels, kill time, lie in wait, linger, mark time, pause, play a waiting game, put on hold, put on ice, remain, sit and wait, sit tight, stand by, stick around, sweat it out, take a moment, twiddle one's thumbs, wait and see, wait and wait, wait around, wait in the wings, wait long enough, wait with bated breath, waste time

**Want** v., see also Need, Require
aim, aspire, be desperate for, be dying to, be greedy for, be in the mood for, be inclined, be itching to, be keen to, be sorely tempted to, be up for, call for, can't wait, choose, covet, crave, demand, desire, fancy, hanker after, have an urge for, have designs on, (only) have eyes for, have need of, have on one's wish list, hope for, hunger for, incline towards, intend, long for, look for/to, plan, prefer, seek, set one's heart on, set one's sights on, thirst for, wish, yearn for

**Warn** v., see also Forecast
advise, advocate, alert, caution, counsel, enjoin, exhort, flag up, forewarn, give a heads-up, give notice, give warning, guide, hint, inform, issue a note of caution, issue a warning, make aware, notify, prompt, put on guard, put on notice, put on standby, raise a red flag, raise the alarm, raise the prospect of, recommend, remind, serve as a reminder, signal, sound/strike a note of caution, sound the alarm, speculate, suggest, tell, threaten, tip off, urge

**Warning** n., see also Advice, Indication
advance notice, alarm, alert, canary in the coal mine, caution, cautionary tale, cry for help, fair warning, foretaste, forewarning, guidance, heads-up, Mayday, note of caution, notice, notification, omen, portent, prediction,

recommendation, red flag, reminder, sabre-rattling, salutary experience/tale, shot across the bows, sign, signal, stark warning, SOS, threat, tip-off, wake-up call, warning light, warning signal, word of warning, writing on the wall

**Way** n., see also Approach, Method
action, arrangement, avenue, channel, conduct, course, course of action, direction, fashion, form, instrument, knack, line, manner, means, measure, mechanism, mode, move, nature, path, plan, policy, practice, procedure, process, road, route, routine, scheme, step, style, system, tack, technique, trick, usage, use, vein

**Weak** adj., see also Inefficient, Negative
ailing, at a low ebb, at rock bottom, below par, crummy, deficient, depressed, detrimental, dire, disappointing, disjointed, dismal, doomed, dysfunctional, exposed, failed, feeble, flawed, flimsy, fragile, frail, half-hearted, hapless, hesitant, ill-equipped, ill-prepared, impotent, inadequate, indecisive, ineffective, ineffectual, inept, insipid, lacking, lacklustre, lax, limited, low, lukewarm, mediocre, not fit for purpose, not robust, not strong, not up to scratch, patchy, poor, poor relation, powerless, rickety, scrappy, second-rate, shabby, shaky, shambolic, shoddy, slim, sluggish, spent, subdued, subpar, substandard, susceptible, thin, uncertain, unconvincing, under par, unconvincing, underperforming, uninspiring, unprepared, unsatisfactory, unsound, unstable, unsteady, unsure, untenable, vulnerable, wanting, wavering, weakened, without strong foundations, wobbly, woeful

**Weaken** v., see also Affect Negatively, Decline
abate, be eroded, be in decline, become weaker, blight, cripple, crumble, damage, debilitate, decay, decrease, depress, destroy, deteriorate, devastate, dilute, diminish, disappoint, disintegrate, dog, dwindle, eat into, ebb, enfeeble, erode, exhaust, fade, flag, get weaker, give way, go downhill, hamper, hinder, hit, hollow out, impair, incapacitate, languish, lessen, lower, make weaker, moderate, niggle, peter out, pressure, put on the back foot, put under pressure, recede, reduce, reduce strength, rock, ruin, sap (energy), shackle, shake, slow down, soften, spell trouble for, stunt, subdue, tail off, take the edge off, undermine, wane, water down, weigh on, wilt, worsen

**Weakness** n., see also Deficiency, Disadvantage
Achilles heel, chink in armour, defect, disappointment, downside, drawback, error, failing, fault, flaw, fragility, frailty, gap, hole, impairment, impotence, inadequacy, instability, lack, lapse, malaise, minus, negative aspect, problem, shortcoming, snag, trouble, vice, vulnerability, weak point

**Wealth** n., see also Asset, Many
1. affluence, billions, capital, combined assets, deep pockets, estate, financial clout, financial muscle, financial resources, fortune, funds, good life, high life, how the other half live, lap of luxury, life of luxury, luxury, means, megabucks, millions, money, net worth, opulence, property, prosperity, resources, revenue, riches, splendour, success, trappings of success, vast wealth, worth
2. abundance, great deal, host, huge amount/quantity, lots, myriad, no end, plenty, vast amount, whole host, wide range

**Wealthy** adj., see also Famous, Successful
affluent, billionaire, comfortable, deep pockets, deep-pocketed, elite, filthy rich, flush, having lots of money, high-end, high-net-worth, in the money, loaded, made of money, moneyed, multimillionaire, not short of money, privileged, prosperous, rich, rich and famous, rolling in it/money, super-rich, upmarket, upscale, well-heeled, well-off, well-to-do

**Well-known** adj., see also Popular, Successful
acclaimed, all-star, best-known, big, big name, blockbuster, box-office, celebrated, celebrity, distinguished, eminent, esteemed, fabled, famed, familiar, famous, famous face, feted, foremost, great and the good, hallowed, hit, household name, iconic, illustrious, in the limelight, in the public eye, in the spotlight, infamous, influential, known, leading, legend, legendary, megastar, memorable, much-discussed, name on everyone's lips, national treasure, needing no introduction, no secret, notable, noted, noteworthy, notorious, of note, pre-eminent, prominent, public, recognised, renowned, reputable, respected, revered, rising star, rock-star, star, star-studded, stuff of legend, superstar, talked about, VIP, widely known, widely respected, world-famous

**Win** v., see also Defeat, Succeed
accomplish, achieve, bag, be awarded with, be crowned the winner, be first, be the victor, be the winner, be victorious, beat, blow (the opposition) away, carry the day, claim, claim first place/prize, claim/retain the crown, clean up, come away with, come first, conquer, deserve, earn, edge it, edge out, finish first, finish in front, gain, gain first place, gain victory, garner, obtain, outclass, outrival, outshine, overcome, overwhelm, pick up, pip (to the post), prevail, receive, romp to victory, scoop, score (a victory), seal victory, secure, sweep the board, sweep to victory, take/claim victory, take home (the spoils), top, triumph, trump, upstage, walk away with, win big, win hands down

**Wise** adj., see also Intelligent, Sensible
advisable, appropriate, astute, aware, canny, careful, clear-eyed, clever, clued-up, common-sense, considered, deep thinker, diplomatic, discerning, educated, enlightened, experienced, far-sighted, good idea, informed, insightful, inspired, judicious, knowing, knowledgeable, logical, mature, perceptive, philosophical, politic, practical, prudent, rational, realistic, reasonable, reflective, respected, right, sage, sane, savvy, sharp, shrewd, smart, sound, suitable, thoughtful, wary, well-informed, well-judged, well-reasoned, worldly

**Withstand** v., see also Continue, Struggle
abide, battle through, be subjected to, be victim to, bear, bear the brunt, bear the scars, brace, brave, carry on, combat, confront, cope with, defy, encounter, endure, experience, face, get through, go through, grin and bear it, hang in there, hold out, keep going, live through, meet with, never say die, oppose, persist, prevail, put up with, remain firm, resign oneself to, resist, ride out the storm, see through, stand, stand fast, stand firm, stand one's ground, stand up to, stay strong, stick it out, stomach, suffer, survive, sustain, sweat it out, take, take on, tolerate, tough it out, undergo, weather, weather the storm

**Work** n., see also Assignment, Employment
achievement, activity, business, calling, career, chore, commitment, craft, drudgery, duties, duty, effort(s), endeavour(s), exertion(s), function, (daily) grind, groundwork, handiwork, hard graft, hard work, heavy lifting, industry, job, labour, labour of love, line, line of business, line of work, livelihood, metier, mission, nine-to-five, occupation, passion project, performance, position, post, practice, production, profession, project, responsibility, role, shift, skill, slog, specialisation, striving, struggle, task, teamwork, toil, trade, undertaking, venture

**Work** v., see also Cooperate, Function
1. apply oneself, be at work, be busy, be employed, be in work, beaver away, burn the midnight oil, busy oneself, carry out, chip away, conduct, dig deep, do a job, do for a living, do work, earn a living, endeavour, exert oneself, forge a career, freelance, go to work, graft, have a job, have one's nose to the grindstone, hold down a job, implement, knuckle down, labour, make an effort, operate, perform, plug away, ply one's trade, practise, practise a profession, pursue an activity, put in a shift, put in the effort, roll up one's sleeves, run a business, serve as, set to work, slog (away), specialise, strive, take on, toil, trade, try, undertake, work flat out, work hard, work one's socks off, work tirelessly

2. be effective, be successful, do the trick, go as planned, go well, operate, run, succeed, thrive, turn out well, work a treat, work as intended, work out

**Worker** n., see also Employee, Personnel
associate, colleague, co-worker, labourer, member of staff, operative, operator, person, staff member, team member, tradesperson, wage earner, workforce

**Worried** adj., see also Cautious, Unhappy
agitated, alarmed, anxious, apprehensive, bothered, concerned, disconcerted, distraught, distressed, disturbed, fearful, frightened, gripped with fear, ill at ease, insecure, jittery, nervous, on edge, perturbed, pessimistic, petrified, racked with fear, rattled, tense, troubled, twitchy, uncertain, uneasy, unnerved, upset, uptight, wary, worried sick

**Worry** n., see also Concern, Problem
agitation, anguish, annoyance, anxiety, apprehension, bad news, care, cause for concern, clouds on the horizon, consternation, discontent, dismay, disquiet, distress, doubt, fear, frustration, headache, hysteria, jitters, misgiving(s), nerves, qualms, reservations, tension, trepidation, trouble, uncertainty, unease, uneasiness, woe, worries

**Worry** v., see also Concern, Trouble
aggrieve, agonise, annoy, badger, be anxious, be concerned, be gripped by fear, be hung up on, be nervous about, be troubled by, be wary of, be worried, bedevil, beleaguer, beset, bother, brood, bug, depress, despair, disconcert, distress, disturb, dog, exercise, feel uneasy, fester, fret, grumble, harass, harry, haunt, have qualms, have reservations, irk, irritate, keep awake at night, make anxious, nag, needle, obsess, panic, persecute, pester, perturb, plague, play on one's mind, rattle, ruffle feathers, scaremonger, spark concern/fears, spook, strike fear into, torment, unnerve, unsettle, upset, vex

**Worrying** adj., see also Serious, Uncertain
cause for concern, chilling, concern, concerning, daunting, disconcerting, disquieting, distressing, disturbing, fraught, frightening, nerve-racking, of concern, perturbing, playing on one's mind, scary, troublesome, troubling, unnerving, unsettling, upsetting, vexing, worrisome, worry

**Worse** adj., see also Deficient, Weak
below par, cannot hold a candle to, cannot keep up with, cannot match, cannot touch, disappointing, eclipsed, falling behind, inferior, lacking, lagging behind, less, less effective, lower, no match for, not a patch on, not as good, not in the

same class/league, outclassed, outperformed, outshone, overshadowed, paling in comparison with, retrograde, smaller, trailing, upstaged, wanting, weaker

**Worsen** v., see also Decline, Decrease
add insult to injury, aggravate, be eroded, be in decline, become worse, collapse, compound, contract, corrode, crumble, damage, darken, decay, deepen, degenerate, descend, deteriorate, diminish, disintegrate, drop, drop off, ebb, erode, exacerbate, fade, fan the flames, flag, fray, get worse, go downhill, go from bad to worse, impact, impair, increase, intensify, lower, make matters worse, peter out, recede, reduce, rot sets in, rub salt into the wound, shrink, sink, slide, slow, slump, sour, spiral down, stall, struggle, suffer, tail off, take a hit, take a turn for the worse, undermine, unravel, wane, weaken, wilt, wither

**Wrong** adj., see also Incorrect, Negative
amiss, appalling, askew, astray, at fault, awry, bad, contrary, defective, dishonest, dubious, erroneous, false, faulty, ill-advised, ill-judged, imprecise, improper, inaccurate, inappropriate, incongruous, irresponsible, misguided, mishandled, misinformed, misplaced, mistaken, no-no, not correct, not legitimate, not right, off-target, out of line, out of order, remiss, reprehensible, skewed, suspect, unacceptable, unbecoming, undesirable, unethical, unfair, unfit, unfitting, unfounded, unjust, unlawful, unprincipled, unsatisfactory, unscrupulous, unseemly, unsound, unsuccessful, unsuitable, untrue, unwise, wide of the mark, wrongful

Printed in Great Britain
by Amazon

21984249R10139